WELCOME

BACK AT LAST!

It's been quite a while, hasn't it? We've all been collectively starved of a good hit of Isle of Man road-racing, but here we are, ready to rumble in 2022.

Of course COVID-19 put paid to the last two years' events, but – now – we can finally say we are going racing again.

When I recall my times at the Isle of Man TT, both as a working journalist and, eventually, a starry-eyed fan, I recall the huge impact watching the race 'live' had on me. As good as the TV coverage is now, you can't beat watching it track-side. As a sports journalist I'd covered Grand Prix racing and world superbikes, so being asked to cover the TT was something I considered, before going, as perhaps a lower formula. How wrong I was.

I still recall that morning practice; feeling a tad jaded (and more than a little hungover) I stood at the bottom of Bray Hill to await the first riders through. I could hear some sort of strangled scream and then Jim Moodie barrelled through the public road next to me, foot-rests sparking as the bike bottomed out before being on his way... It was an introduction to the extreme courage and skill of TT racers (and I mean ANY TT racers) that has never left me. Fair play and much respect to anyone who chooses to test themselves against that historic ribbon of Tarmac. I've been a fan ever since...

With the world having been through so much of late and with us missing out on TT 2020 and TT 2021, we figured it would be good to give Island Racer 2022 a real historic feel, so we've delved into various archives and picked numerous brains to bring you a wide-ranging slice of historic TT features and even a test on an iconic Senior TT-winning machine.

It's not all about history though; we've also done our best to provide the latest information on all the runners and riders for TT22 – although it goes without saying that 'everything was correct at the time of going to press'.

As I write this, we're just weeks away from experiencing all the thrills that the Isle of Man TT event can give us, so it's just left for me to say: 'have a terrific, exciting and safe TT!'

Bertie

CONTENTS

INSIDE
YOUR *ISLAND RACER* | EDITION 2022

008 FLASHBACK!
Revisiting four Isle of Man TT legends whose names continue to resonate through the annals of road-racing history.

016 JOHN MCGUINNESS
The second-most decorated TT winner of all-time once again lays it all on the line in an honest interview before his 2022 return to the Honda family. Can he do it one more time? It would be beautiful...

026 WHO'S WHO IN '22? #1
The top runners and riders in the big-bike classes profiled – can anyone challenge the likes of Hickman, Harrison, Dunlop, Cummins et al? Let's see!

044 WHO'S WHO IN '22? #2
We check out the talent in the smaller classes that will be tackling the Isle of Man TT course.

049 WHO'S WHO IN '22? #3
Focusing on the three-wheeled wonders who attack the TT course year-on-year – can the Birchall brothers actually be beaten?

058 THE CLASS OF '92
Thirty years on, we recall the two greats who battled for the spoils in the Formula 1 and Senior TT races. In a tale of two halves, we hear from Steve Hislop, Norton's Senior TT winner and Carl Fogarty, whose Yamaha set a long-standing lap-record.

070 ABUS NORTON NRS588
Alan Cathcart rides the bike that took Steve Hislop to that historic 1992 Senior TT win.

080 FIRE STARTER!
Back in 1992 a new bike was released that wasn't able to race in many places... then in 1996, the new Production TT class was born. It was o be the start of a long and fruitful relationship between the Isle of Man and the Honda Fireblade.

CONTENTS

CONTENTS

090 FAST, FEARLESS, FEMALES
The Isle of Man TT isn't just a man's world – meet some of the ground-breaking girls who have been very fast around Mona's Isle.

100 DEAN HARRISON
Dean Harrison: the man who won the 2019 Senior TT on how he plans to take more wins around the Isle of Man TT course.

108 SHEENE AND THE TT
Why was it that Britain's greatest motorcycle racer hated the hallowed Isle of Man TT event? We ask why and find the answers.

116 HONDA'S HAUL
The most successful motorcycle marque around the TT course – we check out some of the firm's most famous wins.

124 THE ULTIMATE ROAD TEST
TT winner Michael Rutter tests a KTM over the Isle of Man TT course!

126 THE KNOWLEDGE
Facts, figures, lap records and all the data from races and years gone by.

146 WHAT'S ON WHEN?
What's on and when it's on during the TT event.

148 pages of amazing TT action

EDITOR: BERTIE SIMMONDS

ART EDITOR: CRAIG LAMB

PRODUCTION EDITOR: DAN SHARP

SPECIAL CONTRIBUTORS:
STEPHEN DAVISON/PACEMAKER PRESS, DON MORLEY, BILL SNELLING, STUART BARKER, PHIL WAIN, JOHN WATTERSON, ALAN CATHCART, TIM KEETON, JOHN MCAVOY.

PUBLISHER: STEVE O'HARA
COMMERCIAL DIRECTOR: NIGEL HOLE
PUBLISHING DIRECTOR: DAN SAVAGE

TT 2022 ISLAND RACER

ISBN 978-1-911639-98-5

ALL MATERIAL COPYRIGHT MORTONS MEDIA GROUP LIMITED, 2022. ALL RIGHTS RESERVED.

PUBLISHED BY
MORTONS MEDIA GROUP LIMITED,
MEDIA CENTRE,
MORTON WAY,
HORNCASTLE,
LINCOLNSHIRE, LN9 6JR.
TELEPHONE 01507 529529.

PRINTED BY
WILLIAM GIBBONS & SONS
OF WOLVERHAMPTON.

DISTRIBUTED
BY MARKETFORCE UK LTD.

FOR MORE COPIES OF ISLAND RACER
OR FOR INFORMATION
CALL 01507 529529
OR VISIT WWW.ISLANDRACER.CO.UK

THE BMW
M 1000 RR

RACING LIKE NO OTHER

Your competitive spirit drives you. Your passion dominates and challenges you. The search for more defines every millisecond: pure motorsport. High performance, high-tech materials, the highest-quality workmanship and exclusivity down to the last detail: The M RR is the first M model from BMW Motorrad. Its genes come directly from professional racing. The M RR and M RR with M Competition package offers pure racing technology for the highest performance demands in motorsport and for adrenalin-driven perfectionists on the road. Because #NeverStopChallenging is more than a promise. It's a commitment.

Visit bmw-motorrad.co.uk to book a test ride or contact your local Retailer*

Terms and Conditions:
*Test ride subject to applicant status and availability

#NEVERSTOPCHALLENGING

MAKE LIFE A RIDE

FLASHBACK 1967

WORDS: BERTIE SIMMONDS
PICS: MORTONS ARCHIVE

LUCK OF THE GOD!

For the 1967 Senior TT Mike Hailwood faced a bit a challenge in his bid to score his second hat-trick of wins around the Isle of Man course – but lady luck was smiling.

This was the Diamond Jubilee week for the event and Giacomo Agostini had lapped in practice at 106.56mph. The crowd had been wowed by the Italian's 108.38mph opening lap of the race too – a new absolute lap record. He was now leading Hailwood in the race by 11.8 seconds; surely the Briton couldn't respond? As Mike streaked across the line, fans could see him giving a 'thumbs down' to the pit-wall… Something was clearly wrong with the bike.

Ago and Mike had left the others trailing – this was going to be a battle between two greats. Mike dug deep and set a new record of his own on the second lap: 108.77mph – Ago's lead was now down to eight seconds. By the time the leading pair pitted for fuel at the end of lap three, Hailwood had clawed back a further six seconds – leaving just two seconds between Agostini and Mike at the half-way point in the race.

Almost disaster at the pit-stop: Mike's twist-grip had come loose, hence the gesticulating towards the pits, and – calling for a hammer – Hailwood bashed it into place himself. The 47.8 second pit-stop for Mike helped the Italian to increase his lead back to 12 seconds at the end of lap four, but then disaster struck – Ago's chain snapped at Windy Corner and the great man had to free-wheel his way into the Grandstand: and all on his birthday, too!

Hailwood pressed on, not knowing what had happened to Ago until he reached Ramsey, where the news was conveyed to him by mechanic Nobby Clark, who was working his boards.

Mike could cruise to the win – and all with that broken throttle-grip! He said: "I was lucky – if Ago's chain hadn't snapped, I don't think I could have won. Lap two was about as fast as I could go – I made up a lot of time, but lost it at the pit stop when I had to fix that throttle. It worked loose again on the fifth lap and I was almost riding one-handed! I actually had to stop once to push it back on again and was holding it on for most of that last lap!"

Mike 'The Bike' would retire from motorcycle racing at the end of that year, but would return again in 1978… This would be one of his greatest victories.

FLASHBACK 1982

WORDS: RON HASLAM
PICS: MORTONS ARCHIVE

RON'S REVENGE...

Ron Haslam had paid his dues at the Isle of Man TT and – he felt – 1981 was going to be a big year for him.

"Back in 1981 I knew I had a chance and was confident of an Isle of Man TT victory when I lined up for the start of the Formula One race. Graeme Crosby had a chain problem so wasn't allowed to set off at his allocated time slot: instead he was made to start from way down the field. To me, that meant it was down to Joey Dunlop and myself. In the race, Joey had to change a tyre at the pit-stop but I was flying. Only my bike could beat me now, so I backed off a little bit. Finally I passed the flag and doubled back up the slip-road to celebrate. Ann was there and hugged me. The mechanics were all slapping my back: in all honesty I couldn't have felt any higher.

"My joy was short-lived. Word came through that Suzuki had protested: but I had already stood on the podium. Wasn't that enough? The rest was a blur. I refused to believe it, until that night in the hotel at the function expecting to receive my award and they read out the names and said that Crosby had won. I was numb and the team were furious. They'd removed the four-minute penalty but I would have pushed harder had I known Crosby was in the race. The rules said if you go to the back of the grid, you lose time for each place. But suddenly that had changed.

"In a 226-mile race, there were plenty of opportunities for something to go wrong, so with that supposed big lead I cantered to what I thought was a win. Honda protested, but without success. Instead they painted their bikes black for the Classic at the end of the week and we wore black leathers in a silent protest. I would go back the next year – 1982 – and take an undisputed win in the Formula One race. I think it was a popular win, thanks to what went on the year before. But, after all the relief and joy something had changed. I had wanted the TT win for so long, but once I had it – nothing was the same again."

Island Racer 11

LIKE FATHER...

As the son of trials expert, TT racer, and bike dealer Allan Jefferies, it was clear which way Tony Jefferies' life was heading.

Born in 1948, he left school in 1965 to take up an apprenticeship with the BSA Group. He would finish his apprenticeship with Triumph but left due to personal differences with how unions were behaving and joined the family motorcycle business.

He started racing in 1968 because of very particular circumstances, rather than having a burning desire to take to the track. "My first road race was at Croft on an old Triumph; we'd taken this thing in part-exchange and it was ready to race – so dad said I may as well use it! Dad took me to the circuit too, so for him to later chuck me out for going racing as a bit daft!"

Dad Allan wanted Tony to concentrate on trials, and both he and brother Nick would do well at the discipline. Jefferies would take part in the 1968 Manx Grand Prix but failed to finish the Senior race on his Triumph. In 1969 he took to the TT proper and bagged a best result of 6th place in the Production 750cc class. He took another impressive 6th place in the 1970 Senior TT riding a G50 Matchless.

Tony really made a name for himself in 1971, winning the Junior TT in a very special year for the rider: he'd already won the Formula 750 and narrowly missed out on a third TT win in a week when beaten by Ray Pickrell in the Production 750 race.

He was mixing his racing with his responsibilities at Allan Jefferies Motorcycles, as he had taken over from his father in December 1970 aged just 22. A product of his generation (and having been among the first to liberate Belsen concentration camp during the Second World War) Allan would rail against Tony's decision to take on German manufacturer BMW as a franchise… but time would prove Tony right. Allan Jefferies Motorcycles would become one of, if not THE best, BMW dealers in the UK in the decades to come.

Tony's TT career would peak again in 1973 with his third win in the Production 750cc race, riding the famous 'Slippery Sam' – the Triumph Trident that won a total of five TT races. Sadly, it would prove to be Tony's last TT as he was paralysed in a crash Mallory Park's Race of the Year in September of 1973.

Tony would continue in the motorcycle business as a real leading-light and an astute businessman. Also, his son David would make his own impact upon the Isle of Man TT races…

Tony stepped down from running Allan Jefferies Motorcycles in 2000, with daughter Louise taking over. Despite his own declining health towards the end of 2021, Tony insisted on attending the funerals of his great friends Paul Smart and Peggy Appleyard, wife of Colin Appleyard. Sadly, Tony Jefferies himself died on December 29, 2021,

WORDS: BERITE SIMMONDS
PICS: MORTONS ARCHIVE

FLASHBACK 1973

FLASHBACK 2002

...LIKE SON!

Is it really 20 years since the late, great David Jefferies completed his last Isle of Man TT race?

It seems like only yesterday that the big man – who has inspired so many TT greats since – was up there and winning. His last race on the Island was the 2002 Senior event which (naturally) he won, setting a new lap record at 127.29mph. This was the last of his 2002 treble, which included the Formula 1 race (new lap record of 126.68mph) and the Production 1000 race (seen here as our main shot) on a more standard version of his much-loved Suzuki GSX-R1000.

It was DJ's third triple at the TT in three years (the 2001 event was cancelled due to Foot and Mouth disease). That's nine TT wins in just three years – an unprecedented feat. But the loveable big Yorkshireman was far more than just a TT racer. Between 1990 and 2003 he raced in almost every class imaginable, from British Superbikes to World Superbikes and even 500cc Grands Prix. Think about that for a minute: this means that David raced against the likes of Wayne Rainey, Mick Doohan and Kevin Schwantz in Grands Prix as well as World Superbike talents such as Carl Fogarty, Aaron Slight, Scott Russell et al…

DJ was also British Powerbike TT Production Challenge Champion, Triumph Speed Triple champion, and two-time British Superstock champion. When you consider his background as part of the Jefferies racing dynasty, he really was a chip off the old block.

That said, his 'debut' at the TT itself was less than auspicious! On visiting the 1992 Isle of Man TT event on a road bike he was thrown in jail for his antics: "I blasted down the full length of the seafront promenade on the back wheel, only to be dragged off the bike by the police, who had watched me all the way!" The £100 bail was eventually paid.

We're lucky it was, for he'd make his debut on Mona's Isle in 1996, alongside other debutants such as John McGuinness and Bruce Anstey. That's not to say he didn't have reservations. "I always said I'd never come here – you had to be a nutter to race at this place," he admitted. "But my dad reckoned my style would suit the place and, after a few good results at the North West and Scarborough, I decided to give it a try."

And try he did – winning nine TT races in the process: imagine him out there now, alongside his good mate McGuinness, in his 50th year.

WORDS: BERITE SIMMONDS
PICS: DON MORLEY, MORTONS ARCHIVE

JOHN MCGUINNESS

RETURN OF THE KING!

The second most successful Isle of Man TT rider has had an indifferent last few TT events for many different reasons, but he's back and he's ready to rumble. Can the old lion get one last big-bike win?

WORDS: BERTIE SIMMONDS
PICS: HONDA UK, ISLE OF MAN TT, STEPHEN DAVISON/PACEMAKER PRESS

JOHN MCGUINNESS

2019 wasn't the best for our John!

ABOVE: But saying that, he still got a TT Zero podium placing...

"Hi Bertie, I've got John on the line so I'm just hooking us all up together on our phones…" At last! John McGuinness, 23-time Isle of Man TT winner, is a hard man to pin down and often very evasive unless one uses the might of his 'current employers' to get hold of him. Now, courtesy of Honda PR wonder Becky Simms, he's on the other line and ready to chat.

I say 'elusive' not because John has ever displayed any of the arrogance or ignorance that mark out some (well, maybe two) current top TT-race stars – he's never purposely avoided an interview, but – well – McPint being McPint – he just finds himself busy: a lot. In the old days (we're talking more than two decades back) you'd text him and you'd wait. And wait… and wait. You'd then text again and swear and curse at him. Eventually he'd bell you back and apologise: it would always just take some time…

But times have changed. PR is more advanced so it's better to go through the proper channels than insult the world's fastest bricklayer or is it cockle-picker? More of which later. Becky tells me he's just finished a chat with MotoGP journalist Mat Oxley and that he's: '…on good form!' We exchange pleasantries, he remembers me (many don't, I'm a forgettable kind of bloke) and I ask him how he's doing. "Well," he says, "I'm 50 and I can still get an erection, so I think I'm doing alright!"

Oh yes, McGuinness is on good form alright! Let's recap… 2022 really does mark 'The Return of the King' back into the fold that is Honda Racing UK. And by that we mean a 'proper' return, not the abortive one that ended so badly in 2017. It's fair to say that the last few years have not been good to John McGuinness when it comes to road-racing. The 'new' Honda CBR1000RR Fireblade he rode alongside Guy Martin in 2017 had some sort of electronics glitch that blipped the throttle, spitting him off the Blade at the North West 200, the

JOHN MCGUINNESS

Crossing the line with a big pumper… how we all remember McPint!

injuries from which lingered.

"I know you lot put this in the last *Island Racer*, back in 2019," says McGuinness, "but it's still true – there is no way I wanted to end my Isle of Man TT career all broken up on a bloody golf course or wherever it was I landed; I didn't want my TT journey to end there and I have not forgotten how to ride the TT course." John's recuperation would be slow, so that by 2018 he was still injured, meaning he had to sit the event out again. 2019 should have been special… maybe very special.

"Ahh yes, the Norton," laughs John. "The Norton thing was all Hollywood which went wrong, really. Let's just say that in 2019 I struggled with that silver machine which literally just fell apart all around me: at The Bungalow an engine bolt was actually dragging on the ground and fell out…" John would take 17th and 15th in the two Supersport races that year on a Honda, alongside the two big-bike Norton no-shows (DNFs) as well as a Lightweight DNF (Norton again) but it wasn't all bad, thanks to a 2nd in the TT Zero.

Time then to make amends… and time – or the time – seems right. The stars seem to have aligned: "Yeah, I'm 50 this year," says McGuinness, "it will be my 100th TT start in 2022 as well, which is significant and it's my 30th year of racing so it seems right to get back into the Honda family."

Family indeed: McGuinness's racing career at the Isle of Man has seen 19 wins on Honda machinery and most of those in the big class on the Honda CBR1000RR Fireblade, a bike which is very close to his heart. He likened his main race-winning versions, which hardly changed over the best part of a decade, to a pair of slippers… "And that's what you want," says John. "You need to be comfortable on it, you need to enjoy riding it, it needs to be stable too – you can't fight it. It needs to be consistent and you need it to be reliable, so that you don't have to worry about engine bolts or things dropping off the thing. I never once set off on a race on a Fireblade and worried about that. OK, so sometimes it wasn't the fastest bike out there, but as an all-round package the Blade was the best."

But what about the latest version, considering his issues with the previous incarnation in 2017: "It's a new bike and I look forward to the challenge," he shrugs. "Glenn Irwin my roads partner for 2022 said the 2020-on bike is very good. The whole fly-by-wire thing is new to me, and – while I've used auto-blippers before – I haven't around the Isle of Man. Don't forget there's a new Kawasaki and BMW out this year too… so it's going to be interesting and none of us know how it's going to pan out."

The Fireblade though – for many years – was the bike to beat, even if it really wasn't much more than a Superstock machine at the start of its evolution. McGuinness says: "The base Superstock bike was a

ABOVE: Twenty-three wins have made him the second most successful TT rider ever, behind Joey.

BELOW: "I didn't want to end my TT career on a golf course…"

Waiting for the off...

great package which just went around and around but you can't stand still. When I got 3rd in the 2016 TT I felt that I had done all I could that day so I wasn't unhappy. After all, you can only piss with the dick you have, right? Things have moved on, riders have moved on, so I have to as well – which isn't always easy."

One thing McGuinness can depend on is the team… They've been there, done that and continue to do so – both on the roads and in the British Superbike championship. "That's a weight off your mind at a place like the TT," he says. "You're over there for two and a half weeks so you trust the people putting the bike together and all the crew are on the same page. For that length of time people can get fed up, or lose focus – but not this team. They are the most successful team out there.

"As to the bike itself for the TT, we are going to build a bike that isn't over-complicated as you don't need it. I know some factories spend millions on developing certain gadgets but at a race like the TT it's just something else that could go wrong. With this new Fireblade I'm excited, it really ticks some 'TT' boxes, but we'll finally see what's what when the bike is finished."

But what about his own preparations? With no 'event' itself in 2020 and 2021, will this cause issues? He says: "Well, we're all in the same boat there, aren't we? There isn't much you can do to prepare for things in some ways. You cross the 'Ts' and dot the 'Is' but nothing, NOTHING prepares you for Bray Hill that first time. You just grit your teeth and get on with it. That's why I'm looking forward to putting 'the slippers' back on.

"We'll do some testing with the Superstock bike to get more confident with it. It would have been easy to sit on my arse over the last couple of years, but I haven't! I've been doing enduro riding and then there was the Ducati TriOptions Cup so I've kept on the wave and been pushing hard to keep my fitness up. That Ducati series has been so much fun. Who'd have thought it: me and Chris 'Stalker' Walker, still ripping it up with the youngsters. It's been like going 'back to basics' really.

"Racing is just for fun again. I mean, I used to get my arse wiped for me a little bit back in the past, as a factory rider, but suddenly, with my own little team (which I'm dead proud of) we'd be back to how it used to be. We'd have a beer at night and put the barbecue on and have a laugh: just as it should be. And we all know that your Hickmans and your Harrisons have been doing BSB rounds to keep sharp, too…"

For many it would be a magical return to the TT and Honda if McGuinness could go fast, (well, REALLY fast) but what does the man himself think? "Hey, in 2019 I

BELOW: When John was ejected from his Honda at the North West 200 in 2017, it was left to Guy Martin to take on the roads.

JOHN McGUINNESS

showed I could go fast! I was quick on that Mugen in the TT Zero," he says. "For me, the plan is to line up, aged 50, for my 100th TT start after 30 years of racing and enjoy it. Am I going to do a 135mph lap? Well, hand-on-heart I may struggle, but I will be there at the end of the race, so let's just see what happens..."

John is partnered on the roads this year with BSB winner and established short-circuit star Glenn Irwin. McGuinness has been helping Glenn (see boxout) but having a TT newcomer alongside him also makes him recall his first TT race experience, from way back in 1996. "That year..." he recalls, "...it was my first TT, DJ's (David Jefferies) and Bruce's (Anstey); I think we've got 40 TT wins between us, so it was a good year's intake, that. Obviously, TT racing doesn't suit everybody, but the cream always goes to the top: think of your Hickmans or your Steve Platers, or others. You need to be a different animal to race the TT."

He adds: "I think the race and the organisers of the race have changed, too. Back in the day you were told to consider yourself lucky to get an entry. My preparation was coming to the TT event as a fan and doing laps on my Yamaha TZR125 in 1989 (he'd only just got his L-plates on) and later my Kawasaki KR1-S. You'd go and buy DUKE Marketing's videos, the obvious one being Joey Dunlop's V-Four Victory.

"When you'd turn up for your first race you'd just go and get on with it. Back then – I cut my teeth at the TT on a 250 – I couldn't have imagined going around the course on a superbike – but some do. Now they pick you up from the airport, they take you around the course and talk in depth about each and every section of the track. Is it easier for newcomers now? Maybe, maybe not. The track-side furniture is the same, a few corners are different, but the bikes are faster..."

Is that a worry then? That today's bikes are faster than before? If you think of it, today's superbike that does the RST Superbike/Milwaukee Senior races could have around 200-220bhp. Twenty-five years or so ago, Honda's V4 RC45s had anything between 150-180bhp. Today's 600cc Supersport bikes (often ridden by newcomers at the Manx) are nudging 130bhp, which is

Another result, this time in the Classic TT.

We want him to take another win in 2022... who doesn't?

The happy ride back to the paddock when you've won.

the same sort of power output that a good 750cc superbike made 30 years back.

"I worry about all newcomers," says McGuinness. "Racing is dangerous and that side of it isn't going to go away. For Glenn, well, I can only give him so much information. All newcomers are vulnerable for a few years and Glenn will be no different. Remember, the TT is so different to the North West 200. One is a race against other riders, while the TT is against the clock. I have no doubt in my mind that Glenn could eventually be a TT winner. I know it's also not about the money for Glenn – and that's important."

McGuinness explains that he's been pulling out some of the details of the legendary Isle of Man track for Irwin to focus on. "You can watch all the on-boards you like," says John, "but it's the little bits that you don't see. You don't know where the wind can come from, or affect you

ABOVE: Honda has been the home of most of his triumphs.

on a lap on certain sections of the track. Or how the wind really hits you up on The Mountain, or where you can lose visibility thanks to where the low sun can be during different sessions, catching you out. You can even talk about how some of the gutters are full of shit which can be scary if you go out that wide.

"Glenn's already got the main ingredients to move forward and take part in the TT: there comes a point where I have to step out of the way and he just goes and does it for himself. I also don't think Glenn will mind when I say that I think the COVID break has seen him really grow up a bit and raise his game, being with the Honda Racing UK team has helped with that."

Glenn has a good chance at BSB glory this year on short-circuits within the Honda Racing UK set-up; does McGuinness ever look back at his career and wonder what might have been away from the TT? "Hey, I was

GENTLY DOES IT

Glenn Irwin is looking forward to the Isle of Man TT this year and he says he's missed it, which is strange, for a newcomer.

"I know," he says. "It's hard for me to miss the TT as how can you miss someone you've never met? But that's the truth. We went through a period where we wondered if COVID-19 had killed the North West 200 and TT. I think what would have weirdly hurt me more was if it was delayed for one more year, rather than cancelled forever. I've got a plan for the TT which I have to start no later than RIGHT now… That's because I've stored up all this bank of knowledge that I just have to use and it's refreshing that the work done prior to COVID is still there and can be used.

"I know that my preparation was put away somewhere in my brain and I can access it now and use it. In fact, since the TT was confirmed for 2022, I've had a hard-on for road-racing whenever I've thought about it. The missus has loved it!"

Ahem… apologies, but it seems Honda Racing UK's road-racers seem to be 'erection obsessed' in 2022.

Glenn's 'day job' is to try and claim the British Superbike title for Honda Racing UK. For 2022 they have a four-man team to try to do this. Irwin is joined by 2021 Superstock 1000 champ Tom Neave, while the two Japanese stars Ryo Mizuno and Takumi Takahashi are staying for another go at the UK circuits. Irwin: "That Japanese link has given us a real lift. It's a bit of a feather in my cap for HRC to believe in me. And not many teams get such support; I hope to see some of the big HRC bosses at the Isle of Man TT."

It's understandable that Glenn would get into bike racing, if not the TT. His father Alan Irwin was one of Northern Ireland's most successful riders in the 1980s and 1990s. "I think my dad has a record for the most wins on short and road circuits or something," explains Glenn. "Either way I'm very proud of his record. Dad beat Joey Dunlop from time to time and raced against Barry Sheene. He led North West 200 races – he should have won one – but he never did the TT and maybe that was a ceiling on his fame. I say to him and Brian Reid that they don't tell people enough how good they were! He was better than Phillip McCallen and even Phil says so! Maybe he could have gone to Grands Prix full-time, but in saying no he could stay with my mum. His values have been passed on to his racing sons, my brothers Andrew, Graeme and myself."

Glenn's main focus would initially be on short circuits, from British Supersport and into the Superbike class. He made his debut on the roads at the 2015 NW200 and was straight on the pace. He also impressed on his Macau debut in 2016. The Island promises to be a whole new ball-game.

"John McGuinness has been a great help along the way," admits Glenn. "He's told me: 'get through the first two years…' He'll send me pics of the course at random and ask me what corners they are. I'm competitive and I look up to John, so I want to impress him and get it right! He helps without knowing, too. I've got my training on the static push-bike and I cycle to a lap of the TT, which is his from 2016. Thing is, I reckon I'll have to get his 2016 exhaust on my bike to get the lines right as it sounds right!"

The value of watching TT footage from the masters is not to be underestimated as Glenn explains: "Of course I've got YouTube, but Greenlight who do all the footage have been very helpful. There's also a simulator that's

A kiss for his favourite 'slipper!'

Winning at the TT became almost as much of a disease for John as just taking part.

1999 250cc British champion, I finished 4th in the World Endurance Championship in 2016, I won at Daytona, I did 500cc Grands Prix and other things," he says. "But if you win at the TT you're called a 'road specialist!' OK, sometimes I held back in some races before the TT because that was my focus and often where the kudos was."

So, as an older and wiser man, is John McGuinness the 'McPint half full', or 'half empty?' "Oh I've loved every minute of my career and life," he says. "I never thought I'd get to 50 and have 23 Isle of Man TT wins. Having my time again I wouldn't change a thing. When I was younger, all my mates went to acid parties and stuff – I went to Cadwell Park to watch the racing. Then, later on – when they were going to raves – I would go down to Preston Docks to get some weight off for racing by doing some cockle picking. Well, it was mussels

been made available and the TT organisers themselves have been absolutely fantastic and I go over when I can. I know I've not had my 'exam' yet, but I do think I should get an A-Star for revision alone…"

Chatting to Glenn, while you can sense the eagerness (and fun) he's got his feet firmly on the ground. "I can sit here and say I want two weeks of good weather and that I want X, Y and Z, but I'm there for three weeks all-told and I just want to enjoy it. That's my first target. The potential is to win the Senior race – a fair few years down the line! I want to enjoy the whole thing, the location, the people, the Manx Queenies! I want it to be as relaxed as possible – that's always been my approach to road-racing. Sure, I have some personal goals: I'd be lying if I didn't have dreams either. But it's all about trying to control expectation and let it all happen naturally."

Having a family seems to keep Glenn rooted firmly in reality, which can only be a good thing. "I think my girlfriend Laura is looking for an engagement ring," says Glenn. "People in racing sometimes say it's best to be single, kids slow you down, but I'm like Jonathan Rea. We've got Freddie who is five and Gia who is four months old. I want to work hard for them and for the rest of my career. If I can have a career as long as Jeremy McWilliams – I'll be happy!"

ABOVE: Glenn (2) ahead of Peter Hickman (60). Who will have the upper hand when they go to the Island?

JOHN McGUINNESS

On his beloved Fireblade.

ABOVE: If he can get back onto the top step in 2022 it will be the stuff of legend – it's happened before…

Always stylish.

Knowledge is everything – John's first race on the Island was 1996.

He first pottered round on a road-bike Yamaha TZR125 in 1989.

ABOVE: At Honda Racing UK, John is back with the 'family'.

really, but it always sounded more romantic saying I was a cockle picker…"

John still rates a few of his many successes as special: "It's not fair to pick out one, really," he says. "But clearly the first win was epic for me, my first 130mph lap was epic, the 2015 race where I was written off as an also-ran, that I was too old and past it but I came out fighting and won it. It's always hard to say which one…"

One thing McGuinness does do is have respect for anyone who wants to take on the Isle of Man TT. We have a little chat about one of my good friends – Chris Moss – who was one of the other newcomers in 1996 and never went back. My mate Mossy had the dubious distinction of being the only rider that week to have TWO helicopter rides back to Noble's Hospital during race week… "Anyone who goes to race at the TT – yes even Mossy – gets my total respect," says John. "To finish wherever in a TT race takes a lot of doing, be it 1st, 10th, 15th or 30th but some people just aren't suited to that sort of racing."

It goes without saying that – even from his first TT in 1996, there have been good and bad times. "I hated the TT in practice week that year," he says. "The weather was shit and then Rob Holden and Mick Lofthouse were killed." Mick was a friend and he would lose other great friends David Jefferies (2003) and Ian 'Gus' Scott (2005) at the TT. "It's the people which make this sport," he says. "I was the first at the scene for DJ's crash and – afterwards – DJ's dad Tony was there telling me to get back on the bike. So you do. Despite the weather in practice week, race week in 1996 was brilliant, things just change. And I've really had some brilliant times at the Isle of Man. When you're doing 180mph with your hair on fire and the sun's shining, it's the best. The great bits easily outweigh the shit bits… TT racing and bike racing in general isn't a drug as some people call it, it's a disease."

THE PERFECT HAND

TT 2022

#TEAM**SHOEI**

SHOEI PREMIUM HELMETS

shoeihelmetsuk

shoeiassured.co.uk

WHO'S WHO IN 22!

WHO'S WHO IN 22

We are back! After an enforced two-year break thanks to the global COVID-19 pandemic, we are ready to go racing on the Isle of Man once more, but who do you need to watch out for out on the roads on two and three wheels? Welcome to *Island Racer's* 'Who's who in 22!'

WORDS: PHIL WAIN
PICS: STEPHEN DAVISON – PACEMAKER PRESS

WHO'S WHO IN 22!

TOP 20 RIDERS

PETER HICKMAN
DATE OF BIRTH April 8, 1987
AGE 35
FROM Burton upon Trent, England
RACES Superbike, Senior & Superstock
(Gas Monkey Garage by FHO Racing BMW)
Supersport (Trooper Beer Triumph)
Supertwin
(FHO Racing Norton or Aprilia – TBC)
TT DEBUT 2014
NUMBER OF STARTS 31
NUMBER OF FINISHES 25
NUMBER OF WINS 5
NUMBER OF PODIUMS 14
NUMBER OF REPLICAS 24 silver, 1 bronze
PERSONAL BEST TT LAP 135.452mph

To say Peter Hickman has come a long way since making his TT debut in 2014 would be an understatement and having taken racing on the roads to a new level, he's now, without doubt, the current King of the Mountain. And when you look at his record at the Macau and Ulster Grand Prix events, the North West 200 is the only International road race where he hasn't dominated although he's still won races there too!

What the Burton upon Trent rider has achieved in recent years has been nothing short of superb and if you look at his TT record since 2017, it's simply sensational with his 17 races seeing him stand on the rostrum some 14 times. Five of those have been wins and only a few technical gremlins outside of his control have prevented him winning more. His speed, across the classes, has been consistently at lap record pace and he certainly comes into TT 2022 as the favourite.

It's no small coincidence that the success of 2017-19 all came with the same team, Smiths Racing and although the entire set-up is now owned by Macau businesswoman and TT enthusiast Faye Ho, the support staff, including crew chief Darren Jones, remains the same. The family atmosphere suits him down to the ground and it's an environment that is certainly harmonious.

Thanks to a long-standing relationship with Jones that dates back more than a decade, everyone in the team knows their role and they know when it's time to have fun and when it's time to focus with Hickman remaining laid-back and jovial throughout it all. That relaxed approach has, ultimately, played a huge part in his success which, when combined with his extreme talent makes for a formidable combination, one that the rest of the opposition will again find hard to crack this year.

Racing, and winning, at the TT is never a formality though and red-hot favourites don't always come out on top but, at the same time, it's hard to see Hickman failing to win more races this year especially as he's riding better than ever in the British Superbike Championship. Given the right conditions, upping his outright lap record even further is also more than a distinct possibility while it's also not unreasonable to suggest that he'll dominate for many years to come given he's still only 35.

He won't look at it like that, preferring instead to overlook any such thoughts and keep his feet firmly on the ground whilst he still maintains that the TT is about enjoyment and that the BSB series remains his bread and butter. One can only think what the outcome would be if that outlook was reversed!

The outright lap record holder, Peter Hickman... will that lap be threatened in 2022?

DEAN HARRISON
DATE OF BIRTH January 24, 1989
AGE 33
FROM Bradford, England
RACES Superbike, Superstock, Supersport and Senior (DAO Racing Kawasaki)
TT DEBUT 2011
NUMBER OF STARTS 47
NUMBER OF FINISHES 38
NUMBER OF WINS 3
NUMBER OF PODIUMS 16
NUMBER OF REPLICAS 32 silver, 6 bronze
PERSONAL BEST TT LAP 134.918mph

Dean Harrison won two of the last ten TT races and stood on the podium in the other eight, statistics that would normally have made him the stand-out performer at the TT. But, unfortunately for Harrison, he's found himself competing against and upstaged by Hickman, his nemesis if you like, who he must be sick of the sight of!

WHO'S WHO IN 22!

Dean Harrison and Peter Hickman celebrate after the 2019 Senior TT race which Dean won: are they the cream of the crop for 2022?

LEFT: Vindication at last! Deano bags the 2019 Senior TT win.

The ever chirpy Harrison would never make such a comment however, instead praising the efforts of his main rival and, as things stand, he's the one most likely to defeat the FHO Racing rider. Like Hickman, Harrison has benefited from remaining with the same team, in his case the Silicone Engineering Kawasaki outfit (now called DAO Racing), and the four years with them from 2016-19 saw him establish himself as one of the top three road racers in the world.

It all really clicked in 2018 when he tore out of the blocks during practice week and again on the opening lap of the majority of the races, tactics he'll no doubt employ again in June while competing in the British Superbike Championship. The latter has also played its part significantly. Racing week in, week out against the country's leading short circuit riders has made Harrison a better, more polished rider and, in turn, a better road racer.

He continues to make steps forward in BSB and will be ready to take the fight to Hickman and, it has to be said, others this week – but if there's one area where he still needs to improve, it's the Mountain. This became apparent in 2018 but he did make progress in 2019 and he managed to add a Senior TT win to a multitude of other podium finishes. Three TT wins is no mean feat for any rider but Harrison, now entering his 10th year of TT competition, could and, perhaps should, have won more. He can certainly add to that tally in 2022 though and go on to get himself into double figures for race wins in the years to come but it's all about small margins at the TT nowadays and improving that little bit in each area will ultimately pay dividends.

IslandRacer

WHO'S WHO IN 22!

ABOVE: Can a move to Ducati power for the TT with the successful PBM team bring a big-bike race win for Michael Dunlop?

ABOVE: Can Ducati power put a smile on Michael Dunlop's face for 2022?

MICHAEL DUNLOP
DATE OF BIRTH April 10, 1989
AGE 33
FROM Ballymoney, Northern Ireland
RACES Superbike and Senior (PBM Ducati)
Superstock (MD Racing BMW)
Supersport (MD Racing Yamaha)
Supertwin (SC Project Reparto Corse Paton)
TT DEBUT 2007
NUMBER OF STARTS 66
NUMBER OF FINISHES 49
NUMBER OF WINS 19
NUMBER OF PODIUMS 29
NUMBER OF REPLICAS 46 silver, 3 bronze
PERSONAL BEST TT LAP 133.962mph

Probably one of Michael Dunlop's most challenging years on the island was 2019 and although he took a 19th win with victory in the Lightweight race, he was far from his usual, ebullient self in all of his other races – 4ths, 5ths and 6ths are not what we're used to from the Ulsterman.

There were a number of underlying reasons for his relatively low-key performances, the first of which was almost 12 months out of the saddle with his only race between the 2018 and 2019 TT events being the North West 200. The second reason was a wrist injury sustained in a short circuit crash ahead of the NW200 which he, understandably, played down but which undeniably affected him. And when he needed track time to get up to speed, he didn't get it thanks to the poor weather.

If truth be told, he never looked himself all year and only he'll know the real reasons for that. But what he has done since is get himself back to full fitness and he's now as lean and as fit as he's ever been, which can only mean one thing – he's determined to get his Superbike crown back. And to do that, he's taken the gamble of doing it with Ducati, a brilliant bike and manufacturer on the short circuits, but one whose TT record falls a long way short compared to its rivals. No one knows the Panigale better than the British Championship-winning Paul Bird Motorsport outfit though and Dunlop couldn't wish to be with a better team to aid his latest challenge. Whether this combination of rider and team can make the Ducati a race winner around the Mountain Course remains to be seen but, if they can do it, it will certainly be one of their greatest feats.

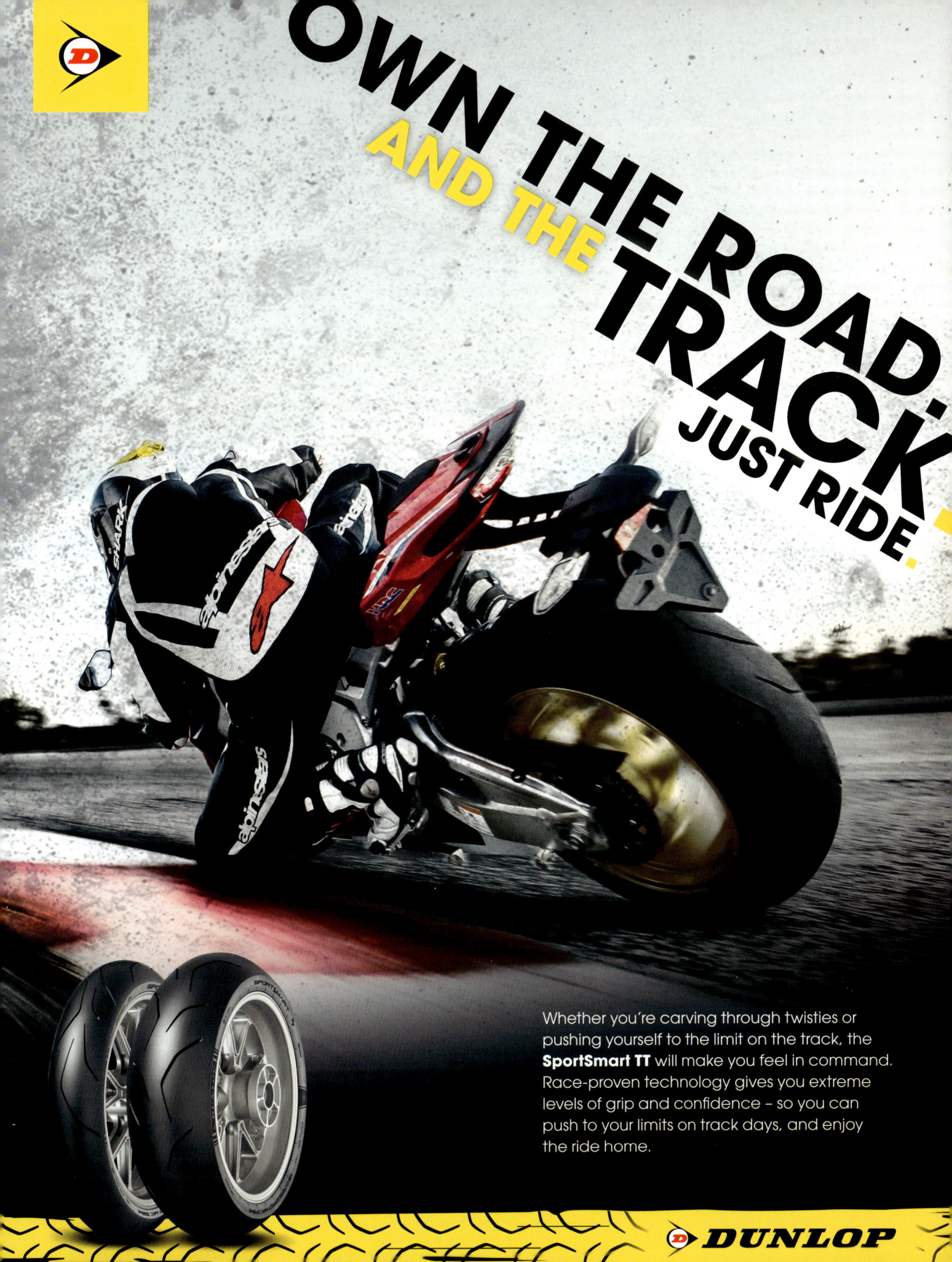

WHO'S WHO IN 22!

IAN HUTCHINSON
DATE OF BIRTH August 12, 1979
AGE 42
FROM Bingley, England
RACES Superbike, Senior and Superstock (Milwaukee BMW)
Supersport (Boyce Precision Engineering/Russell Racing Yamaha)
TT DEBUT 2004
NUMBER OF STARTS 63
NUMBER OF FINISHES 49
NUMBER OF WINS 16
NUMBER OF PODIUMS 27
NUMBER OF REPLICAS 46 silver, 3 bronze
PERSONAL BEST TT LAP 133.115mph

Ian Hutchinson has endured a tough time since he last tasted victory at the Isle of Man and you have to go back to June 7, 2017 to find his 16th and (to date) last TT victory. Just two days later, he was left with another badly broken leg and while he's raced each year since, he's been far from the Hutchy we know.

A practice spill in 2019 at the 11th Milestone, which he was lucky to walk away from, put paid to his chances with 10th place in the opening Supersport race his best result, his two years with Honda Racing not at all how he'd envisaged. But now he's back and more determined than ever to return to winning ways.

Reunited with TAS Racing and the BMW for the three 1000cc races and a Yamaha YZF-R6, with which he's taken four previous victories, for the Supersport class, his TT campaign has a look of familiarity about it and that could work in his favour. Although a lot has happened since his last aforementioned victory, the fact remains that he's still the 4th quickest rider ever to have lapped the Mountain Course.

He'll have to go quicker than that to win another big bike race and his best chances may come on the 600, but his determination remains second to none. He's recently demonstrated good form on the short circuits and he'll enjoy nothing more than proving the doubters, who say his best days are probably behind him, wrong.

JOHN MCGUINNESS
DATE OF BIRTH April 16, 1972
AGE 50
FROM Morecambe, England
RACES Superbike, Superstock & Senior (Honda Racing UK)
Supersport (SMT/Blue Earth Construction Honda)
TT DEBUT 1996
NUMBER OF STARTS 99
NUMBER OF FINISHES 81
NUMBER OF WINS 23
NUMBER OF PODIUMS 47
NUMBER OF REPLICAS 75 silver, 4 bronze
PERSONAL BEST TT LAP 132.701mph

It's fair to say John McGuinness's last outing at the TT was a disaster with the Norton machinery failing to live up to his expectations given the manufacturer's performance in previous years in the hands of Australian pairing Josh Brookes and David Johnson. The 23-time TT winner was unable to get anywhere near Brookes' lap of 131.745mph, set in 2018, with reliability also having dropped significantly and he only managed one race lap on the Norton, a disappointing effort for all concerned.

Of course, the problems on the Island were just the tip of the iceberg for the British manufacturer as they rapidly unravelled later in the year and all their financial issues came to light, some of which affected McGuinness. Desperate not to walk away from the TT on such a low, John carefully considered his options before signing with Quattro Plant Bournemouth Kawasaki as replacement for the departing James Hillier.

Pete Extance's family-run team was the ideal fit for the Morecambe Missile at that stage in his career and there's no doubt they

Both Ian Hutchinson and John McGuinness will be hoping for a return to form in 2022 – will they win a big bike race again?

would have given him every chance of climbing back onto a Superbike podium. Racing has a funny way of changing though and John, like others, has seen his plans change as a result of the pandemic; a return to Honda Racing, in the 30th year of the Fireblade and on his 100th TT start, was just too good an opportunity to refuse.

It's six years since John last finished on a Superbike podium and achieving that this year will be a tough ask given the pace of the leading pack now, something McGuinness is all too aware of. But given the right tools, which he'll most definitely have at his disposal, he's still more than capable of doing a professional job, just as he has done throughout his career.

A win is probably out of reach but at the TT anything can happen and a podium is still well within his grasp – and with rumours of retirement at the end of the season, what better way to bow out? More than anything though, McGuinness wants to enjoy this year's TT and give a good account of himself to repay the faith shown in him by the team and prove – not that it needs proving – that he's still a formidable TT competitor.

Island Racer 33

WHO'S WHO IN 22!

CONOR CUMMINS
DATE OF BIRTH May 27, 1986
AGE 35
FROM Ramsey, Isle of Man
RACES Superbike, Senior, Superstock and Supersport (Padgetts Racing)
TT DEBUT 2006
NUMBER OF STARTS 62
NUMBER OF FINISHES 42
NUMBER OF WINS 0
NUMBER OF PODIUMS 10
NUMBER OF REPLICAS 40 silver, 2 bronze
PERSONAL BEST TT LAP 132.610mph

The quiet man of racing, Cummins is also, arguably, the most laid-back and sometimes it's hard to imagine him tearing round the Mountain Course at breath-taking speeds given his languid demeanour in the paddock! But he most certainly does, and to devastating effect, with the Manxman currently experiencing some of his best ever years in racing.

Having slipped down the pecking order somewhat, Cummins has been revitalised in recent years, something for which he, along with the Padgett's Honda team, must take great credit for. Beneath the quiet exterior lies a steely determination and while Hickman and Harrison may have grabbed the headlines in recent years, Conor has been as good as anyone else. That's more than seen in his run of podiums in the Superbike and Senior races, having finished on the rostrum in all four of those particular races in 2018 and 2019. He's also done similar elsewhere on the roads, particularly at the Ulster Grand Prix where he's been as quick as anyone, and the challenge now is to try to bridge the gap to the front runners.

Of course, the TT is an endurance race where getting to the end is more important than outright pace but it's speed that gets you to the front initially and Cummins' quickest lap, set in the last Senior race to be held, is some 22s slower than Hickman's outright lap record. That gap needs to be reduced if he's to grab that elusive, much yearned for victory.

JAMES HILLIER
DATE OF BIRTH March 17, 1985
AGE 37
FROM Ringwood, England
RACES Superbike, Senior, Superstock and Supersport (Rich Energy OMG Racing Yamaha)
TT DEBUT 2008
NUMBER OF STARTS 60
NUMBER OF FINISHES 56
NUMBER OF WINS 1
NUMBER OF PODIUMS 14
NUMBER OF REPLICAS 52 silver, 4 bronze
PERSONAL BEST TT LAP 132.414mph

Arguably one of the biggest stories after TT 2019 was James Hillier's departure from Bournemouth Kawasaki after more than a decade with the team, a decade that yielded an impressive 14 podiums and a finishing rate second to none. The Hampshire rider completed a remarkable 54 races in his 58 starts with the team (his first two races in

WHO'S WHO IN 22!

2008 came with Jackson Racing) while those rostrums – which could quite easily have been more given his eight fourth place finishes – included victory in the 2013 Lightweight race.

However, the now 37-year old has had a burning desire to try his hand on other machinery, despite his undoubted bond with the team, which made leaving all the more difficult. That move has seen him switch to the Rich Energy OMG Racing team to Yamaha machinery which he hopes will see him close in and, hopefully, overhaul his rivals.

His Supersport form, of late, has been superb and he's been closer to victory here than in any other class but it is Superbike success he craves. Initially, he was due to ride a BMW M1000 RR similar to Hickman's but issues at BSB has seen the team switch to the Yamaha YZF-R1 and so Hillier has had to follow suit. That wouldn't have been his first choice, given the bike's relatively poor record in recent years, but Hillier will see it as a further opportunity to enhance his already strong reputation. Like Cummins, he has a gap to bridge if he's to challenge for the 1000cc wins so only time will tell if the move pays off, with the team having plenty to prove both on and off the track in their debut year on the roads.

One interesting statistic when it comes to Hillier is that only Michael Dunlop has posted more racing laps of the Mountain Course in excess of 130mph, which further highlights his consistency. However, when it comes to laps in excess of 131mph, he slips down to 7th so if he's to challenge for the big bike wins and podiums this year, he needs to up his pace and start lapping at 132-133mph, and above, more regularly.

Can quiet Manxman Cummins get that elusive win in 22?

James Hillier's move from Bournemouth Kawasaki has surprised some people.

WHO'S WHO IN 22!

Old warhorse Michael Rutter may not be able to bag a win on the big bikes, but surely he's in the hunt in the other classes?

MICHAEL RUTTER
DATE OF BIRTH April 18, 1972
Age 50
FROM Brierley Hill, England
RACES Superbike, Senior & Superstock (Bathams Racing BMW)
Supertwin
(Team ILR/Mark Coverdale Paton)
TT DEBUT 1994
NUMBER OF STARTS 77
NUMBER OF FINISHES 63
NUMBER OF WINS 7
NUMBER OF PODIUMS 18
NUMBER OF REPLICAS 59 silver, 2 bronze
PERSONAL BEST TT LAP 131.709mph

Michael Rutter celebrated 30 years of racing and 25 years of competing at the TT in 2019 but he was as quick as ever as he not only took his 7th TT win in the Zero race but also claimed an 18th podium with third and a near 121mph lap in the Lightweight encounter. Equally impressive, if not more so, were his performances in the big bike races. The Midlands veteran brought the exotic Honda RC213V with him for the first time which presented numerous challenges in terms of set up as the bike was most certainly never designed to be competing at the TT! Nevertheless, Rutter and the Bathams Racing team acquitted themselves more than admirably with 5th and 7th place finishes and laps in excess of 130mph. He also took 6th in the Superstock race and those results more than show how good Rutter still is. He's realistic in his ambitions and knows he's not going to be challenging for the race wins, in the 1000cc races at least, but he goes out and does what he does best, which means finishes of 4th, 5th and 6th are always on the cards.

Two days younger than McGuinness, more of the same can be expected this year where, instead of the RC213V, he'll be BMW-mounted for all three 1000cc races, preferring instead to concentrate on one machine and one that's suited to the Mountain Course. And don't bet against him climbing the podium once more in the Supertwin race…

DAVID JOHNSON
DATE OF BIRTH April 16, 1983
AGE 39
FROM Adelaide, Australia
RACES Superbike, Superstock, Senior and Supersport
(Rich Energy OMG Racing Yamaha)
Supertwin (TBC)
TT DEBUT 2010
NUMBER OF STARTS 40
NUMBER OF FINISHES 32
NUMBER OF WINS 0
NUMBER OF PODIUMS 1
NUMBER OF REPLICAS 25 silver, 7 bronze
PERSONAL BEST TT LAP 131.595mph

After a number of years riding for some of the UK's leading privateer teams, Johnson's subsequent years at Norton saw him further impress – but 2019 was when he finally got his first real shot with an established factory team on the roads, something which he grabbed with both hands.

Joining Honda Racing UK (off the back of two turbulent years for the manufacturer) wasn't the ideal time to be doing so and he was seen by many as a number two rider to Ian Hutchinson. Whatever: the Australian didn't see it that way and took a deserved maiden TT podium when he finished 3rd in the Superstock race.

The result in itself was superb but the

ABOVE: Davo Johnson has paid his dues on the Island, getting a priceless podium in 2019.

manner in which he did it, defeating Michael Dunlop in a last lap shoot-out and in the class which the Honda was (supposedly) less suited to, stood out more. The Superbike/Senior races were an even greater challenge but he followed up his TT success with a fantastic victory in the Superbike Classic TT race to mark an excellent year on the Mountain Course.

This year is the likeable Australian's 10th competing at the TT and he now needs to challenge for the podium on a regular basis. The talent and ability is there but it's worth pointing out that his quickest lap was set in 2015 and he needs to improve on that considerably if he's to make podium appearances regular rather than rare. Like team-mate Hillier, he was due to be BMW-mounted this year, on a machine he feels at home with, but will now also line up on the Yamaha YZF-R1. With the new bike and new project, a lot will depend on how the OMG Racing team manage their ambitious TT debut.

36 Island Racer

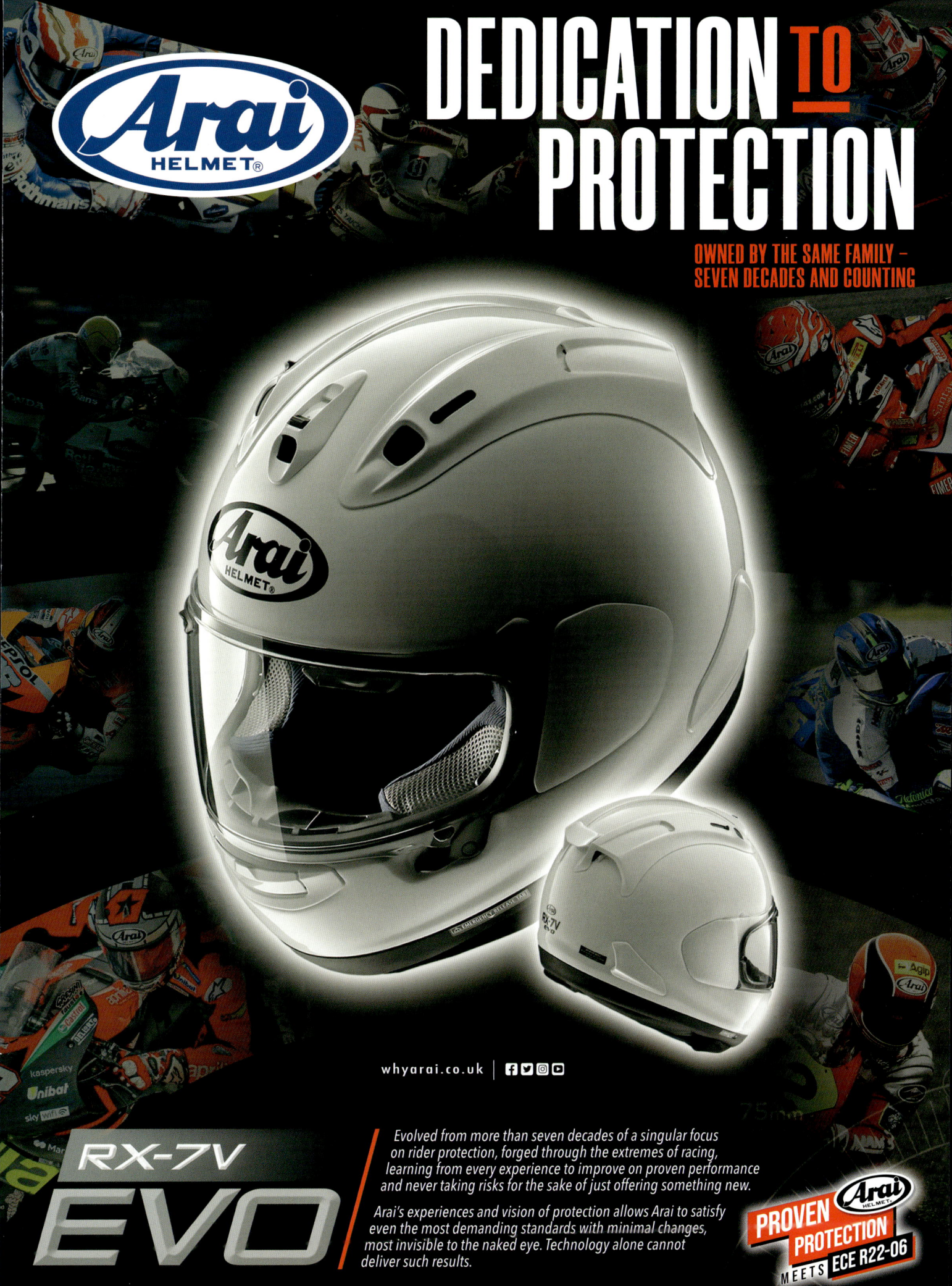

Many rate Todd as the TT's 'coming man.'

DAVEY TODD
DATE OF BIRTH September 14, 1995
AGE 26
FROM Saltburn by Sea, England
RACES Superbike, Senior, Superstock and Supersport (Padgett's Racing)
TT DEBUT 2018
NUMBER OF STARTS 11
NUMBER OF FINISHES 10
NUMBER OF WINS 0
NUMBER OF PODIUMS 0
(best finish – 6th, 2019 Senior)
NUMBER OF REPLICAS 8 silver, 2 bronze
PERSONAL BEST TT LAP 131.491mph

It took Davey Todd just two years of racing on the roads to get himself a factory ride with Honda Racing UK, the most successful manufacturer in the history of the TT, which tells you pretty much everything about the talents of the former Pirelli National Superstock 600cc Championship race winner.

Sadly, the cancellation of TT 2020 meant that ride never came to fruition but without doubt, Todd is the most talented young rider to emerge on the roads since Dean Harrison and Guy Martin before that, and in his two years of racing at the TT he's already taken seven top 10 finishes. The second fastest newcomer of all time, lapping at over 128mph on his debut in 2018, last year saw Todd undoubtedly build on that promise. Riding for the Penz13.com team in the 1000cc classes and for the shrewd, experienced Padgett's team in the Supersport category, he finished in the top 10 in all five of his races, lapping at close to 126mph in the latter to more than confirm his potential and the tag of hottest property in road racing.

However, he saved the best until last and while 6th place in the Senior was an excellent result, so too was his fastest lap of 131.491mph, a stunning effort in just his second year on the Mountain Course. With a win at the North West 200 and podiums at the Ulster Grand Prix, as well as victory in the IRRC Superbike series, it's little wonder he was so highly rated by the end of 2019.

Todd appears to take everything in his stride and keeps his feet firmly on the ground and while his team plans have changed, the fact he's now lining up for Padgett's Racing could well turn out to be a blessing. Time spent away from the factory spotlight and with the Padgett's family instead has helped Conor Cummins and it could help Todd too. He's only going to get stronger and stronger and few would bet against him taking his first podium this June.

Fifteen years into his Island career, Gary has two wins to his credit.

WHO'S WHO IN 22!

GARY JOHNSON
DATE OF BIRTH July 20, 1980
AGE 41
FROM Broughton, England
RACES Superbike, Senior & Superstock (Team Pepsi Gary Johnson Racing BMW)
Supersport (Team Pepsi Gary Johnson Racing Triumph)
Supertwin (Dafabet Racing Kawasaki)
TT DEBUT 2007
NUMBER OF STARTS 63
NUMBER OF FINISHES 45
NUMBER OF WINS 2
NUMBER OF PODIUMS 6
NUMBER OF REPLICAS 41 silver, 4 bronze
PERSONAL BEST TT LAP 130.945mph

It's now 15 years since Gary Johnson made his first appearance at the TT and after making a superb debut he quickly established himself as a front-runner, a trend that has continued ever since. Two wins and six podiums have come in that period, but perhaps it could – and should – have been more.

The amiable Lincolnshire rider has, strangely, never landed a berth with a factory team with his success coming, instead, with his own, privately-run team or with some of the best privateer outfits in the sport. And that's how his 2022 campaign will take place as he reverts to running his own outfit with a variety of machinery in all of the solo races.

Changing teams on a regular basis is, possibly, what's prevented Johnson from achieving more although the last two years of racing saw him have some consistency riding for the RAF Regular & Reserve team. Unfortunately injury each year, particularly last time out, hindered him significantly and while he recorded a whole raft of top 10 positions, eight to be precise, he never really challenged for the podium places.

That led to the partnership coming to an end but such is his pace and experience, he remains a permanent fixture among the seeds, a top 10 finisher and, of course, one of the select group of riders to lap at more than 130mph. He hasn't done the latter enough in recent years though, which is why he's been finishing in the 6th to 8th area, rather than challenging the top three and the Supersport and Supertwin races will again offer his most likely chances of finishing on the podium.

LEE JOHNSTON
DATE OF BIRTH March 10, 1989
AGE 33
FROM Maguiresbridge, Northern Ireland
RACES Superbike, Senior and Superstock (Ashcourt Racing BMW)
Supersport (Ashcourt Racing Yamaha)
Supertwin (Ashcourt Racing Aprilia)
TT DEBUT 2012
NUMBER OF STARTS 37
NUMBER OF FINISHES 26
NUMBER OF WINS 1
NUMBER OF PODIUMS 5
NUMBER OF REPLICAS 23 silver, 3 bronze
PERSONAL BEST TT LAP 130.851mph

Leaving the might of Honda at the end of 2018 to set up his own team was seen as a gamble by many, and some thought he was mad, but Lee Johnston more than vindicated that decision when he became the latest rider to add his name to the winner's list at the Isle of Man TT, victory coming in the opening Supersport race last time out. Riding for Ashcourt Racing, Johnston returned to the British Supersport Championship for the first time in seven years, which immediately proved to be a wise move as he not only became a regular top six finisher, but also finished on the podium. Fully dialled in with the YZF-R6 Yamaha, he grabbed victory in the opening Supersport race at the North West 200 and brought that form to the TT.

The lack of practice hindered him less than others and he was the fastest straight out the traps. James Hillier pushed him close but he got the job done. He also took a podium in the Lightweight class on one of Ryan Farquhar's machines and although the 1000cc classes were a lot tougher, which almost led to him quitting the big bikes at the TT, he'll be back on board the new BMW this year.

Running your own team comes with many different challenges but, with a close knit and experienced group of people around him, Johnston thrived in it and was a new man in 2019. He benefited greatly from the new environment and subsequently took his British Championship performances to new levels in both 2020 and 2021, challenging for the title in the latter after a number of race wins and podiums.

He'll certainly be a contender for the race wins in the Supersport and Supertwin classes but he's aiming to make a greater impression in the 1000cc races this time around too.

Lee Johnston took his first, well-earned win in one of 2019's Supersport races.

Island Racer 39

JAMIE COWARD
DATE OF BIRTH December 24, 1990
AGE 31
FROM Hebden Bridge, England
RACES Superbike, Senior, Superstock and Supersport (KTS Racing Yamaha) Supertwin (KTS Racing Kawasaki)
TT DEBUT 2013
NUMBER OF STARTS 33
NUMBER OF FINISHES 24
NUMBER OF WINS 0
NUMBER OF PODIUMS 1
NUMBER OF REPLICAS 14 silver, 10 bronze
PERSONAL BEST TT LAP 130.317mph

Coward came of age at the 2019 TT when a series of superb performances saw him not only win the TT Privateer's Trophy but also claim his first ever TT podium. That rostrum finish came in the Lightweight race when he pushed Michael Dunlop as hard as anyone else ever has and he was unlucky to miss out on the win when he fell an agonising 1.2s short on the KTS Racing Kawasaki.

Although still at privateer status, riding for the PreZ Racing Yamaha team in all of the other races gave Coward everything he needed to finally showcase his talents across the classes and throughout the week with superb levels of professionalism and reliability seeing the newly-formed team deservedly succeed. The Yorkshire rider finished every race in the top 10 with the main highlights being a brilliant 5th in the second Supersport race and 8th in the Senior.

That closing 8th place not only saw the now 31-year-old break the 130mph barrier for the first time, it also saw him become the fastest Yamaha rider ever to have lapped the Mountain Course. No mean feat indeed but, now riding for KTS Racing in all classes, the challenge this year is to kick on again and post 130mph+ laps and top six finishes on a regular basis.

Jamie Coward's TT progress will be interesting to watch.

PHIL CROWE
DATE OF BIRTH December 21, 1990
AGE 42
FROM Market Rasen, England
RACES Superbike, Senior and Superstock (Crowe Performance BMW) Supersport (Yamaha) TBC
TT DEBUT 2014
NUMBER OF STARTS 25
NUMBER OF FINISHES 16
NUMBER OF WINS 0
NUMBER OF PODIUMS 0
best finish – 9th, 2018 Superbike)
NUMBER OF REPLICAS 4 silver, 7 bronze
PERSONAL BEST TT LAP 129.957mph

Crowe's first three years at the TT saw steady progression but since 2017, he's become a regular fixture in the top 20 of the 1000cc races and pushing hard for the top 10 too. That came to fruition in 2018 when he claimed 9th place in the Superbike race and came agonisingly close to a first ever 130mph lap. That progress halted somewhat last time out though when 14th was his best result while his quickest lap was 127.125mph.

However, 2019 was a peculiar year given the lack of track time during practice week and the shortened races and the Lincolnshire rider is certainly one who gets quicker as the race wears on. Full six-lap race distances seem to suit him better and although his large frame means he's at a disadvantage in the Supersport class, he'll be keen to make his mark again. Indeed, Crowe will be aiming to repeat the top 10 finish of four years ago, get in among the 'factory riders' and finally join the 130mph club.

WHO'S WHO IN 22!

disappointed having not built upon that platform. Given the inclement weather during practice week though, it was an unusual fortnight for everyone and he still took 12th and 13th in the Superbike and Superstock races respectively, results to be more than pleased with given the opposition.

Although still a privateer, West has a good team and infrastructure behind him and now is the time to start turning those consistent 11ths, 12ths and 13ths into regular top 10 positions, something that he's certainly more than capable of. This year will be his sixth at the TT so the experience is there and, having forsaken the Supersport class this year in order to focus his efforts on the bigger bikes, that's exactly what he'll be looking for at TT2022.

DOMINIC HERBERTSON
DATE OF BIRTH March 4, 1991
AGE 29
FROM Hexham, England
RACES Superbike, Senior, Superstock (Rich Energy – machine TBC) Supersport & Supertwin (Cowton Racing Kawasaki)
TT DEBUT 2014
NUMBER OF STARTS 28
NUMBER OF FINISHES 24
NUMBER OF WINS 0
NUMBER OF PODIUMS 0
(best finish – 9th, 2019 Lightweight)
NUMBER OF REPLICAS 6 silver, 17 bronze
PERSONAL BEST TT LAP 129.587mph

Herbertson has soared up the leader-board in recent years with the former Classic TT winner having benefited most recently from the considerable expertise of Davies Motorsport and crew chief Colin Davies who has numerous years as mechanic to Kevin Schwantz among the highlights on his CV. 2019 was their first year together at the TT and Herbertson took full advantage with the main highlight being the Senior race when he took 10th place and lapped well in excess of 129mph.

His best finish at the TT actually came a day earlier when he took 9th in the Lightweight race and TT2019 saw him end

race week with five top 20 finishes, four of them inside the top 15. He's now a formidable competitor in all classes and the 29-year-old will be aiming to become a regular fixture in the top 10, and more, in the years ahead. He lines up with support from Rich Energy this time around but a maiden 130mph lap will also be among his goals for 2022.

BRIAN MCCORMACK
DATE OF BIRTH December 14, 1983
AGE 38
FROM Waterford, Southern Ireland
RACES Superbike, Senior and Superstock (Roadhouse Macau by FHO Racing BMW) Supersport (Triumph) TBC Supertwin (Global Robots Aprilia)
TT DEBUT 2013
NUMBER OF STARTS 38
NUMBER OF FINISHES 28
NUMBER OF WINS 0
NUMBER OF PODIUMS 0
(best finish – 9th, 2019 Senior)
NUMBER OF REPLICAS 4 silver, 21 bronze
PERSONAL BEST TT LAP 128.812mph

A seeded rider for the first time, McCormack has been something of a slow-burner at the TT with his progress steady rather than spectacular since making his debut more than 10 years ago. He immediately broke the 120mph barrier but it's only really been the last few years where the former Irish Superbike Champion has come to the fore in the big bike classes with no fewer than seven top 20 finishes.

Two of those have been inside the top 10 with 9th and 10th taken in the last two Senior races and he appears to have really found his groove on the BMW with a near 129mph lap in 2019 making him the fastest rider ever from Southern Ireland.

Well over 6ft, McCormack wouldn't look out of place on the rugby pitch so he tends to suffer a bit on the smaller bikes but, with a dream berth at FHO Racing and plenty of British Championship racing under his belt recently, he has a golden opportunity to make a serious impression on the top 10 this year.

SAM WEST
DATE OF BIRTH June 9, 1988
AGE 33
FROM Wilmslow, England
RACES Superbike, Senior, Superstock (PRL/Cycle Store BMW) Supersport (TBC)
TT DEBUT 2015
NUMBER OF STARTS 25
NUMBER OF FINISHES 21
NUMBER OF WINS 0
NUMBER OF PODIUMS 0
(best finish – 8th, 2018 Superstock)
NUMBER OF REPLICAS 9 silver, 12 bronze
PERSONAL BEST TT LAP 129.716mph

Having taken his first top 10 finish in 2018 and lapped at close to 130mph while running as high as 6th in the Senior, Cheshire's West, like Crowe, may well have come away from the last TT feeling slightly

WHO'S WHO IN 22!

DEREK SHEILS
DATE OF BIRTH October 6, 1982
AGE 39
FROM Dublin, Ireland
RACES Superbike, Senior, Superstock (TBC) Supersport (TBC), Supertwin (TBC)
TT DEBUT 2013
NUMBER OF STARTS 24
NUMBER OF FINISHES 13
NUMBER OF WINS 0
NUMBER OF PODIUMS 0
(best finish – 11th, 2019 Supersport 1)
NUMBER OF REPLICAS 3 silver, 10 bronze
PERSONAL BEST TT LAP 128.780mph

Dubliner Derek Sheils will be pushing for success this year.

The dominant force in the Superbike class in Irish National road racing, Sheils hasn't yet been able to truly bring that form with him to the TT despite posting top six finishes at the North West 200 and Ulster Grand Prix. A near 129mph lap shows his potential around the Mountain Course but reliability has often prevented him getting the results his undoubted talent deserves, with top 10 finishes and 130mph laps most definitely a possibility.

It's actually the Supersport class that has given him best results at the TT with 11th and 12th coming in the two races last time out and he should be firmly knocking on the door of the top 10 again this year. A lot will depend on the new team and infrastructure he has around him having left the Burrows Engineering/RK Racing with whom he spent four successful years.

SHAUN ANDERSON
DATE OF BIRTH August 7, 1984
AGE 38
FROM Banbridge, Northern Ireland
RACES Superbike, Senior, Superstock (Hawk Racing Suzuki)
Supersport (Wilcock Consulting Honda)
Supertwin (TBC)
TT DEBUT 2012
NUMBER OF STARTS 32
NUMBER OF FINISHES 17
NUMBER OF WINS 0
NUMBER OF PODIUMS 0
(best finish – 6th, 2018 TT Zero)
NUMBER OF REPLICAS 1 silver, 14 bronze
PERSONAL BEST TT LAP 128.672mph

With a decade of experience on the Mountain Course, Anderson has quietly been going about his business and is now a regular fixture inside the top 20 with 2019 seeing him finish no lower than 20th in his five races. Particularly strong in the 1000cc classes, the Northern Irishman can count 12th in the most recent Senior race and 13th in the 2018 Superbike race among his best results although his highest finish, 6th, came in the TT Zero class. A last minute move to the NW Racing team in 2019 paid dividends as he claimed three bronze replicas for 12th, 16th and 20th place finishes on the BMW S1000RR, also lapping in excess of 127mph. However, he's switched manufacturer and team for his return with a dream ride for Stuart and Steve Hicken's Hawk Racing team meaning he's well placed to better his personal best lap of 128.672mph set on his own trusty Suzuki four years ago.

CRAIG NEVE
DATE OF BIRTH October 5, 1990
AGE 31
FROM Immingham, England
RACES Superbike, Senior, Superstock (CallMac BMW)
Supersport (CallMac Yamaha)
Supertwin (CallMac WK Moto)
TT DEBUT 2016
NUMBER OF STARTS 17
NUMBER OF FINISHES 14
NUMBER OF WINS 0
NUMBER OF PODIUMS 0
(best finish – 11th, 2018 Senior)
NUMBER OF REPLICAS 2 silver, 12 bronze
Personal best TT Lap 127.452mph

After one year at the Manx GP, Neve immediately moved up to the TT in 2016 and in the three years he's competed since he's made rapid progression. Indeed, with laps in excess of 127mph, he's firmly knocking on the door of the top 10.

He came mightily close to achieving that in 2018 when he placed 11th in the Senior race but hopes of improving upon that the following year were dashed when he crashed heavily at the preceding North West 200.

That ruled him out of the TT although, crucially, he was on the grid for the Classic TT where he got some valuable miles under his belt.

Since then, he's been competing successfully in the Ducati TriOptions Cup and National Superstock Championship so he'll be more than ready for the resumption of racing on the Mountain Course. In the top 20 for the first time in both the 600cc and 1000cc classes, he has a great chance of setting personal bests in 2022 both in terms of results and lap speeds.

WHO'S WHO IN 22!

OTHER SEEDS: SUPERSPORT AND SUPERTWIN

WORDS: PHIL WAIN
PICS: STEPHEN DAVISON – PACEMAKER PRESS

TOP 20 RUNNERS – SUPERSPORT AND SUPERTWINS ONLY

PAUL JORDAN
DATE OF BIRTH June 7, 1991
AGE 30
FROM Magherafelt, Northern Ireland
RACES Superbike, Senior, Superstock and Supersport (PreZ Racing Yamaha) Supertwin (PreZ Racing Kawasaki)
TT DEBUT 2017
NUMBER OF STARTS 13
NUMBER OF FINISHES 10
NUMBER OF WINS 0
NUMBER OF PODIUMS 0
(best finish – 4th, 2019 Lightweight)
NUMBER OF REPLICAS 4 silver, 6 bronze
PERSONAL BEST TT LAP 125.385mph

MICHAEL SWEENEY
DATE OF BIRTH September 11, 1981
AGE 40
FROM Skerries, Southern Ireland
RACES Superbike, Senior, Superstock (MJR Racing BMW) Supersport (MJR Racing Yamaha) Supertwin (Kiely Heating Kawasaki)
TT DEBUT 2014
NUMBER OF STARTS 33
NUMBER OF FINISHES 28
NUMBER OF WINS 0
NUMBER OF PODIUMS 0
(best finish – 6th, 2015 TT Zero)
NUMBER OF REPLICAS 3 silver, 24 bronze
PERSONAL BEST TT LAP 126.407mph

MICHAEL EVANS
DATE OF BIRTH June 3, 1993
AGE 28
FROM Santon, Isle of Man
RACES Superbike, Senior, Superstock (Heatech BMW) Supersport (Heatech Yamaha) Supertwin (Heatech Kawasaki)
TT DEBUT 2018
NUMBER OF STARTS 6
NUMBER OF FINISHES 4
NUMBER OF WINS 0
NUMBER OF PODIUMS 0
(best finish – 17th, 2018 Supersport 2)
NUMBER OF REPLICAS 1 silver, 2 bronze
PERSONAL BEST TT LAP 123.614mph

ADAM MCLEAN
DATE OF BIRTH March 9, 1996
Age 26
FROM Tobermore, Northern Ireland
RACES Superbike, Senior, Superstock, Supersport and Supertwin (McAdoo Racing Kawasaki)
TT DEBUT 2017
NUMBER OF STARTS 5
NUMBER OF FINISHES 3
NUMBER OF WINS 0
NUMBER OF PODIUMS 0
(best finish – 8th, 2018 Lightweight)
NUMBER OF REPLICAS 3 silver
PERSONAL BEST TT LAP 123.113mph

TOP 20 – SUPERTWIN ONLY
STEFANO BONETTI
DATE OF BIRTH December 23, 1976
AGE 45
FROM Castro, Italy
RACES Superbike, Senior, Superstock
(Speed Motor BMW)
Supertwin (Aprilia RS660)
TT DEBUT 2004
NUMBER OF STARTS 60
NUMBER OF FINISHES 48
NUMBER OF WINS 0
NUMBER OF PODIUMS 0
(best finish – 4th, 2018 Lightweight)
NUMBER OF REPLICAS 6 silver, 40 bronze
PERSONAL BEST TT LAP 127.070mph

JULIAN TRUMMER
DATE OF BIRTH April 25, 1991
AGE 31
FROM Wagna, Austria
RACES Superbike, Senior, Superstock
(WH Racing BMW)
Supersport (WH Racing Yamaha)
Supertwin (WH Racing Kawasaki)
TT DEBUT 2017
NUMBER OF STARTS 9
NUMBER OF FINISHES 9
NUMBER OF WINS 0
NUMBER OF PODIUMS 0
(best finish – 9th, 2018 Lightweight)
NUMBER OF REPLICAS 8 bronze
PERSONAL BEST TT LAP 124.258mph

JAMES CHAWKE
DATE OF BIRTH January 16, 1992
AGE 30
FROM Limerick, Southern Ireland
RACES Superbike
(Emjess Racing/Carl Roberts)
Senior & Superstock
(Chawki Racing Supporters Club)
Supersport (Lyonara Cold Stores)
Supertwin (CBG Contractors)
TT DEBUT 2019
NUMBER OF STARTS 6
NUMBER OF FINISHES 4
NUMBER OF WINS 0
NUMBER OF PODIUMS 0
(best finish – 11th, 2019 Lightweight)
NUMBER OF REPLICAS 1 silver, 3 bronze
PERSONAL BEST TT LAP 122.674mph

WHO'S WHO IN 22!

MICHAEL RUSSELL
DATE OF BIRTH July 15, 1980
AGE 41
FROM King's Lynn, England
RACES Superbike, Superstock and Senior (Russell Road Racing BMW) Supersport (Russell Road Racing Yamaha) Supertwin (Russell Road Racing Aprilia) Sidecar (Russell Road Racing Suzuki)
TT DEBUT 2010
NUMBER OF STARTS 28
NUMBER OF FINISHES 16
NUMBER OF WINS 0
NUMBER OF PODIUMS 0
(best finish – 7th, 2015 Lightweight)
NUMBER OF REPLICAS 1 silver, 14 bronze
PERSONAL BEST TT LAP 124.417mph

JAMES HIND
DATE OF BIRTH December 15, 1999
AGE 22
FROM Scunthorpe, England
RACES Superbike, Superstock & Senior (North Lincs Components –machine TBC) Supersport (Bass Tyre Services Yamaha) Supertwin (Team ILR/Mark Coverdale Paton)
TT DEBUT 2022
NUMBER OF STARTS 0
NUMBER OF FINISHES 0
NUMBER OF WINS 0
NUMBER OF PODIUMS 0
NUMBER OF REPLICAS 0
PERSONAL BEST TT LAP 121.773mph (2019 MGP)

ROB HODSON
DATE OF BIRTH November 2, 1986
AGE 35
FROM Wigan, England
RACES Superbike, Superstock, Supersport, Senior & Supertwin (Dafabet Racing Kawasaki)
TT DEBUT 2016
NUMBER OF STARTS 21
NUMBER OF FINISHES 11
NUMBER OF WINS 0
NUMBER OF PODIUMS 0
(best finish – 14th, 2018 Senior)
NUMBER OF REPLICAS 11 bronze
PERSONAL BEST TT LAP 126.274mph

JOHN BARTON
DATE OF BIRTH June 5, 1969
AGE 52
FROM Rochester, England
RACES Supertwin (Wemoto.com Kawasaki)
TT DEBUT 1990
NUMBER OF STARTS 67
NUMBER OF FINISHES 40
NUMBER OF WINS 0
NUMBER OF PODIUMS 2
NUMBER OF REPLICAS 11 silver, 27 bronze
PERSONAL BEST TT LAP 122.961mph

Where R/World Meets Yours

2022 R7 – New generation Supersport

The 689cc CP2 engine with A&S clutch provides torque-rich acceleration for a truly exciting riding experience. The small frontal area of the R7 ensures the highest level of aerodynamic efficiency, while high specification brakes and suspension give optimum controllability when cornering and braking. This new generation sportsbike is designed for thrill-seeking riders like you – whether you're riding on the track or out on the road.

www.yamaha-motor.eu

YAMAHA
Revs Your Heart

Always wear a helmet, eye protection and protective clothing. Yamaha encourage you to ride safely and respect fellow riders and the environment. Images shown depict professional riders performing under controlled conditions. Specifications and appearance of Yamaha products as shown here are subject to change without notice and may vary according to requirements and conditions. For further details, please consult your Yamaha dealer.

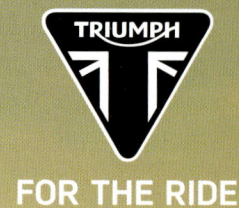

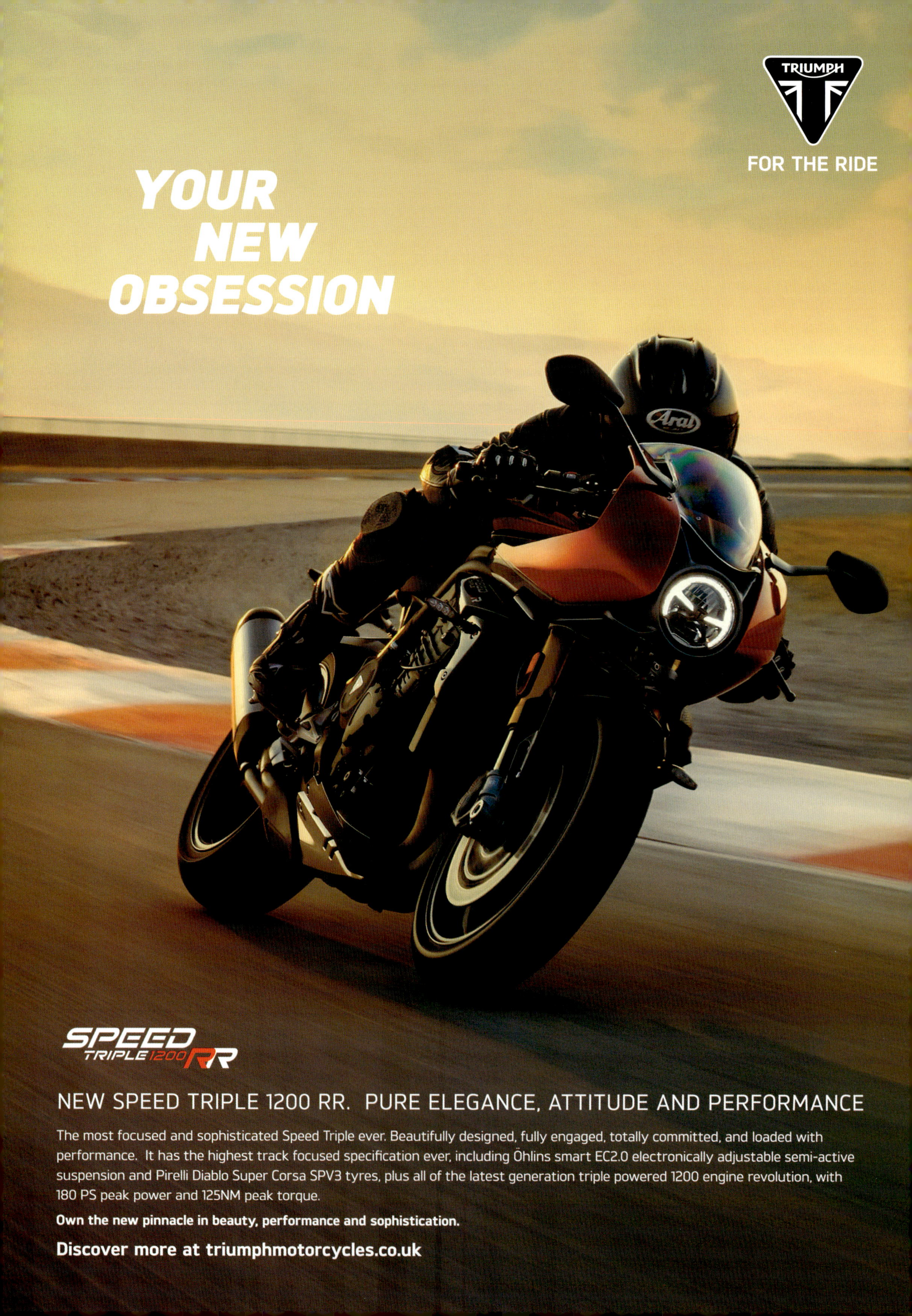
TRIUMPH
FOR THE RIDE
YOUR NEW OBSESSION
Arai
SPEED TRIPLE 1200 RR
NEW SPEED TRIPLE 1200 RR. PURE ELEGANCE, ATTITUDE AND PERFORMANCE
The most focused and sophisticated Speed Triple ever. Beautifully designed, fully engaged, totally committed, and loaded with performance. It has the highest track focused specification ever, including Öhlins smart EC2.0 electronically adjustable semi-active suspension and Pirelli Diablo Super Corsa SPV3 tyres, plus all of the latest generation triple powered 1200 engine revolution, with 180 PS peak power and 125NM peak torque.
Own the new pinnacle in beauty, performance and sophistication.
Discover more at triumphmotorcycles.co.uk

WHO'S WHO IN 22!

SIDECARS

BEN BIRCHALL
AGE 45 (January 21, 1977)
FROM Mansfield, England
PASSENGER Tom Birchall, 35 (December 23, 1986)
TEAM Haith/Live Your Adventure LCR Honda
TT DEBUT 2009
NUMBER OF STARTS 18
NUMBER OF FINISHES 14
NUMBER OF WINS 10
NUMBER OF PODIUMS 12
NUMBER OF REPLICAS 14 silver
PERSONAL BEST TT LAP 119.250mph (1st)

Quite simply, the Birchall brothers are one of the best sidecar crews ever to have competed at the Isle of Man TT. Ben's 10 wins are only bettered by Dave Molyneux which puts him joint second alongside Rob Fisher on the all-time winners list while Tom is already the most successful passenger of all time. Throw in the fact they've won nine of the last 10 races and have held the outright lap record since 2017 and it's easy to see why they're held in such high regard. Those statistics clearly make them the combination to beat and when it comes to making predictions for TT 2022, it's hard to look past them adding more wins to their tally. With commitment second to none, no stone is left unturned when it comes to their preparation either and that will only make them stronger when the flag drops. A first ever 120mph lap is definitely on the cards.

All the information we publish in this section was correct at the time of going to press.

WHO'S WHO IN 22!

Holden will be back in 2022 and with a new passenger, Jason Pitt.

Surely the favourites for the spoils in the sidecar races – the Birchall brothers.

JOHN HOLDEN
AGE 64 (July 13, 1956)
FROM Blackburn, England
PASSENGER Jason Pitt
TEAM Barnes Racing LCR Honda
TT DEBUT 1988
NUMBER OF STARTS 47
NUMBER OF FINISHES 38
NUMBER OF WINS 2
NUMBER OF PODIUMS 21
NUMBER OF REPLICAS 34 silver, 2 bronze
PERSONAL BEST TT LAP 117.878mph (2nd)

It would be grossly unfair to say John Holden is the best of the rest when compared to the Birchalls at the TT as he's far more than that; he's the driver, along with former passenger Lee Cain to have consistently pushed the Nottinghamshire brothers the hardest. On the opening lap, he's always been the closest challenger and although the outright pace of the Birchalls means they've gradually edged clear on laps two and three, Holden has remained the one most likely to deny them the victory. His superb tally of 21 podiums is only bettered by Dave Molyneux's record of 30 and the impressive fact among that tally is that he's finished in the top three in every race since 2014 – that's 12 races in total with the last seven all 2nd place finishes. However, he has a new challenge for 2022 with Cain being replaced by Mountain Course newcomer Jason Pitt.

"HOLDEN HAS REMAINED THE ONE MOST LIKELY TO DENY THE BIRCHALLS VICTORY"

Ninja ZX-10R

FACE YOURSELF

£179 PER MONTH
Plus deposit and optional final repayment.

REPRESENTATIVE EXAMPLE

Based on 2022 Ninja ZX-10R on K.Options PCP

36 Monthly Repayments	£179.00	Interest Rate (Fixed)	5.72%	Customer Deposit	£2,528.72
Total Amount of Credit	£13,721.28	Optional Final Repayment	£9,326.00	Total Amount Payable	£18,298.72
Representative APR	5.9% APR	Agreement Duration	37 Months	Cash Price	£16,250.00
Purchase Fee*	£10.00				

*Included in Optional Final Repayment.

TAILOR THE PERFECT DEAL FOR YOU AT WWW.KAWASAKI-KALCULATOR.CO.UK

Credit is subject to status and is only available to UK residents aged 18 and over. K.Options Personal Contract Purchase (PCP) is only available through Kawasaki Finance, a trading style of Black Horse Ltd, St William House, Tresillian Terrace, Cardiff, CF10 5BH. Finance figures are applicable at time of print and are subject to change. Representative example based on 4,000 miles per annum. With K.Options Personal Contract Purchase (PCP) you have the option after you have paid all of the regular monthly repayments to: (1) Return the motorcycle and not pay the Optional Final Repayment. In this example if the motorcycle has exceeded 12,333 miles, a charge of 7.2p (including VAT at 20%) will apply per excess mile. If the motorcycle is in good condition (fair wear and tear accepted) and has not exceeded 12,333 miles you will have nothing further to pay. (2) Pay the Optional Final Repayment to own the motorcycle or (3) Part exchange the motorcycle subject to settlement of your existing finance agreement; new finance agreements are subject to status.

Kawasaki
Let the good times roll

WHO'S WHO IN 22!

ABOVE: Multiple world champ Tim Reeves will want a return to winning ways at the TT.

TIM REEVES
AGE 49 (August 28, 1972)
FROM Tenterden, England
PASSENGER Kevin Rousseau
TEAM Bonovo Action LCR Yamaha
TT DEBUT 2008
NUMBER OF STARTS 23
NUMBER OF FINISHES 15
NUMBER OF WINS 1
NUMBER OF PODIUMS 8
NUMBER OF REPLICAS 14 silver, 1 bronze
PERSONAL BEST TT LAP 117.729mph (3rd)

One can't help but feel that multiple World Champion Reeves should have more TT wins than just the single victory he took in 2013 and he'll be desperate to ensure that his career doesn't end that way. Up until 2019, the Kent driver was the fastest newcomer ever, having lapped at more than 112mph in 2008 and his record of eight podiums is one to be admired but on too many occasions it's been a case of what might have been. A brace of 3rd place finishes in 2018 and near 118mph lap with Mark Wilkes should have been the springboard to mount a major challenge to the Birchalls but, instead, reliability issues meant he had a torrid time in 2019 and only got as far as the bottom of Bray Hill in race one; 4th place in the second at least salvaged his week, but 2022 won't be any easier as he comes to the island with a newcomer passenger in the shape of Kevin Rousseau.

WHO'S WHO IN 22!

DAVE MOLYNEUX
AGE 58 (November 21, 1963)
FROM Regaby, Isle of Man
PASSENGER Daryl Gibson
TEAM DMR KTM
TT DEBUT 1985
NUMBER OF STARTS 53
NUMBER OF FINISHES 35
NUMBER OF WINS 17
NUMBER OF PODIUMS 30
NUMBER OF REPLICAS 33 silver, 2 bronze
PERSONAL BEST TT LAP 116.785mph (4th)

It's fair to say the last few Isle of Man TT campaigns haven't gone smoothly for Dave Molyneux and while his 17 wins and 30 podiums still make him, comfortably, the most successful sidecar driver in the history of the event, you have to go back to 2017 to find his last podium – and even further back, 2014, for his last victory. Injury to Dan Sayle and then reliability issues affected him in 2017 and 2018 and having ditched his own DMR chassis in favour of an LCR in 2019, Harry Payne couldn't lap at the speeds the Manxman was accustomed to. However, re-energised by the new rules, which see him switch to the 890cc KTM power-plant, he should be back to being a major challenger this year. Catching the Birchalls, let alone beating them, will be far from easy but he'll be hoping the KTM and new passenger Daryl Gibson will help him get back on to the podium at least.

PETER FOUNDS
AGE 44 (August 27, 1977)
FROM Knutsford, England
PASSENGER Jevan Walmsley, 32 (April 13, 1990)
TEAM Trustland Group/Founds Racing Suzuki
TT DEBUT 2015 (competed as a passenger between 1997 and 2007)
NUMBER OF STARTS 10
NUMBER OF FINISHES 6
NUMBER OF WINS 0
NUMBER OF PODIUMS 2
NUMBER OF REPLICAS 6 silver
PERSONAL BEST TT LAP 116.435mph (6th)

Hailing from a family steeped in sidecar tradition, Founds began his Mountain Course career as a passenger, enjoying a decade in the chair with a number of drivers, the highlights being a brace of 5th places in 2007. However, when he moved into the driver's seat in 2015, it was clear his talents weren't just confined to the side of the outfit and, together with Jevan Walmsley, he's now established himself as a regular podium contender. A brilliant 2nd place was achieved in 2016 with another podium, 3rd, coming in 2019 when they increased their personal best lap by almost 2mph. They're also former British Champions having dominated in 2019 with 12 wins from 17 races so expect them to be pushing for more rostrum finishes in 2022.

Passenger-turned-driver Peter Founds will be wanting big results this year.

Will the old war-horse Moly be able to mix-it once more in the two sidecar races?

ALAN FOUNDS
AGE 39 (September 2, 1982)
FROM Little Neston, England
PASSENGER Jake Lowther
TEAM Founds Racing Yamaha
TT DEBUT 2014
(competed as a passenger in 2005)
NUMBER OF STARTS 12
NUMBER OF FINISHES 9
NUMBER OF WINS 0
NUMBER OF PODIUMS 2
NUMBER OF REPLICAS 5 silver, 4 bronze
PERSONAL BEST TT LAP 116.367mph (7th)

Five years younger than his brother, Alan Founds has been equally as successful at the TT, if not more so, with the second son of Des Founds – a podium finisher in the F2 class in 1989 – getting his TT career off to a brilliant start in 2014 when he took a stunning 6th place.

That won him the Newcomers Trophy and he's gone from strength to strength ever since with six top six finishes now having been chalked up. Two of those have been podiums with 3rd place the outcome in the first race in both 2016 and 2019, the latter seeing him, like Pete, break the 116mph barrier for the first time. Together with regular passenger Jake Lowther, he should again be challenging the top three this year while he'll also be looking to up his pace even further.

LEWIS BLACKSTOCK
AGE 30 (July 11, 1991)
FROM Blackburn, England
PASSENGER Patrick Rosney, 26
TEAM TBC
TT DEBUT 2016
NUMBER OF STARTS 8
NUMBER OF FINISHES 7
NUMBER OF WINS 0
NUMBER OF PODIUMS 0
(best finish – 4th, 2017 'B' race)
NUMBER OF REPLICAS 6 bronze
PERSONAL BEST TT LAP 114.145mph (10th)

Blackstock and Rosney have been one of the youngest pairings on the grid in recent times and the duo are back for more this time around. After making a strong debut in 2016, they have improved each year since although their 4th place finish in their second year in 2017 remains their best result. Fifth place was taken the following year and while they, and others, may have expected more than their 6th and 7th place finishes in 2019, a new personal best lap in excess of 114mph showed their continued progression. Coming into their fifth year, Blackstock has enough experience behind him to make a firm podium push with Rosney the perfect foil for him to achieve that.

WHO'S WHO IN 22!

RYAN CROWE
AGE 26 (March 6, 1996)
FROM Jurby, Isle of Man
PASSENGER Callum Crowe, 21 (June 5, 2000)
TEAM Haven Homes/LCR Triumph
TT DEBUT 2019
NUMBER OF STARTS 1
NUMBER OF FINISHES 1
NUMBER OF WINS 0
NUMBER OF PODIUMS 0 (best finish – 5th, 2019 'A' race)
NUMBER OF REPLICAS 1 silver
PERSONAL BEST TT LAP 113.529mph (13th)

Sons of former five-time winner and outright lap record holder Nick, Ryan and Callum Crowe were the revelations of TT 2019 when the newcomers not only went on to finish in a stunning 5th place in race one, they also lapped at more than 113mph – making now 26-year old Ryan the fastest newcomer driver in the history of the event. The feat was even more miraculous due to the fact the inclement weather during practice week meant they only managed two laps of Mountain Course prior to the race! Their fastest lap of 113.529mph bettered the mark of 112.031mph set by Tim Reeves in 2008 and to add to their achievements, it was all done using the 675cc Triumph engine, rarely used in sidecar racing, and whose previous fastest lap around the Mountain Course was just 105mph. Unfortunately, a technical issue meant they were unable to start the second race but they'd already been rewarded for their meticulous preparation and dedication over the winter months. Without doubt, they're ones to watch in 2022.

GARY BRYAN
AGE 57 (January 4, 1965)
FROM North Kelsey, England
PASSENGER Phil Hyde
TEAM GBM/Drury Engineering/Baker Honda
TT DEBUT 1998
NUMBER OF STARTS 36
NUMBER OF FINISHES 30
NUMBER OF WINS 0
NUMBER OF PODIUMS 0 (best finish – 4th, 2010 'A' and 2012 "A' and "B' races)
NUMBER OF REPLICAS 13 silver, 13 bronze
PERSONAL BEST TT LAP 113.196mph (14th)

Having recently celebrated 20 years of racing at the TT, Lincolnshire's Bryan is another driver who not only continues to record consistent top six finishes but also get quicker as seen by a new personal best lap set last time out in 2019. A lap of 113.196mph saw him break the 113mph barrier for the first time and he can now boast an impressive 19 top 10 finishes to his name with 5th and 7th coming his way three years ago when he was again partnered by Phil Hyde. Another former Newcomers Trophy winner, Bryan has fought back from injury on more than one occasion, not always racing related, and his determination cannot be underestimated. Equally impressive on the short circuits, whether in the British F1 or F2 Championships, more top six finishes should come his and Hyde's way this year.

CONRAD HARRISON
AGE 58 (August 30, 1963)
FROM Bradford, England
PASSENGER Andy Winkle
TEAM Printer Roller Services/Bellas Honda
TT DEBUT 1993
NUMBER OF STARTS 47
NUMBER OF FINISHES 35
NUMBER OF WINS 1
NUMBER OF PODIUMS 10
Number of replicas 17 silver, 13 bronze
PERSONAL BEST TT LAP 114.674mph (9th)

A veteran within the sidecar fraternity, Harrison has competed at the TT every year since 1993 and although the heady days of 2010-2015, when he racked up nine rostrums from 12 starts including a dream victory in 2014, are behind him, he's still one of a select number of drivers who's consistently lapping at more than 110mph. His last podium finish came in 2017 with the following two years yielding a brace of 6th places along with an 8th and he should again be operating in this area come June. An eleventh rostrum appearance is probably out of reach, and he'll need some good fortune for that to happen, but together with fellow veteran Andy Winkle, himself a race winner with John Holden, he remains a welcome presence on the TT leader-board.

Subscribe to

Get your FREE digital copy!

SPECIAL OFFER!
Expires 31/12/22

£20 for 6 issues

Fast Bikes is home to the best sportsbike tests on the planet, full of technical insight and hardcore action – all done in our own inimitable style using some of the best snappers in the business.

We love testing the latest and greatest bikes - potentially your next bike – but we cater for every budget too, thrashing everything from £1,000 hacks to £100,000 race bikes! And that's not all. We get to talk to the most important and interesting people in motorcycling – be it world champions like Marc Marquez or the bloke down the road that fixes bikes.

SUBSCRIBE TODAY

Visit: www.classicmagazines.co.uk/FBIR22

Call: 01507 529529 and quote **FBIR22**

Download your FREE digital copy of Fast Bikes! Visit: www.fastbikesmag.com/islandracer

1992
THE CLASS OF '92

Many Isle of Man TT race weeks live long in the memory – but 30 years ago something very special happened and it involved two very special racers. *Island Racer* goes back to 1992…

WORDS: BERTIE SIMMONDS, WITH THANKS TO STUART BARKER, CARL FOGARTY
PICS: DON AND JO MORLEY, MORTONS ARCHIVE

Hislop and Fogarty were in a class of their own in-the Senior TT

It was a perfect storm, the 1992 Isle of Man TT. Two of the greatest exponents of their craft – Steve Hislop and Carl Fogarty – came back to race at an event that, perhaps, they felt should have been part of their back catalogue by this time in their careers.

Hislop was an Island legend already but he really wanted to crack short-circuit racing in the UK and beyond. As 1992 dawned, Hizzy assumed that he would take the Honda Britain ride vacated by Fogarty when the rider from Blackburn decided to move to a private Ducati 888 in the World Superbike championship. Apparently this would have given him two RC30s (by now very long in the tooth) and a full team to back him in the British national series. However, as winter wore on no contract was forthcoming. Eventually it was announced that Honda Britain had opted for young Kiwi Simon Crafar instead. Steve was left in the lurch as the 1992 season loomed large.

The Scot tried to set-up a deal in Britain riding a Yamaha OW-01 for Tillston's Yamaha but that also foundered thanks to shenanigans with the official Loctite Yamaha squad, run by Rob McElnea. What Hizzy needed was a ride somewhere – anywhere – that would give him some money and – just as important – a way to advertise his skills as a motorcycle racer. Steve would eventually get a well-paying ride with Kawasaki France in World Endurance, as would one Carl Fogarty.

By the end of 1991, Fogarty had done all he could with the Honda Britain RC30. Beating the former champ Fred Merkel more often than not when the team competed in World Superbikes, the Briton had decided enough was enough and that he'd fund his own, privately-entered Ducati 888 Corsa – the base version of the bike which had won the 1990 and 1991 WSB titles.

Like Hizzy, Carl was at a crossroads in his career: he wanted to move forward, but – for some reason – riders of other nationalities were getting the plum jobs. It was time to put his own money where his mouth was. Legend has it that Foggy and crew turned up at Bologna to pick up their Corsa around the same time Team Oxford Products picked up the one that they would run with Trevor Nation in BSB in 1992. In his World Superbike season, Carl would beg for spare wheels from other Ducati teams so he could get through practice sessions and – despite being on such a tight budget – Foggy would take his first WSB win in the second Donington Park race that year. This prompted some (notably Nation) to question how 'standard' Carl's Corsa was. Nation told the press Foggy must be Superman if that machine was standard. Foggy's reply was: "Tell Nation my bloody cape is in the back of the van…"

With Carl and his dad George paying £50,000 that year to get him noticed, Foggy – like Hizzy – would take any ride that paid to keep him running in the World Superbike shop window. The Kawasaki France Endurance ride would see him alongside Hislop and fellow Brit Terry Rymer, but Steve's move away from Yamaha following their issues meant Fogarty was offered the Loctite Yamaha bike for the Isle of Man TT. It could mean £10,000 – more if he won. And as he was going to take his 888 Corsa to the Island, his precious WSB machine would be unused.

So, the twists and turns of their respective careers conspired to bring Hislop and Fogarty together at the Isle of Man TT in 1992. Both had given their all in 1991, riding the exotic Honda RVFs (and scaring themselves silly) so riding two different machines, with start numbers far enough apart (Fogarty 4, Hislop 19) meant a re-run of their on-track, side-by-side battle was unlikely. But then both men needed the money and both said they were going back just for that.

The 1992 season was a case of one step back to go two steps forward for Hizzy and Foggy. Their future successes lay before them, but first they had to do battle at the Isle of Man TT.

1992

HIZZY'S STORY

Everyone laughed, when they heard. Some to his face. Even Hizzy himself laughed at the prospect of him riding the Norton in the toughest race of them all. "I actually laughed when Norton's team boss, Barry Symmons, asked me to ride that bike at the TT, but I did. I thought: 'you must be joking, that thing will never last one lap of the Isle of Man.'"

The bike in question was what many felt was almost a 'home-made' superbike: the rotary-engined Norton NRS588. While it had enjoyed major success on the British short circuits with lucrative backing from cigarette company JPS, the bike was often fragile, quirky, difficult to ride and had never managed to win a TT race. JPS did not wish to be associated with the TT because of its inherent dangers but Symmons still had access to a bike and was determined to see it race at the TT – if only he could raise the £25,000 needed in order for this to happen. He had just one month to raise the cash.

Despite laughing at the prospect, Hislop agreed to ride the bike because he knew the publicity value of riding for the British marque that had last won a Senior TT in 1961 when the late, great Mike Hailwood took victory. Hizzy said: "I just felt it would really put me back in the spotlight and that was something I needed badly, if only to secure a solid ride for 1993!" Symmons would eventually raise £20,000 (from Abus locks, EBC brakes and the Isle of Man Tourist Board) but decided it was enough to go racing.

Hislop only had time (and the team only had funds) for one pre-TT test at Oulton Park. Things didn't go well. After just eight laps at Oulton the engine blew up. Hislop told the team bluntly: "Boys, this thing can't even manage 10 laps round Oulton without shitting itself..." But Hislop was stuck – he had nothing else to ride. Quitting his Yamaha BSB team meant that he would not ride for them at the TT. With the TT only a month away he had little choice but to accept Symmons' offer to ride the Norton.

"I had no other offers but inside I was thinking it was a bit of a joke," Hislop said to biographer Stuart Barker. "I'd always seen the Norton as a kind of wacky project bike: after all, it had been developed from a slow old Norton police bike by Brian Crighton in the back of a shed. Surely it couldn't win a TT race?"

Arriving at the TT for practice week, Hislop surprised everyone, including himself, by topping the time sheets in the first night of practice. The rest of the week was a washout weather-wise and the Norton had proved a handful as expected, but outright pace was clearly not an issue.

After his first few laps, Hislop said: "The Norton was tremendously fast in a straight line and I was clocked by a radar gun at 193mph down Sulby straight at one point. But it was the weirdest bike to ride because of its rotary engine. It had very little engine braking and I just got sucked really deep into corners so I had to change all the braking points that I used on other bikes. I remember many times I was hammering down the gearbox and pulling the front brake lever like hell only to find I was still heading into the corners way too fast!"

After the dreadful conditions of practice week, the opening race day was a scorcher; too hot, in fact, for the Norton. With the bike overheating badly, Hislop had his crew rip the front mudguard off during the pit stop to allow more cool air into the engine. When Carl Fogarty's Yamaha broke its gearbox, Hislop chased Phillip McCallen home in 2nd place. Not so bad for an unreliable bike...

BELOW: Hizzy and the Norton were on fire in practice. The rotary motor needed cooling in the F1 race so that front mudguard had to go...

"AS SOON AS I SAW THE CROWDS LINING THE PATH THAT LEADS BACK TO THE PITS I KNEW I'D DONE IT."

Barry Symmons said: "During practice at the TT we allowed Hizzy to make whatever changes he wanted to the bike, rather than telling him how we thought it should be set-up. Steve was just 12 seconds behind Phillip McCallen in the Formula 1 and part of the reason for that was that when he saw Anthon 'Slick' Bass in the pits, he stopped right in front of him. Steve was so used to working with Slick at Honda that he automatically pulled in where he was! When he realised his mistake he had to paddle the bike down pit lane to the Norton pit. Talking to him after that race he said the bike was a real handful so I asked him if he'd let us make some changes to it. While the bike wasn't brilliant for the Senior race, it did handle a bit better and the rest is history."

By Senior race day on the Friday, around 45,000 fans lining the 37-73-mile TT course were daring to dream that Steve Hislop might just be able to pull off a fairy-tale win for Norton. But to make history, Hislop would first have to beat Fogarty who was starting at number 4 – a full three minutes ahead of the Scotsman on the 19 bike.

"The first signal I got was 13 miles out and it told me I was in 2nd place," Hislop said. "I had expected to be 4th or 5th at the pace I was riding but there I was only two seconds off the leader and I knew it had to be Carl. No-one else could touch us at that pace. I started to up my pace on the second lap, having found a rhythm, and I set about trying to catch Carl.

"By the end of the lap I was 2.8 seconds ahead as we pulled in for our first pit stops. I took the precaution of fitting a new rear tyre because I didn't know how badly those speeds would tear up the rubber. Foggy only took on fuel and blasted out of pit lane having retaken the lead with his quicker stop. Once again, I had to do all the work of catching him up and I knew I'd have to ride really hard from then on."

Hislop found that the Senior race required a different style of riding compared to Formula 1. "In the F1 race I'd tried to ride the Norton flat-out everywhere but it was simply too fast on top speed for that and I had been totally out of control," Hizzy explained. "This time I was in control of the bike instead of having it take me for a ride. But I was still hitting bumps and getting lifted up out of my seat and the wind at those speeds was really wrenching at my neck and shoulders, threatening to blow me off the back of the bike.

"Bigger bumps caused the bike to shake its head viciously from side to side while gentle rises in the road sent the front wheel skyward, which is always dangerous because the wind can get under the front wheel and loop the bike over."

By the end of lap three, Hislop had pulled back five seconds on Foggy and was just one second behind. "I knew that would demoralise him and play on his mind but I kept charging all the same." At the end of lap four as the pair came in for their pit stops Hislop was 7.4 seconds in the lead but a slow pit stop of 35 seconds – due to fumbling with the fuel cap – left Hizzy just one second in front as he headed out on the penultimate lap.

Seven miles out, at Ballacraine, Foggy had pulled out a lead of three seconds but by Ramsey Hizzy had overtaken him again and went on to stretch his advantage to 6.4 seconds. Hislop said: "I knew Carl would struggle to pull that back in one lap but I also knew how good he was and that it was still a possibility. I only had to make one slight error and he'd be right back on me. There was no doubt in my mind that he'd try everything he knew on that final lap."

And try Fogarty did. Knowing it was all or nothing, he set a new outright lap record at 123.61mph – faster than even he and Hizzy had lapped at the previous year on their ultra-exotic factory RVF Hondas. This lap record would stand for seven years.

ABOVE: The Norton was fast but wayward – clocked at 193mph in the speed traps.

The rotary had a tendency to 'push on' in turns.

"AROUND 45,000 FANS LINING THE 37.73 MILE TT COURSE WERE DARING TO DREAM THAT STEVE HISLOP MIGHT JUST BE ABLE TO PULL OFF A FAIRY-TALE WIN FOR NORTON."

1992

> With Foggy starting '4' on the road, it took some time to work out if '19' and Hislop's Norton had won.

It was a heroic effort on Fogarty's part but it wasn't enough. As he flashed across the finish line, he now had an agonizing three-minute wait for Hislop before he knew if he had won the race or not. Hislop howled across the line not knowing the outcome either – until he braked heavily and turned left to enter the narrow return road to the pits. "As soon as I saw the crowds lining the path that leads back to the pits I knew I'd done it," he said. "I remember my back being sore from all the slaps I got even though I had a back protector on. My team were ecstatic. They knew the budget was running out and that this might be the last big win for them; it was certainly the biggest they'd ever achieved. But when the press asked Barry Symmons if we'd be having a party to celebrate he replied: 'If we can afford it.' That's how tight things were money-wise. But none of that mattered; we'd silenced a thousand critics and made racing history in what was probably the greatest single race of my life."

Hislop's former (and future) Honda team boss Neil Tuxworth could only shake his head in disbelief at Hislop's performance. Even today he speaks in reverential tones about it: "One of the greatest achievements I ever witnessed at the TT wasn't a Honda win – it was Steve Hislop's win on the Norton in that 1992 Senior. As a Honda man I shouldn't really say this but that was one of the greatest TT wins in history. That bike was an absolute camel to ride and far from being the best bike out there but Hislop managed to keep it going and won that race and it was absolutely phenomenal."

Future TT God John McGuinness – 18 at the time – was also watching. Years later he'd ride that very bike (see our road test on page 70). He says: "I've ridden Hizzy's white charger Norton round the TT course on a demonstration lap and in places I was having a bit of a go on it. It had an oil leak but I gave it the berries in a few sections and, having ridden the bike, I'm now even more amazed that he won on it. It was a very different bike – really quirky.

"It was fast and light, so there were lots of positives but, for example, you couldn't hold part-throttle on it and it required a different style of riding and I'd imagine it took some sorting out during practice week in order for Hizzy to be able to dig deep and push it and do what he did on it. He didn't get the fastest lap but he won the race. But the new lap record Foggy set stood for seven years so that shows you the pace Hislop was having to ride the Norton at. It was an incredible achievement."

Many describe Steve Hislop as a flawed gem; well, that may be the case but on that one glorious summer's day in June 1992, Hislop gave us all a breath-taking glimpse of the mercurial talent that made him one of the purest and fastest riders the world has ever seen. As he himself said: "I don't think anyone in the world could have beaten me that day." How right he was.

Hizzy rated it as one of his greatest ever victories.

FOGGY'S STORY

Foggy really shouldn't have been at the Isle of Man in 1992 because, as he'd said to the press that year: "I've won at the Isle of Man TT, what more can I do?"

Fogarty and his dad George had invested in Carl's talents that year to the tune of more than £50,000. This covered the Ducati 888 Corsa, a small truck and some support in the shape of mechanic Doug Holtom. It was a seismic year for Fogarty; he'd cut himself adrift from Honda Britain when the team had decided to downsize to UK championships only – Carl wanted to ride in World Superbikes. "I'd struggled for a ride in 1992 with all that went on," he says. "I suppose I could have raced in Britain again against those Nortons, but the rules seemed quite different for them and the Honda wasn't that quick and it didn't handle that well either – it was one of the worst handling bikes I rode, that RC30. James Whitham could hardly ride it at all! He suffered worse than me from that front-end. At some tracks it was OK – like Cadwell Park – and at others like Thruxton it became a nightmare."

There was only one thing for Carl to do: "I had to go out and buy the best bike I could… I knew the Kawasaki was pretty good, but the 888 Corsa was good too – even if it wasn't quite up there with the factory bikes. At the second round of the WSB season at Donington Park, I crashed leading one race and won the second. Things were so tight financially we had no spare wheels at the start of that season…"

Money, then, would keep his World Superbike season going and money could be had at riding Endurance… or at the TT. Foggy recalls: "Roger Burnett had gotten me a good deal for World Endurance, something like £10,000 for winning an endurance race. I think I set pole for every race apart from Suzuka – much to my team-mate Terry Rymer's disgust! I even jumped on a YZR500 at the British Grand Prix and made some of the regular riders look a bit daft, but then there was the Isle of Man TT.

"I hadn't planned to do it back in 1991, but I was backed in a corner because that special bike – the Honda RVF – was rolled out to spoil Yamaha's 30th anniversary of racing. People thought that was a classic race event: I was sharing a bike with Joey Dunlop and it wasn't an ideal finish as it was misfiring for the Formula 1 and Joey had the bike for the Senior."

The rumour (and it was only that) was that Fogarty had been lured back to the TT on his privateer Ducati – not a machine that many felt would suit the TT. With low-down torque – handy for coming out of slower corners – Fogarty was known to be strong over The Mountain, where a top-endy power delivery suited. Like what you'd get from a four-cylinder machine, not a V-twin.

"I was having a chat early in the year with Steve Hislop," says Carl. "Steve could be funny in the head sometimes, but we got on really well – no matter what some people thought. I mean, he came to my wedding. I think it was only the World Superbike riders I was up against that I hated… Anyway, Steve told me early on that he'd had a falling out with Yamaha and they came to me not long before the TT itself.

"I was like; 'fucking hell, yeah, OK.' I always rated the Yamaha OW-01 on short circuits so I knew it would suit the TT and I really wanted to try it there. I'd be getting around £6000-£7000 and the same from the tourist board. In the meantime Hizzy said to me: 'I think I'm riding the Norton.' I thought to myself: 'that's one of the fastest riders riding the fastest bike.' But, I never thought that bike would last, to be honest."

Much is made of Steve Hislop's amazing abilities when he was 'in the zone' but also of his frailties when he wasn't. Fogarty said: "I would try and 'get in his head' a little bit. But I would also learn from him how to win a TT. A story I recall was at the TT in 1989; me and Dave Leach set off together, I think we were seventh and eighth and we got tangled up with Steve.

"Watching him showed me how aggressive you had to be to win a TT! I'd lose a bit, gain a bit, but then when I

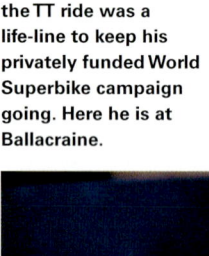

BELOW: For Carl, the TT ride was a life-line to keep his privately funded World Superbike campaign going. Here he is at Ballacraine.

The Mountain was where Foggy was best.

IT'S 30 YEARS AGO NOW, BUT I DO REMEMBER THINKING TO MYSELF THAT I'D GET MY HEAD DOWN AND WIN THE RACE. I KNEW STEVE'S BIKE HAD ABOUT 15MPH ON US THROUGH THE SPEED-TRAPS AND I KNEW HE WAS ONE OF THE BEST GUYS AROUND AT THE TT, BUT I THOUGHT STEVE ON THAT BIKE WOULD STRUGGLE..."

ABOVE: Carl's lap record would last for seven years.

with Hislop 2nd and Joey Dunlop 3rd. Foggy adds: "For me, looking back, if I could go back in time and put one race 'right' in my career, and this covers some of my Grand Prix races too, it would be that Formula 1 race that would have stopped Honda winning 10 in a row…" Fogarty would have a DNF in the Supersport 400 race, leaving everything banked on the Senior, at the end of the week.

"The scene was set," recalls Carl. "It's 30 years ago now, but I do remember thinking to myself that I'd get my head down and win the race. I knew Steve's bike had about 15mph on us through the speed-traps and I knew he was one of the best guys around at the TT, but I thought Steve on that bike would struggle…"

Come the race, come the legends. Fogarty says: "So off I went, I remember getting P1: +0 or +1 at Kirkmichael, and I'm thinking it may be McCallen: he was on a bike he knew well and was a bit nuts, but maybe not as quick as me or Steve yet, back then. It then came to Ramsey and it's still +1 but it was coming up to The Mountain and I loved it up there… here was where I was going to pull some decent time on whoever was following me, I'd done it in the Formula 1. But – this time – it wasn't happening. I'd been pegged back to +0.

"I started to realise: 'It's him! He's only gone and got to grips with that Norton…' It was confirmed when I got into the pits for the first time: 'It's Hislop,' I was told. I was like: 'Oh fuck!' Sure, sometimes things could get to him, but he could also do things that could shock you – and this was one of those times, I knew I was in for a battle."

As the lead see-sawed over the six laps thanks to pit-stops and other issues, Fogarty realised that his got to The Mountain, I was like: 'right you fuckers, this is my territory now!' It was effectively between me and Dave, but I looked over my shoulder and there was Steve! I waved at him as if to say: 'Eff off, you can't win this,' so he backed off! He taught me how to win at the TT and – I think it was that very year – he was the man and took the record through the 120mph barrier. Much is made of the 1991 battle on the RVFs where I had a misfire but – if I'm honest I wasn't in the right frame of mind and wouldn't have beaten him anyway. I do think that – at the TT – I learned from him, I learned from the best."

With all that happened with the pair of them in 1991, where they scrapped it out together over the TT course in close proximity, neither wanted a repeat of that. Foggy recalls: "We chatted at a UK race meeting and I told him I was on the Yamaha with number four, he told me he was going with 19. I said: 'Fuck, that's a ways back, Steve?' I wanted to start with four: I didn't want to be around him and he didn't want to be around me."

Both Hizzy and Foggy would take their 'strange' bikes up to Jurby for some sort of 'bedding in' as Carl explains: "I had no previous time on the Yamaha, but I was pretty good at jumping on most things and going fast. In practice we were all over the place: Rob McElnea said: 'Make it stiffer!' I was like: 'how will that work?' We lost time and sessions because of the weather too. We did go softer on the settings and I went out on the Friday morning practice and did a 120mph standing start lap. I thought to myself: 'We mean business here!'"

Come the Formula 1 race, there was disappointment for Hizzy and Foggy. Carl says: "As we all know, in that race I was leading by a mile when the gearbox went at The Bungalow." He was leading by around 40 seconds at one point, the race would be won by Phillip McCallen

Loctite Yamaha was beginning to fall apart. "Oh man, the screen got broken somewhere," says Carl, "some of the clocks fell off, the exhaust started to blow around Ramsey one lap, the rear shock was knackered, the rear brake lever was bent and I think on the last lap I may have been nine seconds down or something but the daft thought in my head was 'the quicker you go, the sooner you get off this thing!'

"Not the cleverest thing to think at the TT. So I got my head down, I may have lost a bit of time with an incident on that last lap, but I still got the lap record. To be honest, Steve was happy with the win, and I was happy with that lap record – 123.61mph – and that was on a well-used tyre. I always wanted to be the fastest around the TT course and it stood for another seven years, I think only one of Hailwood's records stood for longer."

And where's the bike? Surely it should have been kept forever by Yamaha? "They should have just thrown a cover over it and left it as it finished that race," says Fogarty. "As it was, I guess Rob Mac is the only one who knows where it went. He always took the best bits off for his BSB bikes! I would have loved to have ridden one of those in the UK in 1989-1990, it was a good bike. I doubt the bike exists anymore."

As to Hislop, what did Fogarty think of Steve's achievement? "At the time, Steve was never a rival around short circuits. I'd take the piss out of James Whitham and say to him: 'You can't even beat Hislop on short circuits now!' James would say to me: 'You dickhead, he's going really fast now!' And that was Hislop all over: when things were right – wherever he was racing – he was the fastest man out there and I was always in a battle with him at the TT."

Fogarty was happy enough with the lap record – or so he says!

"AND I WAS HAPPY WITH THAT LAP RECORD 123.61MPH AND THAT WAS ON A WELL-USED TYRE."

By the last lap, the Loctite OW-01 was falling apart around him.

Hislop would become a two-time BSB champ, proving the doubters wrong on the short circuits.

POSTSCRIPT

Both riders would go on to great things. Foggy would become one of the most successful British riders of all time if not the most popular since Barry Sheene with his four WSB titles – he'd later go on to become something of a TV star, winning the 2014 I'm a Celebrity, Get Me Out of Here title in Australia. Once a prickly character, the man has mellowed somewhat but is still good for a juicy quote or three.

Stevie would crack the short-circuits in the UK, winning two BSB titles in 1995 and 2002, but he would never get the chance he deserved, truly deserved, on the world scene – many who watched him closely felt he could have been a handy 250 or even 500cc GP rider. Many who raced against Hizzy knew that – on his day – he was one of the best in the world. Anyone who witnessed his 2002 BSB qualifying lap of Donington Park on a customer Ducati 998 RS where he beat the MotoGP lap record set by Valentino Rossi that year on a works Honda RC211-V would agree.

Following his sacking from McElnea's Virgin Yamaha squad in early July 2003, Hizzy was set to return on his old 2002-title winning Ducati at Oulton Park, in August, a bike now owned and run by ETI Ducati. It was not to be. Robert Steven Hislop would die on July 30 when the helicopter he was flying crashed near Teviothead, not far from his birthplace of Hawick.

ABOVE: Fogarty would take four WSB titles: his 1992/TT investment in himself paid off!

THE 'OTHER' CLASS OF 1992

It would be unfair to not shine a light on the other amazing achievements at the TT that year.

First and foremost, Joey Dunlop equalled Mike Hailwood's 14 TT wins thanks to beating brother Robert in the Ultra-lightweight 125cc TT. Robert himself would add that 2nd place to his 3rd in the Junior and his impressive 3rd in the Senior. Two solo riders would bag a brace of wins: Phillip McCallen would take his in the Formula 1 and Supersport 600 with Brian Reid taking the spoils in the Junior and Supersport 400 races. The chairs double would be won by Geoff Bell and Keith Cornbill.

Joey would match Mike Hailwood's 14 TT wins at the 1992 Isle of Man TT event: he was only just starting!

MAKE US YOUR FIRST CHOICE

When it comes to insurance, our competitive quotes cut prices, not corners.

At Bikesure we pride ourselves on insuring motorbike riders from every walk of life. We can find you a specialist policy that's tailored to your own riding history and personal requirements.

POLICY BENEFITS AVAILABLE CAN INCLUDE:
- Modifications Cover
- Great Value Multi-Bike Rates
- Cover for Convicted Riders
- Free Legal Expenses

Bikesure
Freethinking Insurance

CELEBRATING OVER 30 YEARS

5 STAR INSURANCE

bikesure.co.uk
Authorised and regulated by the Financial Conduct Authority

CALL US ON FREEPHONE
0808 1001 294

ABUS NORTON

An old legend! But enough about Sir Alan – the Norton NRS is a piece of British TT racing history!

A beautiful machine, etched into the history of the TT forever.

ABUS NORTON

SENIOR
Service!

Alan Cathcart rides one of the Isle of Man TT's legendary machines: the Senior TT-winning ABUS Norton NRS588 of the late, great Steve Hislop.

WORDS: ALAN CATHCART
PICS: KYOICHI NAKAMURA, MORTONS ARCHIVES

Thirty years on, the magic of it all still thrills the spirit – especially in the memory of those privileged to have witnessed it personally.

The closest, fastest, most exciting and most enthralling Isle of Man Senior TT ever run resulted in a long-awaited all-British victory for super-Scot Steve Hislop and the Norton Rotary, painted an unaccustomed white to reflect the support of Steve's personal security equipment sponsor ABUS, rather than the more usual black of Norton's mainland cigarette sponsors, John Player Special.

JPS management must have kicked themselves when they heard the result for not finding the extra budget to support Norton's quixotic, shoestring assault on Japanese supremacy in the world's oldest and most famous road race, one that Norton hadn't won since 1961.

ABUS NORTON

ABOVE: Alan would get two rides on the Norton, some 18 years apart.

BELOW: Note missing front mudguard: a change made after the F1 race when the bike needed better cooling.

Back then the Senior TT was confined to 500cc GP racers, and a spotty kid named Mike Hailwood brought his single-cylinder Manx Norton home first after the all-conquering MV Agustas uncharacteristically self-destructed. Laudable as Mike the Bike's win was (and both he and fellow Norton rider Derek Minter lapped at over 100mph for the first time ever on single-cylinder machines), Norton got that win by default – something you could never accuse Hislop of doing this time around.

For to win the 1992 Senior TT, Hizzy had not only to contend with the perennial Honda threat, led by factory-supported TT maestro Joey Dunlop and Honda Britain rider Phil McCallen, but also with another graduate – like himself – of the Honda school of TT talent, and another former TT F1 World champion, same as Yer Maun Joey: future four-time World Superbike champion Carl Fogarty.

Later that same year, Carl would clinch the World Endurance title on a Kawasaki, only, like Hislop, Carl wasn't riding a Kawasaki on this occasion, nor a Honda – but instead a tricked-out OW-01 Yamaha, with lots of special parts sourced from the factory race shop. And of course, there was always Joey Dunlop's kid brother Robert – Hislop's Norton teammate – riding a Rotary racer in JPS colours that he'd leased for the event with sponsorship from an array of Ulster supporters, thus giving the cigarette company a free ride in terms of exposure, since Robert couldn't be bothered to repaint the bodywork. Not an easy race to win, this one…

So it proved. The pace was electrifying right from the start, with the lead see-sawing between Fogarty and Hislop, neither of them ever more than eight seconds ahead of the other on corrected time throughout the entire six-lap/226-mile race. The ABUS Norton rider lost time at his second fuel stop with a filler cap that wouldn't close, leaving him three seconds behind the Yamaha at Glen Helen on the penultimate lap.

A superhuman effort saw Hislop retake the lead by six seconds starting the final 37.73-mile lap, in which both riders broke the outright lap record, with Fogarty leaving it at 123.61mph to close to just 4.4 secs of the Norton at the flag. But it wasn't enough – and Norton had won its first Isle of Man TT race since 1973, when Peter Williams took victory in the F750 race on the JPN Monocoque, defeating Jack Findlay's Suzuki triple in a race more comparable with Hislop's great victory than Hailwood's 1961 Senior win.

Norton's 1992 Senior TT win was achieved against the odds, judging by the bike's performance in the Formula 1 race at the start of that year's TT Week. The motor of Robert Dunlop's JPS-liveried Rotary racer had seized thanks to being jetted too lean, and Hislop's ABUS bike ran too hot, causing the team to lose time in the pits removing the front mudguard. Even so, he still finished runner-up to McCallen's Honda by just 12 seconds!

Having had five motors blow up at the NW200 two weeks earlier, Norton team manager Barry Symmons knew his team had a problem, so for the Senior race they fitted a third float chamber to the Keihin flat-slides, in order to increase the fuel supply to the motor, and also maxed out the jetting to 240, compared to the 210s used before. That gained them six-degrees C, but they also dropped the compression ratio slightly, fitted a smaller nozzle to the ejector system on the Micron exhaust to draw more cooling air through the centre of the engine between the rotor housings thanks to an

72 Island**Racer**

ABUS NORTON

It's all black and white: JPS couldn't sponsor the TT ride so in came ABUS et al to the tune of £20,000! Ron ahead of Alan here…

ABOVE: Oh yes… this is 'The One' alright!

increased vacuum effect, and again removed the front mudguard for the second race.

Some extra vents in the fairing and internal ducting maximised the flow of cooling air to the outside of the engine, while to leave nothing to chance they also used a front tyre with a softer construction. This improved flexibility and minimised the chance of heat transfer rearwards. It all worked – and with a master craftsman of the TT course at the controls in the shape of Steve Hislop, Norton achieved the victory they and every Brit-Bike fan in the world had been praying they'd earn.

Snetterton race circuit in Eastern England is a poor substitute for the TT Mountain Course, but then it's better than tight, twisty Mallory Park, where I'd previously ridden the 1991 Norton NRS588 – certainly in terms of track testing a bike that will clock close-on 190mph in a straight line. So when Barry Symmons invited me to sample Hislop's TT-winning bike – complete with engraved plaque to prove it was 'The One' – at the Norfolk circuit just a month after Steve's hard-fought win, it gave me a chance to keep my Norton Rotary education properly up to date.

Having ridden each version of the Rotary racer, during the years it had progressed from an after-hours pet project for Norton technician Brian Crighton, the man who first gave the Rotary its racing opportunity, to a full-on factory race effort with tobacco sponsorship and high-profile TV coverage, I'd been able to appreciate how much had been achieved on resources that would barely keep a 500GP team in tyres for a full season.

And with phenomenal success, too, for Norton won the British Superbike title in 1989 with Steve Spray, repeated the feat the following year with Trevor Nation, then finished 2nd in the UK Supercup series in 1991 with star recruit Ron Haslam who, fresh from 500GP racing, set lap records galore with the revamped Rotary racer now wearing its all-new Harris-built, Ron Williams-designed Maxton chassis.

That year Norton returned to GP racing officially for the first time in four decades when permitted by the FIM to race the Rotary in the British 500GP at Donington, then in 1992 reached the pinnacle of success with Steve Hislop's victory in the Senior TT, matched by Robert Dunlop's win later that year in the Ulster GP. Even Norton's rivals, or those who denigrated the Rotary engine concept, had to admit this was quite an achievement, especially considering the dire financial straits of the parent company during most of this time, thanks to the depredations of the smart suit City brigade who milked it dry of vital cash.

FAREWELL TO ARMS:

Sadly, had I but known it, my ride on Hislop's TT-winner was a farewell to arms, for immediately after my test the bike travelled straight to the NMM/National Motorcycle Museum in Birmingham where it now resides – a museum piece that should have been swooping round the Island the following June, to wave the British flag in an effort to repeat its 1992 Senior TT victory, if only Norton could have found the resources to continue racing in the Isle of Man and mainland circuits. But it didn't, so instead, look at these photos and remember the Way it Was 30 years ago, while we take a lap or two

LEFT: Hislop on the Norton at the 1992 Isle of Man TT.

Island**Racer** 73

ABUS NORTON

Black tank courtesy of the JPS machines.

37mm Keihin flat-slides helped power delivery and a 147bhp top-end.

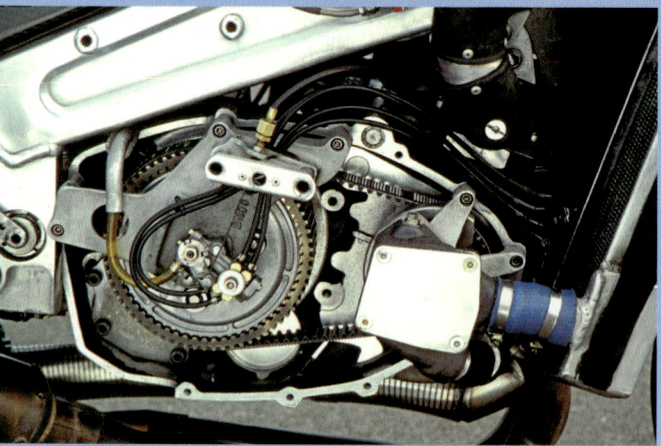
Twin-rotor motor gave power, speed and not much engine braking!

> "WHY? WELL, BECAUSE IT WAS FAST, TOO – VERY FAST."

round Snetterton on Steve's Senior-winning mount.

Compared to Ron Haslam's short-circuit bike, which I also rode the same day at Snetterton, the Hislop machine couldn't have been more different. Even with the settings he used in the IoM only approximated for Snetterton, it was like the difference between a GP racer and a (very powerful) street bike. Haslam's Norton felt taut, low-slung and compact, with hard suspension and a ground-hugging ride height, as well as a distinct forward weight bias that had the rear wheel waving in the air everywhere I used the very effective front brake cocktail of 310mm cast iron PVM discs mated to AP four-piston calipers, to something like max effect.

It felt like what it was: a Rotary racer set up like a 500GP bike for a rider who'd spent the past decade riding such machines on purpose-built circuits at World Championship level. "To be honest, the first time I rode the Norton in TT practice, I thought I'd made a terrible mistake," the late Steve Hislop once told me ruefully. "The way Ron had it set up was completely unsuitable for the Island, and it was actually quite a battle to persuade the team that it had to be altered very drastically in terms of handling to make it rideable at race-winning speeds there. But I got my way in the end – just as well, really!"

Too right: basically, Steve needed the bike set up with much softer suspension settings, and a higher ride height front and rear, which you noticed immediately when you sat on his Norton in the pits – it was longer but also measurably taller off the ground than Haslam's short-circuit racer, with a softer ride and more suspension travel. With a 50mm longer wheelbase than the 1991 version of the same Maxton chassis, it was also much more stable round fast sweepers like Snetterton's Coram Curve (or the 33rd Milestone on the TT Course), at the expense of some understeer in slower corners with the power on – although the more conservative 23.5-degree head angle Steve had opted for (versus 22-degrees on Ron's bike) might have had something to do with this.

On the other hand, the longer wheelbase also meant it didn't wheelie quite as easily out of turns as the other bike, and traction was better out of slower bends like the Snetterton chicane under something approaching full power. Parliament Square, Ramsey Hairpin, Waterworks, the Gooseneck – all easy meat for the ABUS Norton in TT-mode, especially with that lovely, linear power delivery from the twin-rotor engine.

However, another factor in the improved traction may well have been the auxiliary damper unit that Maxton's

ABUS NORTON

Brakes were the effective 310mm cast-iron PVM discs with AP-Lockheed four-piston calipers.

ABOVE: Stripped, the bike looks even meaner!

TOP: By 1991-92, Harris had fabricated the Norton's chassis.

Ron Williams had grafted on to the modified Koni rear shock for 1992. "The problem was the inherent surge of the Rotary engine running on a closed throttle," explained Ron. "When that happens the engine speed varies, which loads the gearbox and winds up the rear shock, then unloads it again. By using an additional damper unit that comes into play after about 40mm of travel on the main shock (which can run a lighter, more sensitive spring as a result), we can control this unusual problem. On a bumpy circuit, too, like the Isle of Man, the second damper comes in earlier to stop the rear end squatting too much, which improves traction, so there's a double benefit."

The system worked well out of the chicane at Snetterton, or at the Esses, where you were using hard acceleration in a low gear – but it must really have come into its own in the Island over the bumpier sections, especially when taking a fast turn like Bungalow or Windy Corner on a closed or trailing throttle, where the Rotary engine's traditional hunting trait due to the uneven firing rotation, might upset the traction.

The suspension also seemed very sensitive, despite being softly-sprung, and this could have been be due to the auxiliary damper system – I could feel the ripples left by the cars in Riches Bend, as the rear wheel moved smoothly over them without chatter. Haslam's bike didn't like the dip on the exit there at all: shaking its head every lap as the stiffer forks got upset at having to cope with what by TT standards was just a wee bump! Hislop's softer-sprung bike took it all in its stride, with just a slight dip and dive as the White Power upside-down fork did its job. Following Japanese Supermono ace Shinichiro Ohura on the Haslam Norton through there on his guest test ride for the JPS team (they must have been trying to interest some Japanese sponsors) confirmed the difference in behaviour between the two bikes: horses for courses.

However, different as the two set-ups were, both Nortons had one thing in common – the twin-rotor engine's liquid-smooth power delivery and unbelievably meaty torque at almost any point in the rev-range. It was surely one of the great motorcycle power units of its era in racing form, and as effective as the similar but two-thirds as powerful engine in the Norton F1 Sport rotary road bike was frankly underwhelming by comparison.

Barry Symmons' team refined the engine heaps during the 1992 season, fitting bigger 37mm Keihin flat-slides which gave a very immediate but still controllable response, and helped unlock the waves of torque in the motor at almost any point between 6000 rpm and its 11,500rpm appointment with the rev-limiter. The biggest difference, though, was the power delivery. Although power rose to 147bhp at 10,000rpm for 1992, the way it came through was indeed more linear and progressive than on the 1991 bike, which was much peakier than previous Rotary racers, in an effort to wrest more Japanese-beating performance from the engine. This must again have made a big difference to riding it in the TT, coupled with the crisp carburation and improved throttle response offered by the Keihins compared to the Amals fitted to previous Rotaries I'd tried. Just a twist of the wrist, at almost any revs in almost any gear, and the Norton delivered. What a great Island engine!

Why? Well, because it was fast, too – VERY fast. As luck would have it, I spent half a dozen laps running with ex-500GP racer Rob McElnea on his Loctite Yamaha OW-01 Superbike, presumably not too far removed from Carl Fogarty's TT racer in terms of performance, and the Norton just romped away from the Yamaha down the straights.

It was an educational comparison. "You can see what we're up against," said Rob afterwards. "I couldn't stay with you in a straight line, because the Norton really packs a punch out of turns, and weighs about 80lb (36kg) less than our bikes. That's a huge advantage!"

In contrast to 1991, the British bike also had a gearbox that worked – a six-speeder lifted (oh the irony) straight from the FZR1000 Yamaha, mated to a Gates Kevlar toothed-belt primary drive to deliver a smooth, precise change that now allowed you to ride the bike like a two-stroke if you wanted (and as Ron Haslam certainly did), by standing on the brakes and zapping down two or three gears at a time with the clutch home in a way that would have been unthinkable with the harsh-shifting, semi-vintage, five-speed Triumph gearbox fitted previously.

You did need to be very precise working the gear lever though, else it was all too easy to get a false neutral. But with zero engine braking on a rotary engine, two-stroke style, this was indeed the approved manner of riding the ABUS Norton, especially as the only disconcerting

Auxiliary damper allied to normal suspension and swingarm improved the 1992 bike.

76 Island**Racer**

thing I found about the engine's behaviour was its very high idle speed, which combined with the hunting effect to make the engine run on into slow turns. As a result you sometimes ended up missing the apex.

Holding the clutch in seemed to be the best way of coping, but Ron Haslam had a better idea: "I don't like that either, so what I do is use the back brake to lock the rear wheel when I have it off the deck under braking," he said. "That stops the engine, then when the wheel comes down again, it restarts OK – but you've not been pushed past the apex of the corner by the engine running on. It's definitely the best way to solve that problem." Thanks, Ron – but I'll leave you the exclusive on doing that!

Eighteen years later, I was asked to ride the Senior TT-winning NRS588 ABUS Norton once again, by demonstrating it for the NMM at Donington Park's big 2010 International Historic race meeting, in company with Trevor Nation, Terry Rymer and the rest of the Rotary racers on the actual bikes they raced back then.

I was honoured to be standing in for Steve Hislop, sadly no longer with us after his fatal helicopter crash in 2003 – and I couldn't help but think back to the year before he passed away, when I'd talked with the 11-time TT race-winner about his Senior TT victory on the Norton, on the 10th anniversary of his win. "I've been fortunate to have a lot of success in the Island, but that win on the Norton was the best race I ever had there," said Steve. "Foggy was such a determined competitor, and I knew he'd not stop trying till the very last yard of the very last lap. I wasn't sure to be racing in the TT that year until right at the last minute, when ABUS came up with the cash to fund Norton bringing over a bike for me.

"We finished 2nd in the Formula 1 race at the start of the week, and that proved the Rotary could last the distance. But in the Senior race which is the one you really want to win, I had a problem closing the filler cap at my second pit stop. I put my head down and went for it, and managed to just edge Carl on corrected time at the end. We never saw each other during the race, because I started no.19 and he was up at the front, so signals were vital, and I owe it to all the people around the course who kept me in the picture with what was happening on time. If not for them, I'd have had no clue how I was doing, and how a win was still on the cards. I'd never ridden so hard in the Isle of Man as I did in that race – and I never did again!"

But that was the rotary Norton's final appearance in the Isle of Man for 17 years, until Robert Dunlop's son Michael's ill-fated attempt to race one for Norton's then owner, Stuart Garner, in 2009. But at least, thanks to ABUS, the late and very definitely great Steve Hislop was able to add to his glorious TT career in 1992 – and Norton could remind us all that it was still, as its company slogan used to say, Simply Unapproachable. Well, by 4.4 seconds, anyway!

Top-end speed was incredible on the Norton: 193mph at Sulby Straight.

A lack of engine braking means you need to plan ahead and use those AP-Lockheed anchors…

RIGHT: 2010 and Alan is riding the ABUS Norton at Donington Park alongside other Rotary dignitaries.

BELOW: Soft suspension was the order of the day on Hizzy's Norton: making it much more compliant over the Island's bumps.

ABUS NORTON

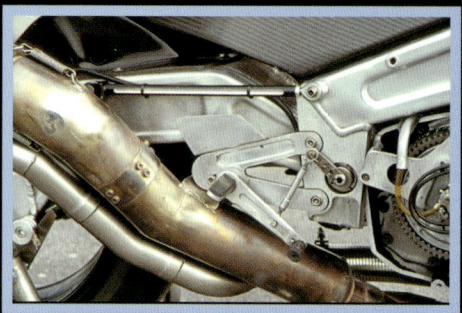

LEFT: The liquid-cooled rotary was a compact unit in the Harris frame.

RIGHT: While the Norton was considered somewhat 'Heath Robinson' many big names worked in the team and would go on to great things – such as Chris Pike and Tony 'Slick' Bass. Look at the detail…

ABUS NORTON

1992 ABUS NORTON NRS588 SPECIFICATION

The 'White Charger'
IN ALL HER GLORY!

One machine – forever linked to the 1990s – proved itself in the crucible of road-racing. Honda's CBR900RR FireBlade would go from road bike legend to road-race winner, paving the way for many wins in the future.

WORDS: BERTIE SIMMONDS
PICS: HONDA UK, MORTONS ARCHIVE, DOUBLE RED

FIRE

When the FireBlade could finally be unleashed in anger, there was only one man to race it: the development test rider, Phillip McCallen. Note the flex in the 16-inch front tyre!

FIREBLADE

STARTER

As a race machine for pure road racing, the Honda CBR900RR FireBlade was a case of the wrong bike at the wrong time… At launch in 1992, it just wasn't the right capacity for the more popular production racing classes, these being mainly 400cc, 600cc and 750cc superbike classes. There wasn't anywhere – save for the USA's Formula Xtreme – where the 893cc inline four-cylinder FireBlade could really stretch its legs.

It was the king of the current road-going superbikes but this wasn't enough for Honda; the company wanted to prove the CBR's credentials on the toughest race-track of them all – the Isle of Man TT circuit. There was a problem though: it was the wrong capacity for both the Formula 1 and the Senior TT. The bike couldn't enter these prestigious races and there hadn't been a production TT race for larger capacity sports machines for some years.

This was thanks to a well-publicised tragedy at the 1989 1300cc Production TT race on the Isle of Man TT course. Two extremely popular racers – Phil 'Mez' Mellor and Steve Henshaw – died during the second lap in two separate incidents just nine miles apart. Tragedy struck when Mellor's Suzuki GSX-R1100 crashed at the 110mph Doran's Bend, both he and the machine hitting the wall. He died later in hospital.

Meanwhile Mellor's team-mate Jamie Whitham had crashed at the notorious Quarry Bends, with Henshaw and Mike Seward colliding as they tried to avoid the crash debris. Henshaw was killed instantly and Seward badly injured in the incident. These accidents highlighted the fact that the big, powerful, unwieldy

ABOVE: Honda UK bike manager Bob McMillan used his influence with the TT organisers to get the new Production TT instigated.

The original Honda CBR900RR FireBlade had no equal as a road machine but it would take time before it could hit the tracks.

Island Racer   81

FIREBLADE

ABOVE: Baba-san knew his Blade better than anyone… a few calculations and he was confident that a win was on the cards.

BELOW: Could Yamaha's longer, more stable (and maybe faster) Thunderace be better at the TT?

machines of the day on the tyres of the time were a handful on short circuits, let alone the most demanding road course in the world, where mistakes or even a wobble can lead the rider to make the ultimate sacrifice.

TT photographer, fan and journalist Don Morley had no doubt as to the cause. He said: "I campaigned hard against the 1989 1300cc Production TT. Although there had been a race for up to 1300cc machines before, the powers that be decided to make it compulsory to use road tyres for the 1989 race. Myself and some of the riders thought this was dangerous, considering how big, heavy and powerful the bikes were at the time. Using my monthly column in *SuperBike* magazine at the time, I criticised this decision and was virtually blacklisted by the ACU and TT organisers. Were the crashes tyre-related? I suppose we will never know…"

The fallout would not just see big capacity production bikes stop racing on the Island, but on the UK's short circuits too. By the mid-1990s, however, things were about to change.

Honda UK was a powerful force at the Isle of Man TT back then – as it is now – always entering a strong line-up of men and machines for most of the categories. Big names such as Joey Dunlop, Phillip McCallen and Nick Jefferies, as well as a raft of quality privateers on Honda machinery, helped the manufacturer become the dominant force in road-racing during the decade.

Honda UK's motorcycling supremo of the time Bob McMillan used his not inconsiderable influence with the Isle of Man TT organisers to get a new 1000cc production class ready for the 1996 event. The machines had become lighter by now – though just as fast – while tyre and suspension technology had moved on somewhat.

By late 1995 it was announced that four-stroke machines of 701-1010cc would be allowed to complete in the new Production Race for the 1996 Isle of Man TT. The event would become a three lap race of some 113.19 miles. The old production rules at the TT meant almost no changes at all to the bikes, but for the new Production class more nods to safety were allowed. This meant rear shock absorbers could be changed, as could all fork internals; a steering damper could also be fitted. In the motor, carburettors had to be standard but jetting could be altered and the air-box and air-filter itself had to be as supplied by the manufacturer. The exhaust's silencer could also be changed.

Tyres had to be 'production-based', which meant street legal and available to all over the counter, but by the mid-1990s good, grippy, durable tyres were available in a number of sizes, even the 'quirky' 16-inch front which the FireBlade used.

Bikes that were eligible included the new Yamaha Thunderace, of some 1002cc, the flighty Suzuki GSX-R750 WT SRAD and Honda's CBR900RR FireBlade…

The FireBlade was the best-selling large capacity sportsbike in the UK at the time. Designed by Tadao Baba, it became known as the best-performing sports machine thanks to the 'light is right' and 'mass centralization' concepts. Baba and his team had made the lightest but most powerful machine they could, with a well-balanced chassis. This meant the bike could go around corners like a proper race machine and was therefore perfect for the TT. Or was it?

Some felt the longer, more powerful Thunderace could have the edge, or perhaps even the heavier – but faster – Kawasaki ZX-9R. Either way, Honda and McMillian weren't taking any chances and the entry list was flooded with both Honda UK and dealer-backed riders, including Phillip McCallen on a Motorcycle City-backed machine. McCallen was actually one of the FireBlade's development riders – few knew the bike as well as he did.

While the race was for 'production' bikes – Honda UK weren't taking any chances: this meant testing the FireBlade on a number of short circuits first. Once more McCallen and Honda UK/Honda Europe test rider Dave Hancock were brought in. Hancock said: "Just before the TT we were testing all sorts of forks and suspension set-ups at Brands Hatch in preparation for the bumps that the Island would throw at us. We tried so many things in the rules, changing to heavier springs, thicker oil and the like, but they were all pretty bad, to be honest. We finally found that the best thing was a brand new set of the standard forks. For that sort of road surface you couldn't really beat the standard forks!"

Many of the riders that were selected to ride the

> HONDA UK WAS A POWERFUL FORCE AT THE ISLE OF MAN TT BACK THEN – AS IT IS NOW – ALWAYS ENTERING A STRONG LINE-UP OF MEN AND MACHINES FOR MOST OF THE CATEGORIES.

ABOVE: Dave Hancock: "We were worried about how the FireBlade would consume fuel over the three laps..."

CBR900RR would actually try and lengthen the wheelbase of their FireBlades to give a bit more stability over the Islands' notorious lumps and bumps.

Come the race a total of 23 of the 53 entrants were mounted on CBR900RR FireBlades, alongside 11 Yamaha Thunderaces, seven Suzuki GSX-R750s, three Kawasaki ZX7-RRs and two of the bulky ZX-9R Ninjas. The 750cc machines would basically be battling in their own 'class' for honours, but everyone was looking to the big bikes to see what would win. Riding the big Yamaha would be a number of seasoned roads campaigners, including Tim Leech, Nigel 'Cap' Davies and Lee Pullan, so it was not a forgone conclusion that the Honda would win. The Kawasaki wasn't going to be really in the fight – although one of the ZX-9Rs did take the honours for being the fastest through *Performance Bike* magazine's speed trap at around 170mph. Worryingly for Honda, some of the GSX-R750s were as fast as the FireBlades.

Practice week was hit by changeable weather, meaning it was hard to get an accurate picture of the class. FireBlades did fill five of the first seven places on the leaderboard, but surprisingly it was a Yamaha – one belonging to Dennis Winterbottom – which led the practice times, with McCallen some 2.4 seconds behind. Despite being behind, McCallen was quietly confident and on race morning he was hoping to complete a hat-trick of the four wins he'd get that week. But first of all there was a question that needed answering: "Could the FireBlade and its 18-litre tank do two laps on one tankful?" It was an important question as a 'splash and dash' in between every lap would see them lose the race.

Dave Hancock remembers just who worked it out: 'Mr FireBlade' himself, Tadao Baba. "At racing pace and consumption, what could we get out of that 18 litre tank around the 37.73 mile circuit?" recalled Hancock. "Baba simply asked us what the lap length was, how many laps the race was and worked it out himself. He had all the relevant information on specific fuel consumption for this that and the other jet sizes in his head. He just went up to a blackboard and worked it out. It was remarkable to watch. It showed he knew the bike inside and out. At the end of it all he simply said, 'It's OK, the bike will do two laps,' and, of course, it did. All he needed was a cup of coffee, a cigarette, an ashtray and something to write down his calculations on."

Everything was ready and as the bikes rolled forward to the startline Hancock watched McCallen's Motorcycle City-liveried number 12 machine get ready for the off. "Watching Phillip just before the start of that production race, I could see that he wanted to win it as much for Honda, Baba-san and me as for himself," Dave recalled. "I think as he was part of the test team he wanted to prove that this bike was the best machine in the world on the harshest road track in the world."

On the opening lap, the first battle was between the FireBlades of McCallen and Scot Iain Duffus, with Duffus holding a 3.6 second advantage over McCallen. Davies, on the Yamaha, was a further 3.6 seconds down the road. In 4th at the end of the opening lap was CBR-mounted Colin Gable with Leech and Pullan close behind. Second time around both Duffus and McCallen lapped at more than 118mph – but Phillip was just faster with an average of 118.93mph. By the end of that second lap the roles were reversed with McCallen holding a 3.1 second advantage over Duffus with Pullan, Davies, Alan Bennallick (FireBlade) and Nick Jefferies (FireBlade) following. Leech retired at the end of that lap in the pits, with Gable dropping to 9th.

At the end of the third lap, over the line came McCallen to take the win – his third of race week –

ABOVE: McCallen took his Motorcycle City-backed bike to the win in 1996 and 1997.

watched by Honda staff including Baba-san himself. He'd completed the three laps and 113.19 mile distance with a race average of 117.32mph – a new lap record. Just 6.1 seconds back was Duffus, with Davies in 3rd. following close behind were Gable, Pullan and Honda's Derek Young, which rounded out the top six, with Jefferies eventually finishing 7th, just ahead of Bennallick.

Baba's help proved vital. Leaning off the bike a little meant that McCallen could make it home, when several riders had run out of fuel. Even Davies had to nurse his Yamaha home. Honda had proved a point – it was the ultimate test ride for the FireBlade and it had succeeded…

McCallen was overjoyed: "For me the picture that sums it all up from that first race was a great shot taken by James Wright of Double Red photographic. I'd always told Baba-san and the engineers that because a 16-inch front wheel has a higher profile, you'd probably get some sort of tyre flex. You can see in the shot that front tyre deforming to keep on the road as the bike's trying to push wide. You can see I was trying hard!"

The following year's race proved to be another win for the FireBlade – and Phillip McCallen – although this time pushing him hard in the controversial race was Scotsman Ian Simpson on a production Ducati 996SPS. Poor weather saw the original three laps cut to just two, and this race would prove to be a struggle for both riders.

The Scotsman had led up until Glen Helen on the first lap, and then McCallen used all his knowledge of both course and machine to reverse this into a 11.5 second lead at the end of the first lap. Simpson would claw some time back on the second and final lap to finish 7.6 seconds adrift.

For McCallen, it was a wonder he finished at all, as he'd had a scary moment on the first lap: "I landed with the steering a bit out of line at Ballaugh, I think it was, and that fired me almost over the top of the bike and the landing twisted the forks in the yokes.

"From then on I raced with the steering twisted to one side to compensate and whenever the front wheel came up or I hit a jump I had to guess if the front wheel was in line, otherwise I would have been tank-slapped off the bike. Despite this problem in one lap between Glen Helen and Ramsey I was able to make up the gap between me and the leader Simpson and take the win.

Again, I had to go for the win and prove the Blade was the best."

Following the race, there was an inquiry into whether the fuel McCallen's Motorcycle City-backed bike was using was legal. In the rules it states that the fuel must be pump unleaded available in garages, but the fuel they were using was of a higher RON rating than normal pump unleaded and apparently only available from one service station in the UK. The protest was eventually thrown out and FireBlades would take seven of the top 13 finishes.

The arrival of Yamaha's YZF-R1, as well as an updated Kawasaki ZX-9R, should have been the biggest threat to the Blade's dominance in the Production class in 1998. Practice showed that the also improved FireBlade was in for a struggle. The highest placed Blade was that of Michael Rutter down in 7th place. At the front, Alan Bennallick's R1 just had the edge on Nigel Davies' ZX-9R. Kiwi rider Shaun Harris had sneaked his GSX-R750 ahead of the Hondas, too. In 8th was Jim Moodie, who'd eventually take another victory for the FireBlade – and a memorable one at that – as it proved to be Honda's 100th TT win (see boxout).

By 1999 the pressure was beginning to tell on the FireBlade and a Honda UK plan to produce a limited-edition version of the bike to run in both production class short circuit and road race events backfired when it was decided it wasn't eligible. With the new rules allowing big four-strokes such as the Yamaha YZF-R1, FireBlade and Kawasaki's ZX-9R to join the more established race machinery in both the Formula 1 and Senior classes, it was a V&M Yamaha YZF-R1 which took the F1 and Senior race wins.

David Jefferies would take both these important victories as well as the Production TT win with a more standard R1; R1s filled the Production podium that year, with Welshman Jason Griffiths and McCallen, now on a Yamaha. The first Blade home was Adrian Archibald in 4th.

Come the new millennium, the new rules, new machines and new riders would see the baton passed between the major manufacturers as each battled for glory. Honda continued with the RC45 750cc V4s in open TT races until the SP1 and SP2 V-twins arrived at the turn of the century. So, part two of the Fireblade's story as an Isle of Man TT Superbike and Senior machine really begins when John McGuinness

ABOVE: Phillip McCallen was a test-rider in the CBR900RR project and a very handy roads racer.

FIREBLADE

re-joined Honda in 2006 and Honda UK got serious about turning the Blade into a proper TT race bike.

Neil Tuxworth – a handy TT racer himself – and Honda Racing UK manager from 1989-2017 said: "When we saw the performance the bike was putting up in production races we decided, let's just build a slightly better road bike. So at first we didn't build a full-blown superbike. Some people get it wrong and try to build short-circuit bikes for the TT, which doesn't usually work. We said, we're racing on public roads in all kinds of conditions, so you don't need the quickest thing – you just need something that handles well and has really linear power, which the Blade had at that time."

In the 10 year period between 2006 and 2015 Honda's Fireblade would chalk up 20 victories in the Superbike, Superstock and Senior classes – helped in no small part by the talents of John McGuinness, who returns to Honda for 2022.

McGuinness won his first Fireblade TT in the 2006 Senior and his last in the 2015 Senior. During that period he won a total of 12 Fireblade victories – six Senior TTs, five Superbike races and one Superstock.

"The Fireblade has been a massive part of my journey," said McGuinness. "It was a consistently good package. I always knew how the bike was going to react, so it was a bit like putting on an old pair of slippers. It was stable, which is what you need on the Isle of Man – you don't want to be fighting a bike over there, you want to enjoy it." Tuxworth worked with McGuinness throughout his time at Honda, during which Bruce Anstey, Michael Dunlop, Ian Hutchinson and Steve Plater also won TTs on Fireblades.

Tuxworth explained: "One of the comments a lot of riders made was that the Blade often felt slow but it did the lap times. It's always had nice, linear power all the way through, which is much better than an aggressive power delivery, even if it doesn't feel as fast. John loved riding it because he always knew what it was going to do and it always performed as he expected. It was a very

John McGuinness has enjoyed a long and fruitful relationship with Fireblades over the years at the TT.

Honda UK's build of a 'special' SP Blade backfired in 1999.

Island Racer 85

Honda's V4 race machines – such as this RC45 – were dominant on the Island for so long.

FIREBLADE

easy motorcycle to work with."

McGuinness won his 12 Blade TTs on several different iterations of the machine. The first few came with the eighth-generation Fireblade, with the under-seat exhaust, including the 2007 Centenary Senior TT, during which he rode the first 130mph lap. "That was such a sweet package," recalled John. "I used to walk towards the bike and think, nobody's going to beat me on this thing. I always felt really confident with it. I won the double-double with that bike: the 2006 and 2007 Superbike and Senior races.

From 2008 to 2016 McGuinness stuck with the ninth-generation machine – because he was confident with the bike. "From 2008 through to 2016, it's basically the same bike," said John. "We kept it the same – same ride-height, same wheelbase and so on – all that time, because it worked." OK, so the Blades were the same, but – any favourite moment? "2013 and the Senior that year," said McGuinness. "I remember hitting every spot and every apex and the pit stops were perfect. The Fireblade didn't use a lot of fuel. Everybody thought we were better in the pits, but it was just that we were putting less fuel in, because it used less fuel than the other bikes."

In 2017 Honda launched an all-new Fireblade, but the machine wasn't a success. McGuinness had a serious accident at the North West 200 when the race kit ECU caused an unexpected throttle blip, leaving him with a badly broken leg. Meanwhile team-mate Guy Martin was ruled out of the TT after a big crash in practice.

The global COVID-19 pandemic has seen the last two TTs cancelled, but now – with updated 2022 Honda CBR1000RR-R SP Fireblades – both McGuinness and newcomer Glenn Irwin are looking forward to the event. Honda Racing UK team boss Havier Beltran said: "We've not raced the bike on the roads yet, but everything Glenn tells us about the machine suggests that it will be a real weapon at the TT. Hopefully everything will be pretty much back to normal in 2022 and we can get back to the Isle of Man to continue the Blade's TT story."

McGuinness on the later Blade, his 'pair of slippers' at the 2009 Superbike TT.

McGuinness is back on a Blade for 2022!

Island**Racer** 87

FIREBLADE

JIM MOODIE – 100TH HONDA TT WINNER

Jim Moodie had never ridden a FireBlade before 1998's TT fortnight, but he still ended up coming home with another FireBlade Production Race win and – more importantly for Honda – the marque's 100th ever Isle of Man victory. The Scot was ecstatic to get the win – watched as it was by Honda top brass, including Soichiro Honda's widow. "I was so pleased to be the rider who got the 100th win for Honda on the Island," he said, "especially when you think of the greats who rode for them in past years."

On his second lap while on his way to the win, he also picked up the lap record for the class for the time, taking the FireBlade to a lap record of 18 minutes 45.3 seconds – a lap of 120.70mph. It shattered the old record of 19m 02.2s – 118.93mph, which was set by McCallen in 1996's Production race. It was a dominant win, with Moodie leading every one of the three laps and winning by a margin of almost 30 seconds.

Baba-san was again delighted, especially in view of the competition during that year in the form of Yamaha's YZF-R1 and Kawasaki's ZX-9R. "We are all very pleased," Baba said, "There was a lot of strong competition this year from Kawasaki and Yamaha." Nigel 'Cap' Davies took 2nd on his Kawasaki ZX-9R, Michael Rutter was 3rd on a FireBlade and David Jefferies came 4th on a Yamaha YZF-R1. For Jefferies, the result in only his second TT would be a taste of what was to come the following year.

BELOW: Tough Scot Jim Moodie takes another Blade win – Honda's 100th at the TT. Seen to the right are Sanyo Honda's Mick Grant and Russell Savory.

ABOVE: Jim Moodie and the Blade in full flight.

TT WOMEN

FAST, FEARSOME, FEMALE!

Despite the fact that women were banned from competing at the TT for much of the event's existence, there's been no shortage of ladies who have put in impressive performances on the TT Mountain Course. This is their story.

WORDS: STUART BARKER
PICS: MORTONS ARCHIVE, DON MORLEY, HONDA RACING UK, LIDIA LEWSKA, LARA PLATMAN, BURGOS PICS

Beryl Swain was the main trailblazer for fast females racing at the Isle of Man TT.

TT WOMEN

This year marks the 60th anniversary of the first time a woman raced solo in the Isle of Man TT.

Women have not always been welcomed in the sport of motorcycle road-racing. Original regulations laid down by the FIM (Fédération Internationale de Motocyclisme) in the early days of racing dictated that competitors must be "male persons between 18 and 55 years of age". Can you imagine – in today's society – such a thing happening?

Thankfully, by 1962 the FIM had changed its rules and allowed women to race. Beryl Swain became the first female solo rider at the TT, finishing 22nd in the 50cc race at an average speed of 48.33mph – although her 50cc Itom lost top-gear on the second lap. The race was won by eventual world champion Ernst Degner on a Suzuki at an average speed of 75.12mph.

TT WOMEN

ABOVE: Beryl was stylish on the bike.

RIGHT: Beryl's career at the TT was curtailed by male ignorance.

In a sport that was so male dominated, there was an outcry about Swain's participation and, folding under the pressure from groups such as the Motorcycle Joint Advisory Committee, the FIM back-tracked at their next annual conference and reinstated the ban on women in the sport. Beryl would not race at the TT again, instead going on to a career working for Sainsbury's in her native London.

It wasn't until 1978 that the ban was lifted and the first to take advantage of this was Hilary Musson, who entered the world championship Formula 3 TT race that year. Musson stated that she would rather have entered the Manx Grand Prix in order to gain some experience on the Mountain Course before tackling the TT, but women were banned from competing in the Manx right up until 1989 so that wasn't possible.

Undeterred by this illogical thinking (which allowed her to enter a faster, more dangerous race, but not a slower one with riders of similar experience) Musson went on to finish a highly credible 15th out of 22 finishers at an average speed of 74.77mph. Better still, she was just one place behind her husband, John, who averaged 77.68mph. It was the first time a husband-and-wife team had ever competed at the TT, let alone in the same race. Hilary would continue racing at the TT for the next six years, with a best result of 23rd in the 1984 Production 250 race. Her daughter Gail would later race in the Manx GP and would set a lap at over 90mph on a 125c machine.

Civil servant Sandra Barnett finished in an impressive 5th place in the 1993 Newcomers Junior race at the Manx Grand Prix before stepping up to the TT proper the following year, taking an equally impressive 15th place in the Supersport 400 race that was won by Scotsman Jim Moodie. While Moodie's average speed for the race was 108.21mph, Barnett averaged 100.13mph and beat 11 other riders – all of whom were men.

There was better to come in 1995 when Barnett finished 11th in the Singles TT and her ride to 12th place in the 1996 Junior was even more impressive, beating, as she did, riders such as David Jefferies (a newcomer that year) and Michael Rutter. In the 1997 Junior TT, Barnett set the fastest ever lap by a female rider at 114.87mph.

That same year saw the personal best result for another female rider when Kate Parkinson finished 16th in the Lightweight TT. Parkinson was a talented two-stroke racer and – in 1997 – took up the offer of riding a four-stroke for the first time, an offer from *Bike* magazine journalist Olly Duke; it was his CBR600F she would ride in the Junior but she wouldn't gel with the four-stroke. In the Junior race itself, she would retire after three laps.

She said: "The Honda seemed to move around more than the Yamaha TZ250 I normally race, so I never felt confident on it. It felt it was going to let go in every corner and I told my friend Gail that during the pit-stop. She said I should pull in if I wasn't enjoying the race so on the third lap that was in my mind. Then I came across a crash at May Hill: there was a lad being stretchered away and his bike was badly smashed. It made me think that I didn't want to fall off. Then I had a nasty moment of my own when I took the wrong line through the Mountain Box Corner – probably because I wasn't concentrating and I ran far too near the edge of the kerbs. That shocked me. When you're not riding right – it's dangerous on the Island. So I recalled Gail's words and pulled in…" Male or female – the Island is a tough mental test.

Both Barnett and Parkinson last raced at the TT in 2000, with Barnett taking a best result of 9th in the Lightweight 400 race and Parkinson beating her demons and taking a superb 18th in the Junior race.

ABOVE: Barnett would ride a variety of machines at the TT, mainly Hondas, including CBR600Fs, FireBlades and the V4 RC30. She's on the 600F here.

LEFT: Sandra Barnett would be the Island's fastest female rider for many years.

ABOVE: Kate Parkinson on her favoured Yamaha TZ250.

By the turn of the millennium, Maria Costello had been racing at the Manx GP for three years with a best finish of 10th in the 1996 Newcomers Senior. By 2002 she had moved up to the TT and she continues to race to this day. Costello made history in the 2005 Manx Grand Prix when she became the first female to finish on a podium in any solo race around the TT Mountain Course. Riding a Honda RVF400, the Northamptonshire rider took 3rd place in the Ultra Lightweight race and set a new standard for female riders at the TT.

Four years later, more history was made at the Manx, when Carolynn Sells took the first ever race victory for a woman on the TT Mountain Course. Sells won the Ultra Lightweight race on her Yamaha FZR600RR at an average speed of 106.02mph and rode a clever race by conserving her fuel so she didn't need to make a pit-stop. Not that it would have made any difference – her winning margin of 62 seconds would have allowed plenty of time to refuel. Sells described what it felt like to achieve such an historic win: "When I crossed the finish line, I was shouting and screaming inside my helmet," she said. "I have been so near, and so far, a few times and you never know if it's just going to remain a dream." Carolynn retired from racing soon afterwards – and why not? She'd achieved her dream. She later became a rider liaison officer for the Manx Grand Prix. Respect!

Maria Costello took another podium at the Manx in 2011 when she finished 3rd in the Classic 250cc race. But her finest hour to date was finishing 3rd behind TT

TT WOMEN

legends John McGuinness and Dean Harrison in the 2016 Senior Classic TT on her Paton 500. She said: "To end up on the podium in such company was amazing. All the owners of the bike had wanted was a finish, so it was like a fairy tale, both for me and them. I stayed in my leathers with my laurel around my neck for hours that day. It was just brilliant. I didn't even get a taste of the champagne though – I gave it to my team."

Costello became the fastest female rider in TT history in 2004 when she set a lap at 114.73mph in the Production 1000 race. But the honour of being the fastest female would pass to Cheshire's Jenny Tinmouth when she made her TT debut in 2009 and set a lap of 116.83mph. The following year she went even faster in the Senior and set a new woman's record of 119.94mph on her Honda Fireblade. "When I finished the Senior and got back to the pits to be told that I had just set the fastest ever lap of the TT course by a female, I was absolutely chuffed to bits," Jenny said. "I hadn't gone to the TT with any goals, other than to learn the course and enjoy myself, so to have come away with that record was amazing. I was over the moon: it's quite a cool record to have!"

Time now to mention Anita Buxton: she would come 14th in the Manx Grand Prix Newcomers race in 1996 and would race at the TT itself off and on from 1998-2005. While her best result was 27th on a Kawasaki ZXR400 at the 2002 Lightweight TT, she would have a great claim to fame by being the first woman to ever win an international road-race. Her time came at the Ulster Grand Prix's 400cc lightweight race in 2004. She led that race from start to finish on the Dundrod circuit, just beating Joe Phillips by a tenth of a second.

Jenny Tinmouth only raced at the TT in 2009 and 2010 before going on to be the first female racer in the British Superbike Championship and then the first to be signed by a factory team, when she signed for Honda Racing UK in 2015. In her two years at the TT, Jenny scored a best finish of 4th in the 2010 TT Zero race, and she remains the fastest woman in TT history some 12 years later.

Maria Costello achieved another first in 2019, becoming the first woman to race in both solo and Sidecar TTs. Alongside her passenger, Julie Canipa, she finished in 21st place and set another landmark for female TT racers.

When it comes to taking risks at the TT, it seems the women are every bit as courageous as their male counterparts. One female racer who sadly paid the ultimate price for pushing the boundaries was Pam Cannell, who was killed during practice for the Manx Grand Prix in 1997. The hazards of road-racing are no kinder to female competitors, and tragic accidents like Cannell's prove just how hard these pioneering women are pushing to blaze new trails in motorsport.

Over more than two decades of racing, Maria Costello has broken no fewer than 24 bones but always comes back for more. Two of her most serious accidents happened on the TT Mountain Course she has been riding since first entering the Manx Grand Prix in 1996. She explained: "I had a big crash during practice at the TT on my Honda CBR900RR FireBlade in 1999. Another rider clipped me at the bottom of Bray Hill, and I rattled up someone's fence! I was thrown from the bike and knocked out, so I don't remember it – and I don't want to

TOP RIGHT: The eyes have it: Kate eventually made a successful switch to four-stroke power for the 1998 Junior.

TT WOMEN

ABOVE: Maria would eventually become a very successful TT rider.

RIGHT: Two and three wheels – Maria would ride anything!

BELOW: Maria would earn an MBE for her efforts to support females in racing.

GIRL POWER:
FEMALE FIRSTS AROUND THE TT COURSE

FIRST FEMALE SOLO COMPETITOR: Beryl Swain, 1962 50cc TT

FIRST SIDECAR PASSENGER PODIUM: Rose Hanks, 1968 750cc Sidecar TT

FIRST SOLO PODIUM: Maria Costello, 2005 Manx Grand Prix Ultra Lightweight

FIRST SOLO WIN: Carolynn Sells, 2009 Manx Grand Prix Ultra Lightweight

FASTEST EVER FEMALE LAP: 119.94mph, Jenny Tinmouth, 2010 Senior TT

remember it either. I broke my pelvis, my leg was in a plaster cast, I popped my shoulder out but popped it back in, and I took all the skin off my knuckles. I had another accident at the TT on a Honda RVF400 when I crashed on oil at Keppel Gate in practice and ended up deep in the heather on the banking. I broke my femur and my scapula in that one and because it was the 'neck' of the femur – the angled part at the top of the bone – I was out of action for six months."

While acknowledging the dangers of the TT course, Jenny Tinmouth learned to compartmentalise her fear. "I never worried about the dangers," she explained. "Sometimes it's not good to think about things too much. Like when you were a kid and you thought you were invincible – you would try anything because you didn't think about the consequences. It's a similar thing with the TT, it's just best not to think about it too much."

In the 60 years since Beryl Swain became the first woman to race a solo machine around the TT course, the lap times set by the ladies have gone from 48.33mph to 119.94mph and, as more and more girls take to road-racing, it's only a matter of time before the magical 120mph barrier is breached. One can only imagine what the men who once banned women from racing at the TT might have thought about that.

Tinmouth's impact on the Isle of Man TT races was immediate.

Jenny would rise to a factory ride in the BSB championship with Honda Racing UK.

TT WOMEN

A BIT ON THE SIDE

The rules banned women from racing solo machines at the TT for many years but female sidecar passengers have been competing since 1954, when Inge Stoll-Laforge finished in fifth place alongside driver Jacques Drion. Sadly, Laforge was killed four years later in a crash at the Czech Grand Prix.

Rose Hanks made history in 1968 when she became the first woman ever to stand on a TT podium when she partnered Norman Hanks (the elder brother of her future husband Roy) to second place in the 750cc Sidecar race.

In 1982 Julia Bingham stood on the podium for the first of five times, as passenger to her husband Dennis. Four second places and two third places between 1982 and 1987 was an incredible achievement, but sadly that elusive win never quite happened.

The French crew of Estelle Leblond and Melanie Farnier became the fastest all-female sidecar team in TT history in 2017, lapping at 109.39mph. The pair were awarded the Susan Jenness trophy for the most meritorious performance by female competitors at the TT but went even faster the following year when they cracked the 110mph barrier with a lap at 110.22mph.

ABOVE: Rose Hanks with Norman Hanks in 1967.

BELOW: Rose in the chair with husband Roy Hanks in 1970.

98 Island**R**acer

MoreBikes

CHECK OUT THE MOREBIKES WEBSITE

VISIT TODAY!

The latest motorcycle **news**, every bike **spy shot**, the newest **riding kit** and EVERY important **motorcycle tested!** **PLUS** the **hottest videos**, **opinions** and **gossip**

WWW.MOREBIKES.CO.UK
IT'S THE SAME...BUT BETTER!

DOWNLOAD THE FREE EASY TO USE APP FOR ON-THE-GO ACCESS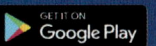

DEAN HARRISON

SENIOR CITIZEN

He's the reigning Senior TT winner and he's looking for more of the same in 2022 – but how has Dean Harrison kept himself sharp during these 'lean' road-racing years?

WORDS: JOHN WATTERSON
PICS: STEPHEN DAVISON/ PACEMAKER PRESS, TIM KEETON/ IMPACT IMAGES, KAWASAKI UK

Deano did it! Finally getting a 'big bike' win gets the monkey off his back… expect more in 2022.

When you win a Senior, you celebrate!

LINING UP, READY FOR THE OFF.

Dean Harrison finally made his dream (and Kawasaki's) come true in the 2019 Senior TT on the Isle of Man.

Not only was this his third overall win, following his first victory in the 2014 Lightweight on an ER-F 650 twin and a Supersport race win on the ZX-6R in 2018, this was his first 'big bike' win. It was also Kawasaki's first Senior TT win since fellow Yorkshireman Mick Grant's in 1975 – a full 14 years before Deano was even born.

"It was almost overwhelming to be honest," explains 31-year-old Harrison. "The thing is, it's the biggest trophy you'll ever win in road-racing. I'd won other TT races and to win in any class is such an achievement, it's unbelievable, but to win the Senior was so special. With the TT being the biggest event of the season, to finish the week off like that feels like the weight of the world lifted off your shoulders." He'd finally bagged a big win and things were looking up and then fate took a hand, blanketing the globe in a pandemic of the sort not seen in a century.

He says: "It's been so surreal and you just find it hard to believe what's happened. Doing the British Superbike Championship has filled a bit of the gap, so at least we've been riding some bikes, but it's like there's been a piece of the jigsaw missing. Hopefully we can finish the jigsaw off this year!"

Rather than go from short circuit racing to road-racing, Deano has been enjoying doing things the other way around, albeit being forced to thanks to the cancelled road-racing calendar of 2020/2021. "Yes, going to British Superbikes only really came about because we didn't have any road races on the calendar," he admits. "The team boss suggested we do the BSB season just to keep us sharp. The bike and all the equipment we had from 2019 was just sat there, so we thought we might as well put it to good use. Most racers start in BSB and go to roads, but I've done it the other way around. BSB is so competitive and it's a brilliant championship. I really enjoy doing it and I'm looking forward to doing more this year, in 2022. Having said all that, my heart will always lie in road-racing. That's what I do. It's what I grew up around and it's what I know."

Oh yes, Deano grew up around road-racing alright (see boxout). He first visited the Isle of Man in 1993 at the age of four in what was his father Conrad's debut year in the Sidecar TT. The family camped in the paddock. His memories of that first visit are understandably limited, but the TT became a regular destination for Conrad, a Royal Mail postal worker from Bradford and his young family.

As the years went on, Dean was greatly inspired by David Jefferies. "He lived next door to my science teacher in Baildon and the family business (Allan Jefferies Motorcycles) is about two miles down the road from me in Shipley," Harrison explains. "I saw DJ ride at a lot of places, including the TT. I remember watching him on the V&M Yamaha R1 battling it out with Ian Lougher on the two-stroke 500 Honda twin in 1999. So yes, DJ was top notch and a big favourite of mine!"

Young Deano's first bike was a Yamaha DT50 'field bike' as he described it, but unlike many lads he never raced off-road in moto-cross. Nowadays he enjoys observed trials and even the odd enduro event – but more of that later. His first proper road bike was a Honda CBR600F that he sourced and fettled himself. He started racing in 2007 at the age of 18 riding Auto 66 events at venues including Elvington and Cadwell Park.

A chance meeting kick-started his career and Billy McKinstry provided machinery for him to contest the 2010 Support Road-Racing Championships in Ireland. He clocked up numerous victories in what was his first year on public road courses, notably a win over Ryan Farquhar at Oliver's Mount, Scarborough. The Manx Grand Prix seemed the obvious route for him to take, but Dean chose the TT in 2011 as it was simply more affordable: "Entries were free and there was the chance to also earn some prize money," he explains.

The then-22-year-old rode a YZF-R6 Yamaha supplied by Ian Bell Motorcycles in the two Supersport races and a Yamaha R1 in the Superstock.

His best result was 12th in the second Supersport race, but he had a fastest lap of 122mph on the Stocker. He used the R6 for three years and scored his first win in the Southern 100 on it in 2014. Still very much a privateer, he scored three top-15 finishes at the TT in 2012, the best of which was a 9th in the Superbike race when he lapped in excess of 126mph on an Ice Valley BMW. Soon afterwards he was signed by RC Express of Avonmouth, a partnership that followed for two-and-

DEAN HARRISON

ABOVE: Harrison at Hillberry during practice.

BELOW: Teamwork is vital at the TT – Harrison is more than happy with the Silicone Racing (now DAO Racing) team, he's been with them for years.

half successful years. Dean finished 11 of the 12 TT races he started, all inside the top 11 – six of them in the top five.

After taking second place in the 2013 Lightweight and 2014 Superstock races he claimed his maiden victory in the 2014 Lightweight. A podium finish also followed at the Ulster Grand Prix and he was becoming the dominant figure at Scarborough.

A move to Mar-Train Yamaha in 2015 didn't quite yield the rewards he was expecting, although he did win the coveted Gold Cup race at Oliver's Mount: "The R1 was a good bike, but I struggled with it," he admits, but change was afoot. A chat with Johnny Bagnall of Silicone Engineering Racing late on in the year led to an offer being made for him to join the team for 2016 and he has not looked back since. "I thought to myself that I'd like to ride a Kawasaki, and its proved the best thing I've ever done," Dean says.

Three podium results were achieved at the 2016 TT, plus two more top-five finishes, in addition to which he racked up numerous more podiums at the Southern 100 and Scarborough. After his maiden podium finish at the North West 200, he claimed 3rd places in both the Superbike and Senior TTs in 2017, raising his personal best lap speed to 132.019mph.

One month later he won the Southern 100 Solo Championship title for the first time, and another few weeks on he won the Superbike race at the Ulster, setting a new outright lap record in the process. He swept all before him at Oliver's Mount, winning the Gold Cup for a third year with a new course record. Dean's career continued on an upward trajectory in 2018 with a second and a third in the Superbike and Superstock races at the North West 200, followed by a brace of 4th places in the Supersport class.

These results set him up nicely for the TT that year when he produced the fastest qualifying lap of all time to that point with an average speed of 133.462mph. On a roll, he established a new outright lap record from a standing start in the Superbike race at an average of 134.432mph to open up a healthy advantage, but a clutch problem with the ZX-10R forced him to retire on lap four. Two days later he secured a brace of podium finishes with the runner-up spot in the first Supersport race and 3rd place in the Superstock.

The eager young Yorkshireman's second TT win came in the Supersport 2 race when pipping arch-rival Hickman.

The same two riders then fought out one of the most exciting Senior TTs in history that ultimately resulted in Hickman snatching the lead on the final trip over the mountain. He crossed the finish line three seconds ahead on corrected timing after Harrison had led for

ABOVE: On it! Dean had to stay focused, despite the issues facing Hickman in the Senior race.

virtually the entire distance.

The Bradford ace was gracious in defeat and had the consolation of setting a new personal best lap of 134.918mph to confirm him as the second quickest rider to date over the hallowed Snaefell course. Five wins out of five at the Southern 100, including the feature race, capped an excellent year alongside a Superstock race win at the Ulster and a Superbike success in the Classic TT on a 1991 ZXR.

His fourth season with the Silicone Engineering team opened in 2019 with a second place in the Supersport class at the weather-hit North West 200. The inclement weather continued at the TT, resulting in slower speeds and reduced distances for virtually all of the races. Harrison took three 3rd place finishes in the Superbike, Superstock and second Supersport races, each time behind nemesis Hickman. He finally got the result he relished most when Hickman ran into trouble on the penultimate lap of the Senior and Harrison took advantage… Hickman led Harrison by a third of a second at Glen Helen on lap one – with the pair already almost six seconds clear of their main chasers.

Harrison had nudged ahead at Ballaugh by two-tenths of a second but by Ramsey Hickman was back in front by a tenth. A standing start lap of 134.284mph – the fastest lap of the entire fortnight – gave Hickman a 2.2s

FAMILY FORTUNES!

The Harrisons of Bradford are the only family to achieve victories in all the main capacity classes of the TT in its 115-year history.

They achieved this feat in a comparatively short period of six years. Conrad Harrison, Dean's father, won the Sidecar TT as a driver in 2014, with Mike Aylott. The pair had previously enjoyed six podium finishes on the same Shelbourne Honda, plus one more 3rd place in 2015, Conrad having made his TT debut in 1993 with Lee Patterson.

Conrad, now 58, continues to compete in the sidecar class with John Holden's former passenger Andrew Winkle and now has a grand total of 20 top-10 finishes, including three 2nd and six 3rd place results from 47 starts. Dean's first solo win came only six days after his father's maiden success when he rode to victory in the 2014 Lightweight on the RC Express ER-6. With successes on a 650 twin, Supersport 600cc and 1000cc classes for Dean, it completes a modern day full-house for him and his father Conrad in current-day TT capacity terms.

Dean's elder brother Adrian (who Dean set up an engineering business with) is a regular and competent road racer in his own right. The 37-year-old made his debut in the Manx Grand Prix in 2012 and has competed in the TT since 2014 with a best result of 15th in the 2016 Lightweight. Benjamin Binns, Conrad's godson, was outright lap record holder for the chairs in 2015 when teamed with Dave Molyneux. Dean and Conrad scored another unique double at the Southern 100 in 2014 when the latter won the Sidecar championship race with Jason Crowe and Dean scored his first big-bike wins on the Billown Course.

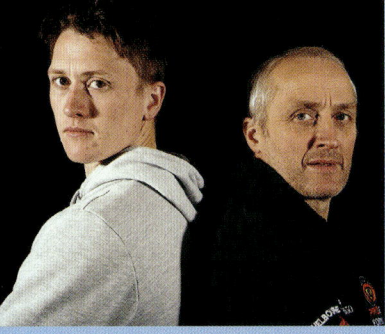

Father and son both love the Isle of Man event.

It's a good haul for father and son at the Isle of Man TT.

DEAN HARRISON

Harrison wins Kawasaki's first Senior since 1975.

OFF THE BEATEN TRACK!

Dean admits that he's doing more off-road training than ever before. He said: "I bought a Kawasaki KX250X so I'm doing a lot of enduro riding now. I've dabbled in a bit of enduro here and there, but never anything serious. When I found out that Kawasaki had the new KX250X coming, I thought 'I'll have one!' It turned up and I was straight in at the deep end, but I'm excited to get to work with the bike and see what it can do. It has so much potential."

Harrison plans to take in some races. He explained: "I'm taking part in some rounds of the British Enduro Championship, then I'm hoping to finish the season off at the Sea to Sky race in Turkey. My plan is to race and develop the bike as the year goes on and really put a bit of effort into it.

It's a brand-new motorbike, I've never really ridden a four-stroke off-road bike and it's totally different, so I thought I need a bit of time here. It's not that I'm not taking it seriously, but I don't have to take it too seriously so it's a little bit more relaxed for me. What with road-racing, BSB and enduro – I'll be keeping myself busy in 2022!"

Not just a play-thing: Deano keeps bike-fit with the Kawasaki KX250X and will be planning some enduro races in 2022.

DEAN HARRISON

Eyes not on the prize...

You never stop learning.

lead over Harrison, with Conor Cummins now more than 14s adrift of the leading pair. Harrison had reduced his deficit to Hickman by four tenths at Glen Helen on lap. Hickman's lead had grown to 10s by Glen Helen on lap three and was 13.5s at half-distance.

By the second round of pit stops Hickman was 18 seconds to the good, but he was then forced to reduce his pace as the Smith's bike began to overheat because of a water pressure issue. Harrison's sector times became seven or eight seconds quicker than his rival's as the lead came tumbling down. On Sulby Straight, Harrison's bike was clocked at 189mph – some 30mph quicker than Hickman's. Inevitably the lead was back in Harrison's possession by Ramsey. A trouble-free final lap secured Harrison his third TT win by 53.062s. Hickman managed to hold onto second place by 5.8s from Cummins on the Padgett's Honda.

It was a dream come true for Dean and Silicone Engineering Racing, who, having been appointed Kawasaki's official road racing team for 2019, received the manufacturer's award. "As the saying goes, to finish first, first you have to finish," said Dean at the time, quipping that he had just won a Dunlop-sponsored race on a pair of Metzelers. "I actually thought I was heading for my fourth runner-up result of the week, but anything can happen at the TT," he added.

More dominance at the Southern 100 was to follow

Island Racer 105

ABOVE: Cummins, Harrison and Hicky were your 3-1-2 in the 2019 Senior.

four weeks later with six wins out of six, including the feature race for a third year in succession.

But Dean again had to settle for three runner-up rides behind Hickman's Smith's Racing BMW at the Ulster GP in August. He reflects: "Clarissa Beadman and the Silicone team have been massively influential in my career. I wouldn't be where I am today without them. They are all genuinely nice people and want to win. Clarissa understands racing. She's the team owner, but also a friend."

Little wonder that Deano signed a new two-year deal with the now-renamed DAO Racing team. Once more Harrison will take part in a full BSB campaign, as well as their commitments as Kawasaki's official 'Road-Racing' team, meaning the North West, TT and Ulster GP – any COVID resurgence allowing, of course.

BELOW: Enjoying the moment.

So what of BSB, Deano? "I think it's helped me and the team," he explained. "When you ride together and work together, you're finding things out about the bike all the time. You're riding all the time, so you're bike fit and your head is in the game. I think that has a knock-on effect, big time. It will help us as we go back into the road-racing season. I can't wait to get back to it now. I'm just looking forward to getting the whole season going, to getting to the North West, to the TT, all of it. I've missed it a lot and I just want to get my teeth back into it now: a bit of normality. I think BSB-wise I've improved year on year and short-circuit stuff comes naturally to be honest. The North West is very good for getting up to speed and acclimatising to riding between the hedges, past the lamp posts and trees. Scarborough helps with that too."

The big thing is: how stressed will you be defending the Senior TT crown? "Do you know what," he said. "I actually feel quite relaxed about it all. The only thing I feel a bit apprehensive about is what the track's going to be like. It changes year-on-year and it's been three years since we raced there. It might take a bit of time to get up to speed, it might not. I'll just take it as it comes."

No hard feelings! Deano cops the bubbly in the face from Hicky!

Britain's favourite bike racer was no fan of the TT and helped play a part in it losing world championship status in 1977. But why did Bazza hate the TT so much? Sheene biographer Stuart Barker looks for answers.

ABOVE: A rare shot indeed! Chas Mortimer (4) leads Barry Sheene (1) at Barry's only Isle of Man TT event.

WORDS: STUART BARKER
PICS: MORTONS ARCHIVE, SUZUKI GB

Barry Sheene's issues with the Isle of Man started early. His dad Frank was a keen supporter of the TT races and it was when he took five-year-old Barry to the island that the youngster found himself having serious health traumas which were blamed on the Manx climate.

Being set in the middle of the Irish Sea, the Isle of Man's wet and misty climate is not particularly suited to asthma sufferers, as Barry was to find to his peril when he suffered such a severe attack that he quite literally turned blue and was rushed to Noble's Hospital and detained for three days until his breathing returned to normal. It was the start of an unhappy relationship with the Isle of Man which would have far-reaching consequences in later years.

It was also on the island that Sheene got drunk for the first time, but even that landmark moment wasn't the happy memory it might have been. It happened at the TT in 1960 when Sheene was only 10-years-old and he guzzled two glasses of champagne, given to him by Gary Hocking, who had just finished 2nd in the Junior TT. Barry was instantly inebriated, and the experience was enough to put him off touching another drop of alcohol until he was 16 (ironic as he smoked from the age of nine despite the asthma!).

By the time he was 21, Sheene returned to the Isle of Man to race for the first, and last, time. He had decided to race there to try and score some valuable points for his 125cc Grand Prix world championship campaign (the TT counted as the British round of the world championships until 1977). After the first two rounds of the Grand Prix season, Sheene was just five points

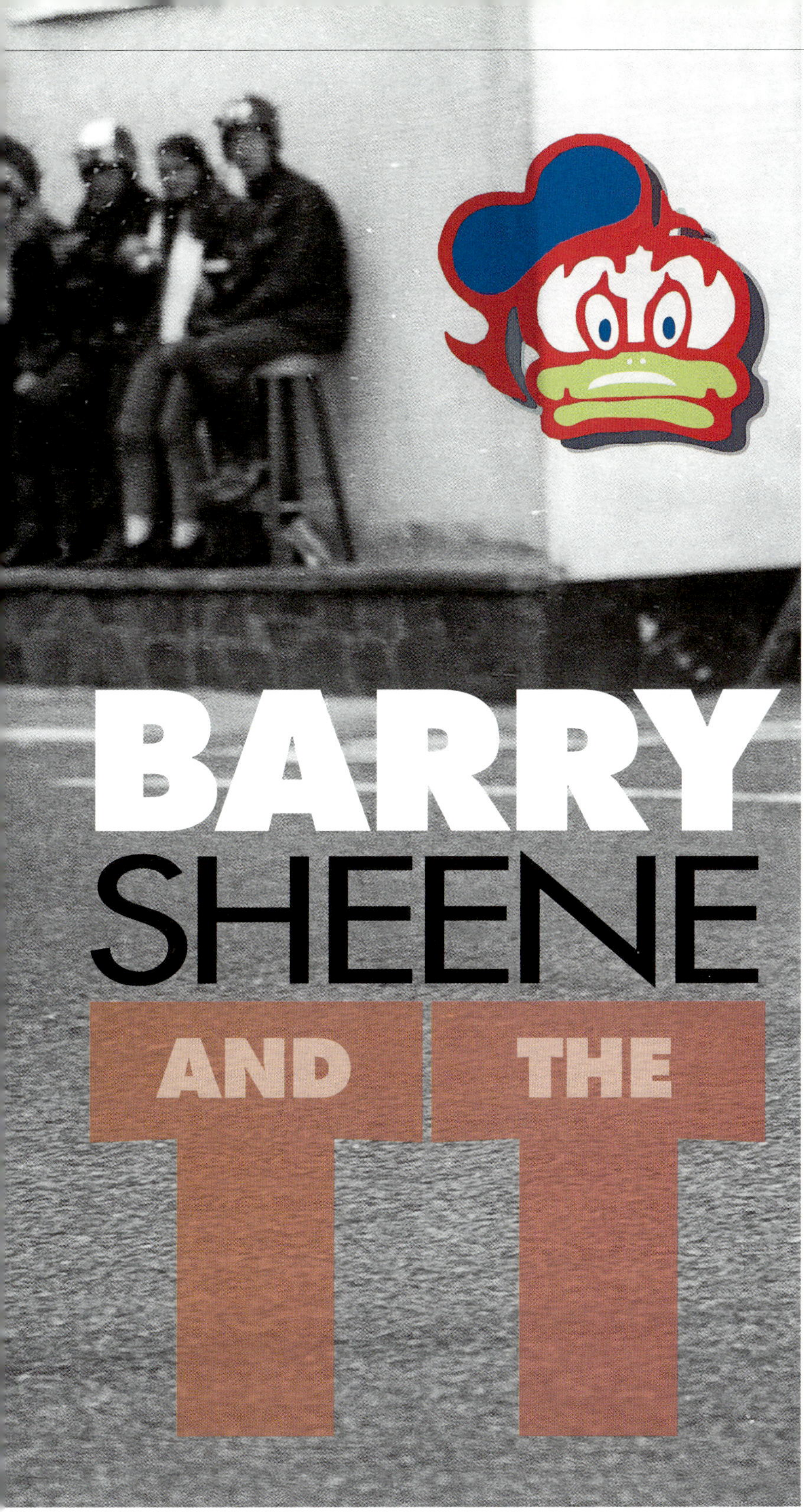

BARRY SHEENE AND THE TT

one point on the opening lap until he hit thick fog and eased off the throttle. When his overworked clutch bit too hard just after the start of the second lap, Sheene was tossed from his bike at the slow, first gear Quarterbridge corner and his race was run – much to Barry's relief as he'd been hating every minute of it.

But that wasn't quite the end of Sheene's TT career: he still had an outing in the Production 250 event, also on a Suzuki. Again, he had posted respectable times in practice, but after suffering a massive tank-slapper during the race, parts of his machine started working themselves loose and Barry pulled in after just one lap. He never raced on the Island again.

One rider's decision not to race at the TT would never normally cause any kind of commotion – it is a free world after all, and no-one forces racers to take part in the TT. But Sheene wasn't content just to stay away from the Island; instead, he embarked upon a sustained one-man attack on the event over the next few years and played a major part in the TT eventually being stripped of its world championship status, a crime for which some never forgave him.

Racing fanatics fall into one of two camps over the whole Sheene/TT issue. If you love the TT, you hate Barry Sheene and if you hate the TT, you tend to agree with Sheene's actions and opinions. Barry's major bone

behind Angel Nieto, who Sheene knew would not race at the TT because of the dangers. If he could score good points at the TT, Sheene knew he could close down the points gap on Nieto and maybe even take the lead in the championship (he would eventually lose the title by just eight points to the Derbi-mounted Spaniard). It was a move which would consolidate Sheene's views on the event, and which would make him many enemies among traditionalists who continued to support the TT despite its dangers.

Those traditionalists have always scoffed at the fact that Sheene crashed out of his first race on the island, but he had actually been on the leaderboard before that incident. He posted the third fastest time in practice on his four-year-old, ex-Stuart Graham, factory Suzuki RT67 and was leading the Lightweight 125 TT race at

RIGHT: Barry Sheene: double world 500cc champion and hater of the Isle of Man TT races – but why?

BARRY SHEENE

Barry at Silverstone in 1971 – the same year he took the RT67 to the Isle of Man.

ABOVE: Barry at Cadwell Park in 1970: you needed balls to ride around Cadwell, too.

RIGHT: While it was little bikes (125, 250cc) at the Isle of Man – Barry's calling and future championships would be on bigger machines. Here he is in 1971 on a Suzuki TR500.

of contention was that riders shouldn't be asked to race on such a dangerous track, just to gain championship points. He never wanted the TT to be banned as such, he just wanted riders to have the choice of whether or not to race there; his thinking being that when valuable points are at stake, riders may be tempted to push their luck to earn a few more. Sheene didn't feel that any rider should be encouraged to race there if they didn't want to, while TT supporters claimed that the throttle works both ways and riders can take things as easy as they want to, thereby reducing the dangers.

Many supporters of the event have said that Barry was just too scared to race there, or that he couldn't be bothered spending the usual three years to learn the course well enough to win on it. The second argument falls down when you consider that Barry was leading his first TT race before he crashed out, and Barry himself responded to the first accusation by saying: "The Mountain Circuit did not frighten me in any way. No circuit frightens me. I just couldn't see the sense of riding around in the pissing rain completely on your own against a clock. It wasn't racing to my mind."

Don Morley, a professional photographer and journalist since 1955 and one of the most respected photographers in the business, has a different take on Sheene's aversion to the TT. Morley has probably taken more pictures of Sheene than anyone else and was always privy to the gossip and chatter in the paddocks of the racing world. "Barry made a bit of a name for himself slagging off the TT, but it was more to do with money than the dangers of the place," Don says. "A normal Grand Prix lasted three days, whereas the TT was a two-week event, and it cost the riders an awful lot of money to compete there. There was very little prize money, and it was awkward for the GP riders to get to the Isle of Man from the Continent. They had to drive to a port, get a ferry to England, drive again, and then get another ferry to the Isle of Man, which was a lot more difficult than just driving from the Spanish GP to the French GP, for example. Then they had to pay for a hotel for two weeks instead of just three days, as well as all the other expenses. It was good for the organisers, but not the riders. This was in the days before lots of long-haul Grands Prix, and it just didn't make financial sense."

Whatever the arguments, they have long since been settled as the TT was struck from the Grand Prix calendar after the 1976 event, much to Sheene's approval. In 1972 Giacomo Agostini (who went on to win 10 TTs and 15 world championship titles), had joined Barry's protest after his close friend, Gilberto Parlotti, was killed on his TT debut. Like Sheene, Parlotti had only decided to race at the TT in a bid to steal world championship points away from Angel Nieto, who always refused to race on the island. Ago said he would never race there again, and he kept his word. He was joined by Phil Read who, five years later, went back on his word and raced at the TT again, thanks to a healthy financial inducement. He was pelted with stones during practice for his troubles.

Sheene's name would be dragged up in the press for more than a decade whenever there were calls for the TT to be banned outright, and to this day there is still a lot of resentment among TT fans towards Barry. But it's worth remembering that, while Sheene hated riding at the TT ("why bother when it's so much easier just to shoot yourself and get it all over with?"), it didn't stop him racing on other pure roads circuits, most notably Oliver's Mount in Scarborough – a treacherous, narrow, and bumpy parkland circuit. Many Grand Prix circuits like Spa-Francorchamps in Belgium, and Imatra in

ABOVE: At Brands Hatch on a Bultaco in 1969.

BELOW LEFT: Barry cut his teeth on father Franco's Bultacos: here he is in 1969 at Snetterton.

BELOW: Sheene's early taste of Yamaha power in 1971.

Island**Racer** 111

BARRY SHEENE

Look at this spectator and tree-lined course: Barry did well at the likes of Oliver's Mount, so surely it wasn't a lack of bravery.

Barry is quicker than the rest of the field with the push-start here at Mallory Park in 1973!

At the same race, going for the win…

SHEENE'S FAVOURITE BIKE: THE SUZUKI RT67

The bike that Barry Sheene raced in his only appearance at the TT was one of his prized possessions, perhaps the most prized of all.

It was the first bike he ever raced in Grand Prix, finishing 2nd to Angel Nieto on it in his GP debut at Monjuich Park in 1970. He also finished a close runner-up to his great friend Nieto on the bike in the 1971 125cc world championship.

Sheene had bought the ex-factory RT67 in 1970 from Stuart Graham (son of the first ever 500cc world champion, Les Graham) who had finished 3rd in the 1967 world championships on it behind Bill Ivy and Phil Read. It cost Sheene an eye-watering £2000 and he worked 14 hours a day driving a lorry to pay for it but would still never have managed without a loan from his dad, Franco (he insisted he paid every penny back). The bike – which was also the one Sheene raced in his only appearance at the TT in 1971 – was restored in the spring of 2020. It was Sheene's favourite bike in his collection and it took pride of place in his house in Queensland, Australia.

Barry's long-term mechanic Martyn Ogborne – who helped restore the RT67 – has his own thoughts on Sheene's attitude towards the TT. He says: "Barry fell off this bike at the TT, but if he hadn't fallen off that day, he might have had a very different view of the TT. He only just lost out to Angel Nieto in the 125cc world championship that year and that's why he took umbrage with the TT. He said he couldn't see where he was going because of the mist. He was running off the road up the mountain and all sorts. He literally couldn't see and didn't know the course well enough. He said to me: 'What is the point of a circuit that you can't even bloody see?' That's what got to him and that's why he never went back. People say: 'Well, how come he races at Scarborough then?' But he wasn't actually racing at Scarborough – he was just performing. And he knew the circuit and could see where he was going, unlike the Isle of Man."

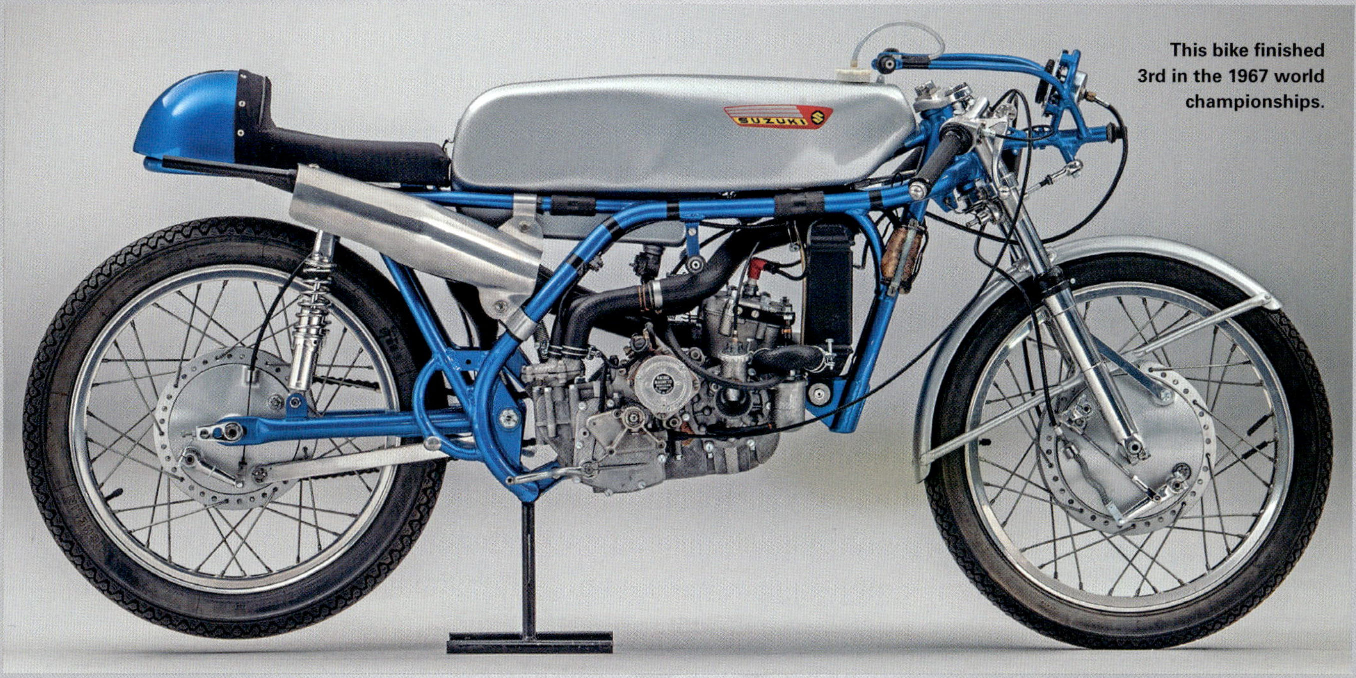

This bike finished 3rd in the 1967 world championships.

Sheene's favourite bike? Many think so… He took the British 125cc title on it in 1970.

This was Sheene's first Grand Prix racer

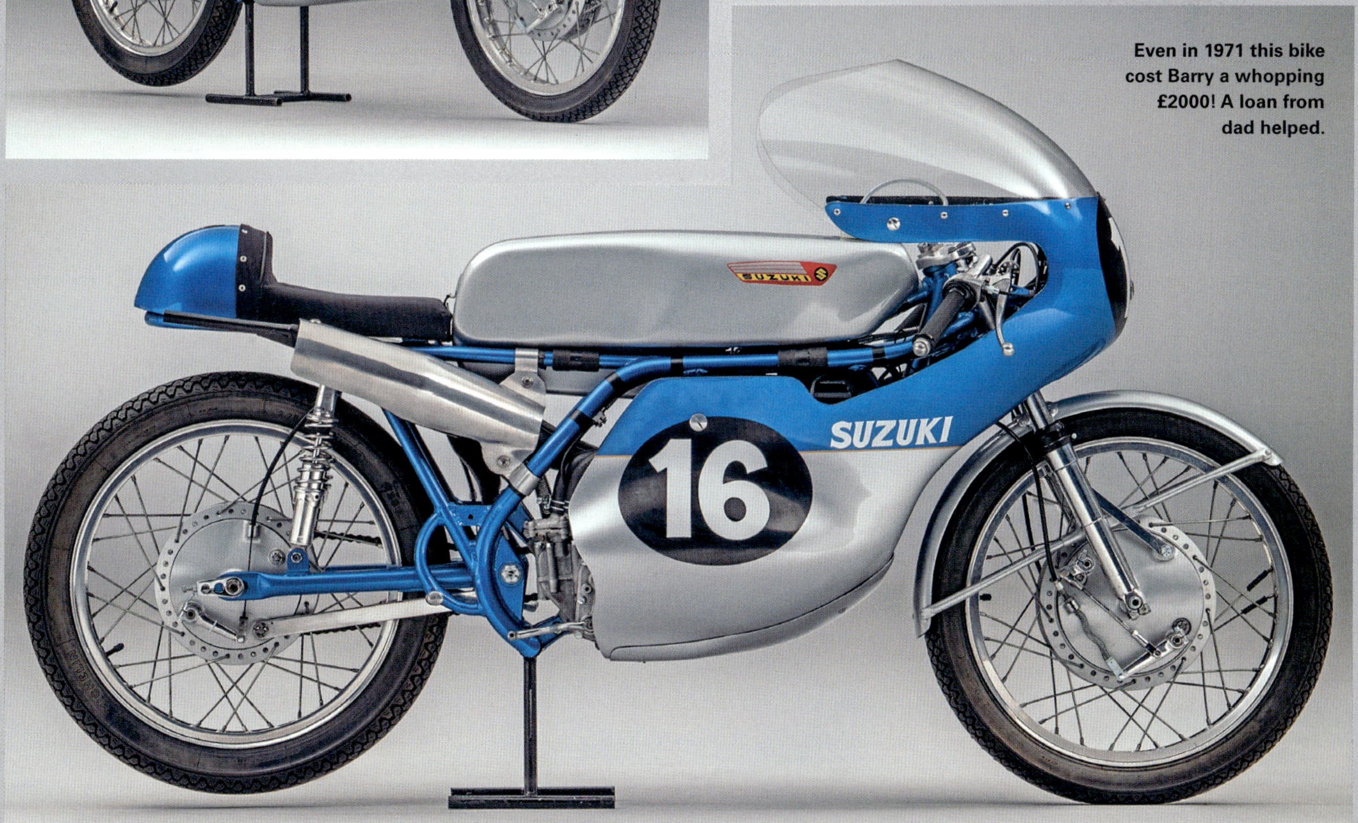

Even in 1971 this bike cost Barry a whopping £2000! A loan from dad helped.

BARRY SHEENE

"THE MOUNTAIN CIRCUIT DID NOT FRIGHTEN ME IN ANY WAY."

ABOVE: Let's remember him this way: on the Suzuki TR750, going for it!

BELOW: Sheene's Suzuki links proved strong: here with Rex White, on Barry's Suzuki twin, as Sheene picks up a little something for mum Iris!

Finland, were also Armco-lined pure roads circuits too.

Sheene's criticism of the TT circuit ran somewhat contradictory to his outlook on those other dangerous circuits. In justifying his decision to continue racing at Oliver's Mount he said: "As with any other circuit, if there are sections which you can't tackle with confidence, it's up to you to ride through those sections at the pace best suited to you. You can make up for lost time in other stretches, where there is less likelihood of hurting yourself." Surely that same theory would apply to the TT circuit as well as any other?

Mick Grant, himself a seven-times TT winner and a staunch supporter of the event, was one of Barry's fiercest rivals in the 1970s. He testifies to Sheene's abilities on road circuits, despite his aversion to the TT. "Although Barry knocked the TT, we never actually spoke about it together. My regret with Barry was that he didn't continue with the TT. Certainly, the way he rode on pure roads circuits like Scarborough and Imatra, there was no way that he couldn't have done the TT. I mean, bloomin' hell, Scarborough requires all the road racing skills you'd ever need, and he could do it. He certainly wasn't slow round there!"

Ron Haslam – himself a TT winner and successful short-circuit champion – agrees. He says: "I went to the Isle of Man because I wanted to be a Grand Prix racer. To some – like Barry Sheene, who was a long-term leader of the anti-TT brigade – the two were poles apart. Sheene went to the Island once and crashed at Quarter Bridge. His view was that it was too dangerous and that if you made a mistake you could end up dead: he had a point, but his stance didn't go down well with those who loved the TT. I could see both sides, but what I do know is that Barry Sheene was never afraid of anything. He rode on other road circuits like Oliver's Mount, which had claimed the life of my brother, Phil, so you can't pretend that Barry wasn't a brave rider. All I can say is that I fell in love with the place very early on. The Isle of Man TT is a one-off, it's about bikes going at breakneck speeds along country lanes…"

So, it clearly wasn't a lack of ability or a lack of courage that set Sheene against the TT. It was the nature of the racing – alone and against the clock, rather than a mass start – that he disliked, coupled with what he perceived as the unacceptable dangers when races were held in heavy fog and mist. He also didn't believe riders should have been forced to ride there just to gain a few championship points. And he resented the time, money and additional effort it took to compete at the TT compared to all other races.

But consider this: the TT might still be a race against the clock, but almost everything else that Sheene complained about has since been changed. Races are no longer held in wet or foggy conditions, the TT is no longer part of a championship, so riders don't have to race there for any other reason than that they want to, and the length of time the TT demands of riders and teams has been repeatedly called into question many times over the years, so it clearly wasn't just Sheene who considered that a problem.

The event simply wasn't to his liking and, had he been any other rider who decided not to take part, there would never have been no-such controversy. But then, asking Sheene to keep his opinions to himself would have been to deny his very character. It's why we loved him, after all.

114 IslandRacer

HONDA

HONDA'S HAUL

WORDS: BERTIE SIMMONDS
PICS: BILL SNELLING/TT RACE PICS, MORTONS ARCHIVE

With 189 wins at the Isle of Man TT, Honda is easily the most successful manufacturer in the history of TT racing. We chart how a motorcycle manufacturing minnow from the late 1940s, became the most successful of all by the Noughties…

A statement was issued by the Honda Motor Company on March 20, 1954, declaring a bold intention to build a racing motorcycle and take it to the Isle of Man TT with the aim of winning the gruelling event.

While not actually written by him (apparently his Honda co-founder Takeo Fujisawa wrote what 'the Old Man' felt) it was attributed to Soichiro Honda himself and this abridged version sums up his determination perfectly.

"Some five years have passed since the founding of our Honda Motor Co., and I never cease to rejoice that the efforts of all our employees have taken form in the achievement of our epoch-making advances.

Since I was a small child, one of my dreams has been to compete in motor vehicle races all over the world with a vehicle of my own making, and to win. Now that we are equipped with a production system in which I have absolute confidence, the time of opportunity has arrived. I have reached the firm decision to enter the TT Races next year.

Never before have the Japanese entered this race with a motorcycle made in Japan. It goes without saying that the winner of this race will be known across the globe, but the same is also true for any vehicle that completes the entire race safely. It is said, therefore, that the fame of such an achievement will assure a certain volume of exports, and that is why every major manufacturer in Germany, England, Italy, and France is concentrating on preparations with all its might. I will fabricate a 250cc racer for this race, and as the representative of our Honda Motor Co., I will send it out into the spotlight of the world.

I address all employees!

Let us bring together the full strength of Honda Motor Co. to win through to this glorious achievement. The future of Honda Motor Co. depends on this, and the burden rests on your shoulders. I want you to turn your surging enthusiasm to this task, endure every trial, and press through with all the minute demands of work and research, making this your own chosen path. The advances made by Honda Motor Co. are the growth you achieve as human beings, and your growth is what assures our future.

We must gauge the true worth of the Japanese machine industry, and raise it to a point where we can display it proudly to the entire world. The mission of Honda is to enlighten Japanese industry. With this, I announce my determination, and pledge with you that I will put my entire heart and soul, and turn all my creativity and skills to the task of entering the TT Races and winning them.

This I affirm.
Soichiro Honda
President
Honda Motor Co., Ltd.

John McGuinness has a long and successful relationship with Honda.

116 Island**Racer**

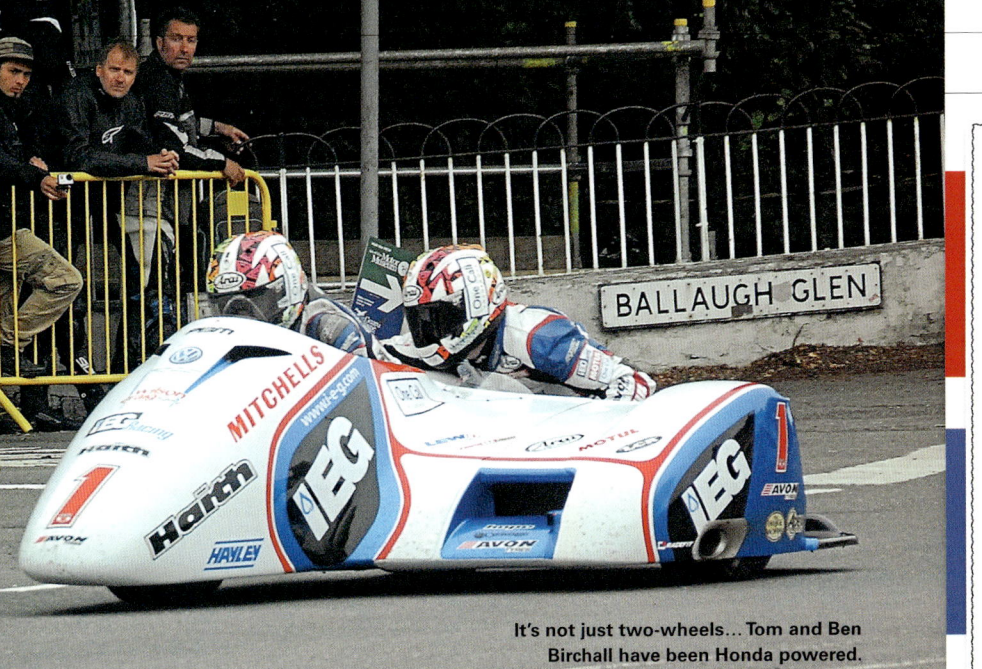

It's not just two-wheels… Tom and Ben Birchall have been Honda powered.

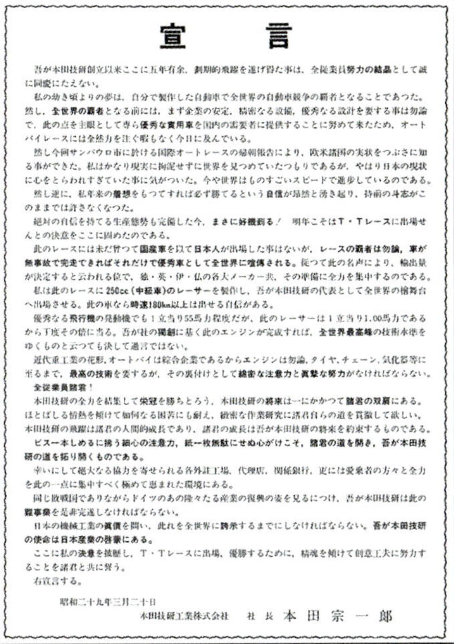

宣　　言

吾が本田技研創立以来ここに五年有余、劃期的飛躍を遂げ得た事は、全従業員努力の結晶として誠に同慶にたえない。

私の幼き頃よりの夢は、自分で製作した自動車で全世界の自動車競争の覇者となることであつた。然し、**全世界の覇者**となる前には、まず企業の安定、精密なる設備、優秀なる設計を要する事は勿論で、此の点を主眼として専ら**優秀な実用車**を国内の需要者に提供することに努めて来たため、オートバイレースには全然力を注ぐ暇もなく今日に及んでいる。

然し今回サンパウロ市に於ける国際オートレースの帰朝報告により、欧米諸国の実状をつぶさに知る事ができた。私はかなり現実に拘泥せずに世界を見つめていたつもりであるが、やはり日本の現状に心をとらわれすぎていた事に気がついた。今や世界はものすごいスピードで進歩しているのである。

然し逆に、私年来の**着想**をもつてすれば必ず勝てるという**自信**が昂然と湧き起り、持前の斗志がこのままでは許さなくなつた。

絶対の自信を持てる生産態勢も完備した今、**まさに好機到る！**　明年こそは**T・Tレース**に出場せんとの決意をここに固めたのである。

此のレースには未だ嘗つて**国産車**を以て**日本人**が出場した事はないが、**レースの覇者は勿論、車が無事故で完走できればそれだけで優秀車として全世界に喧伝される。**従つて此の名声により、輸出量が決定すると云われる位で、独・英・伊・仏の各大メーカー共、その準備に全力を集中するのである。

私は此のレースに**250cc（中級車）のレーサー**を製作し、吾が本田技研の代表として全世界の檜舞台へ出場させる。此の車なら**時速180km以上**は出せる自信がある。

優秀なる**飛行機**の発動機でも１立当り55馬力程度だが、此のレーサーは１立当り1.00馬力であるから丁度その倍に当る。吾が社の**独創**に基く此のエンジンが完成すれば、**全世界最高峰**の技術水準をゆくものと云つても決して過言ではない。

近代重工業の花形、オートバイは綜合企業であるからエンジンは勿論、タイヤ、チェーン、気化器等に至るまで、**最高の技術**を要するが、その裏付けとして**緻密な注意力と真摯な努力**がなければならない。

全従業員諸君！

本田技研の全力を結集して**栄冠**を勝ちとろう、本田技研の将来は一にかかつて**諸君の双肩**にある。ほとばしる情熱を傾けて如何なる困苦にも耐え、緻密な作業研究に諸君自らの道を貫徹して欲しい。本田技研の飛躍は諸君の人間的成長であり、諸君の成長は吾が本田技研の将来を約束するものである。

ビス一本しめるに払う細心の注意力、紙一枚無駄にせぬ心がけこそ、諸君の道を開き、吾が本田技研の道を拓り開くものである。

幸いにして絶大なる協力を寄せられる各外註工場、代理店、関係銀行、更には愛乗者の方々と全力を此の一点に集中すべく極めて恵まれた環境にある。

同じ敗戦国でありながらドイツのあの隆々たる産業の復興の姿を見るにつけ、吾が本田技研は此の**難事業**を是非完遂しなければならない。

日本の機械工業の**真価**を問い、此れを全世界に**誇示**するまでにしなければならない。**吾が本田技研の使命は日本産業の啓蒙にある。**

ここに私の**決意**を披瀝し、T・Tレースに出場、優勝するために、精魂を傾けて創意工夫に努力することを諸君と共に誓う。

右宣言する。

昭和二十九年三月二十日

本田技研工業株式会社　　社 長　本 田 宗 一 郎

Honda's historic announcement was made both publicly and to the company in 1954.

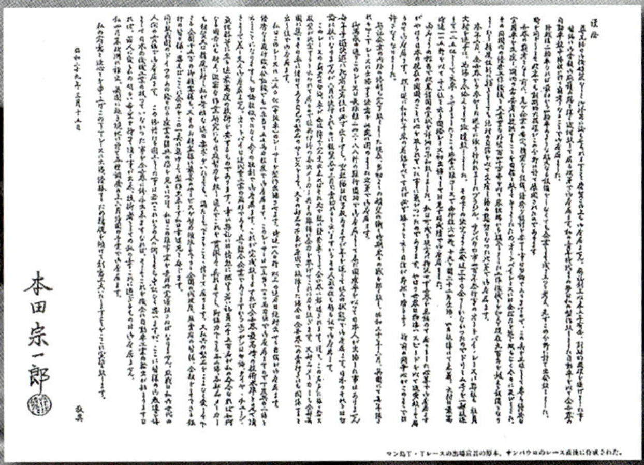

本田宗一郎

マン島T・Tレースの出場宣言の原本。サンパウロのレース直後に作成された。

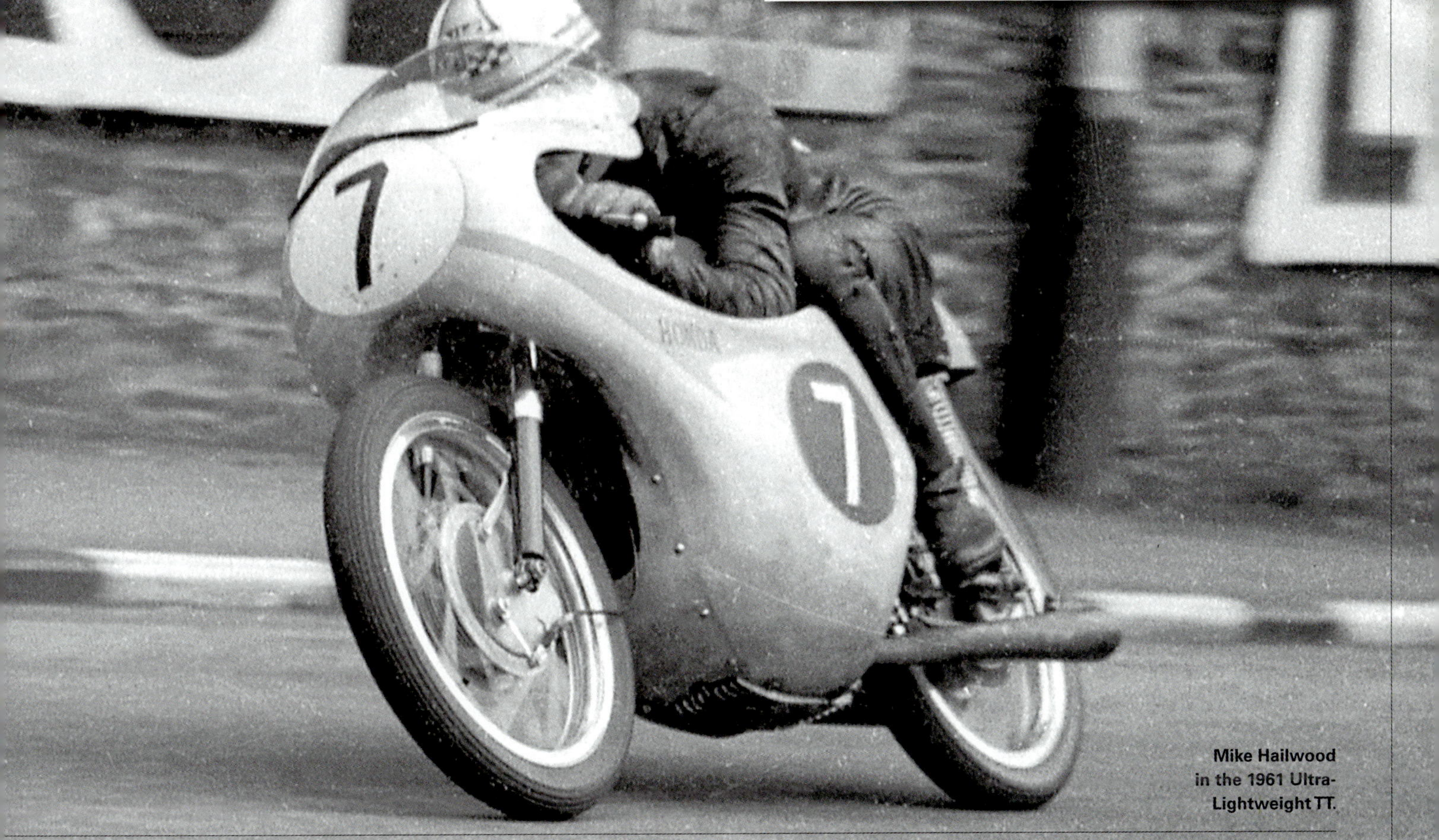

Mike Hailwood in the 1961 Ultra-Lightweight TT.

HONDA

ABOVE LEFT TO RIGHT:

Hailwood at the 1961 Lightweight TT.

Luigi Taveri at the 1962 Ultra-Lightweight.

Taveri at Ballaugh in 1964.

Jim Redman in action at the 1965 Junior TT.

Ralph Bryans on the 50cc Honda in 1966.

Mike Hailwood wins the 1966 Senior TT for Honda.

Motorcycles – cheap, easy-to-produce transport – were burgeoning in post-war Japan. In fact there were 40 Japanese motorcycle manufacturers in business in 1949 alone; Honda would become the biggest.

The company made its debut at the Isle of Man TT in 1959, following a big visit to the previous year's TT races. The machines would be 125cc four-strokes and – on the Clypse Course (used for the last time) the five riders (Japanese, Junzo Suzuki, Giichi Suzuki, Naomi Taniguchi, Teisuke Tanaka and American Bill Hunt) would win the manufacturer's award (not the individual race win) at their first attempt. Not a bad start!

Honda brought a 250cc four-cylinder machine to race alongside the 125cc twins in 1960. Results saw a further improvement, with 4th in the Lightweight race with Bob Brown on the 250 and Moto Kitano and Taniguchi in 5th and 6th. In the 125 class, Honda riders filled the 6th-10th positions.

FINALLY, A WIN

Honda's progress wasn't going unnoticed by the TT's big names. So, for the 1961 races Honda's entrants included the likes of Mike Hailwood, Bob McIntyre and Luigi Taveri. Hondas had dominated the Ultra-Lightweight (125cc) practice and this bode well for the race itself. The winner – Honda's first – would be Hailwood, averaging 88.23mph over the three laps. Hondas would fill the top five, with Taveri and Tom Phillis joining Hailwood on the rostrum. Incredibly, Honda would lock-out the top five in the Lightweight 250cc race too, with Hailwood, Phillis and Jim Redman in the first three placings. Just seven years after his vow, Soichiro Honda had delivered.

Throughout the 1960s more wins came thick and fast

1960s
1970s

in the smaller classes: the 1962 Lightweight TT (Derek Minter), Taveri took that year's 125cc race, while Redman took 1963's Lightweight event and took a 350cc Honda to the win in that year's Junior TT too. There would be more wins in the 125, 250 and 350 classes in 1964, with yet more in 1965 joined by a new 50cc class win, with Swiss ace Taveri in the saddle.

1966 would see a first for Honda – the company's first win in the 'big bike' 500cc class also marking its first Senior TT win. Once more it was Hailwood in the saddle, taking his ninth TT victory in the process. The event's diamond jubilee in 1967 – didn't disappoint: Hailwood took three race wins (250, 350, and 500cc/Senior) with the latter being a classic race and battle against Giacomo Agostini.

HONDA PULLS OUT... HONDA BRITAIN MOVES IN

Some would argue that Honda's golden era at the TT ended with Mike the Bike's classic Senior TT win in 1967. So, with Honda now looking towards Formula 1 car racing rather than bike Grand Prix or TT wins, Hailwood was paid off (£50,000 so he couldn't be a threat if he went bike racing, but he also moved onto four wheels) and there would be no more two-wheel Grand Prix racing for the company until 1979.

Competition on Honda motorcycles would continue at the TT however, albeit not at the previous levels. There

HONDA

LEFT Alex George at the 1979 Classic 1000 TT.

BELOW LEFT TO RIGHT:
Hailwood at the 1967 Junior.

Graham Penny at the 1969 Production 500 TT.

John Williams in 1971.

Bill Smith in the 1973 Production race.

The legendary Phil Read in the Formula One TT of 1977.

Alan Jackson would be victorious on a Honda in the F2 races.

would be no wins in 1968, but 1969 would see Graham 'Bill' Penny take the Production 500 race victory. Moving into the 1970s the production classes would see a number of victories for TT luminaries such as Bill Smith and John Williams.

Honda would finally return 'officially' in 1977, albeit with a national set-up called 'Honda Britain' headed up by Gerald Davison, who was the first director of Honda International Racing Company – which would later become 'HRC' or Honda Racing Corporation. He would appoint Barry Symmons as team boss.

At the same time the TT Formula World Championships were introduced, joining the TT programme following the loss of the event's Grand Prix status. Honda would win all three events. Most notable was a return of Phil Read in the Formula One on the 820cc Honda, with a 97.02mph lap. Formula Two winner would be Alan Jackson, with John Kidson winning Formula Three. Jackson would repeat his F2 feat the following year, with Bill Smith taking the F3 race.

Island Racer 119

HONDA

ABOVE LEFT TO RIGHT:
Joey Dunlop at the 1983 F1 – he'd win most of his TT races on Honda machinery.

Joey once more in the 1984 F1.

Steve Hislop in Production 750 action, 1988.

Joey launches off the line in 1988.

600cc Hondas would be successful racers too: this is Hislop on a CBR600 in 1989.

Hizzy, seen here in 1989, would take the lion's share of his 11 TT wins on Honda machinery.

THE EIGHTIES AND JOEY

Alex George would win the F1 and Classic 1000cc in 1979 and it was a classic, taking on the legend that was Mike Hailwood, who returned to the TT the previous year. The 1980 F1 winner would be popular Yorkshireman Mick Grant, who won despite the controversy of Suzuki's Graeme Crosby taking up the number 11 start position of Alex George who had crashed in practice.

Another 'Crosby controversy' would occur in 1981, when the Kiwi was given the F1 win despite Honda's Ron Haslam being already up on the podium, receiving his garland. What followed was Honda's famous 'black' protest, where bikes and riders would ride the rest of the races in that colour as a protest.

Thankfully, Haslam would get his revenge by winning the 1982 F1 race on his 999 Honda, with a lap record of 113.33mph. This was a start of an amazing run of 17 consecutive F1 wins by Honda.

Honda at the Isle of Man TT will be forever linked with Joey Dunlop. His own string of F1 victories began with his win in the 1983 race (114.03mph record lap) up to the 1988 F1 race – making it six in a row! By this time he'd taken the lap record in the class up to 116.25mph. Of course, Joey would win 24 of his 26 wins with Honda across all classes and – most notably – take one of his most distinguished (and last) big-bike wins on the unfancied VTR1000 SP1 in the 2000 F1 race just weeks before his tragic death in Estonia.

1980s
1990s

RIGHT: Dunlop would win 24 races for Honda.

HONDA

1990S DOMINANCE

During the 1980s and 1990s Joey would be up against a new wave of Honda's rising stars, with 'official' team-mates and talented privateers using Honda machinery, based out of Louth, Lincolnshire since 1990.

This would be Honda's new 'golden age' where their strength in depth in every class would shine through. Successive bosses at Honda UK – most notably Bob McMillan – would put much effort into winning across all classes and this was reflected in many works bikes seen on the start-line. Whether the bikes were 'Silkolene Honda' or 'Castrol Honda' or garbed in any of the many dealer-supported liveries of the time, they would fill the grid and often the podium placings too. In the lightweight two-strokes, Honda's RS125 and 250s were often at the top of the podium, often being ridden by Joey or his brother Robert, who was a demon himself on the 125. With classes changing over the years, the new 'Junior' class would use production based 600cc machines and Honda's CBR600F would be the cream of the crop, not just on road circuits but on short circuits too. Winners in this class would include Hislop, Jim Moodie, Iain Duffus, Ian Simpson and Michael Rutter.

By the end of the 1980s, Honda's pure race bikes would eventually be replaced by production-based machines, as short-circuit racing dictated a move to more road-bike based racers. This would result in machines such as the VFR750RR RC30 V4 – a motorcycle built to win the World Superbike championship (it won that series in 1988-1989) but one that was also suited to the Island's unique stresses. Its successor – 1994's RC45 – would take a little longer to make its mark on the short circuits but would also win on the Island in the hands of Steve Hislop in 1994. Hizzy's battles with the likes of Carl Fogarty in the early 1990s were the stuff of legend. With Honda wanting to spoil Yamaha's 1991 birthday party on the island, Carl, Steve (and Joey) would share two exotic race-only RVFs for that year in the big bike classes.

What followed was another classic in the F1 race as both Fogarty and Hislop battled it out 'on the roads' even if they were separated on final time. With machine problems dogging Foggy, Hizzy would take the F1 win. The RVF was then vacated by Carl (who had to race in World Superbikes at the end of TT race week) to Joey for the Senior, but Hislop would take that win too. The prospect of a 125mph lap was on the cards but instead the Scot could take the new record to 121.09mph.

Phillip McCallen took his first TT win in the F1 on the RC30 in 1992 – he'd be one of Honda's big winners for the rest of the decade. 'SuperMac' would be seen by many as the natural successor as 'King of the Roads' to Joey, as well as taking up the mantle of Steve Hislop, who ended his TT career in 1994 when he won the last of his 11 TT wins. McCallen would not only win with the RC30, RS250 and CBR600 across the classes, but would also champion Honda's CBR900RR FireBlade in the newly-restored Production TT class in 1996 and 1997. The Northern Irishman would win 11 TT races before his retirement in 1999 thanks to injury. Always aggressive out on the course, his highlight would be a four-race win streak at the 1996 event.

The 1990s also saw the start of an impressive tally of Honda wins in the sidecar class, thanks to the move towards the FIM's Formula 2 Sidecar regulations, which would see two-stroke outfits of not more than 350cc take on four-stroke chairs of not more than 600cc.

In 1991, legendary pairing Mick Boddice and Dave Wells took a start-to-finish win (and Honda's first) when they won that year's Sidecar TT – racing with an outfit powered by a 600cc Honda CBR engine. They'd secure the double later that week. Currently Honda sits in second position with 26 TT Sidecar wins.

BELOW LEFT TO RIGHT:
A hard-charging Carl Fogarty at the 1990 TT.

Mick Boddice and Dave Wells would be Honda's first sidecar winners.

Hizzy on the exotic RVF in 1991.

Phil McCallen would become a big TT winner, again mainly on Honda machines. He'd take four wins in 1996 alone!

A popular Honda winner was Nick Jefferies. The Yorkshireman won the F1 race in 1993.

McCallen flies in the 1995 F1 TT race…

Jim Moodie would take Honda's 100th TT win in 1998 in the Production TT race aboard a FireBlade.

IslandRacer 121

HONDA

ABOVE LEFT TO RIGHT:

Joey's final big-bike win: the F1 of 2000.

McGuinness at the 2006 Senior TT.

Moly and Rick Long in 2007.

A Superbike class win for McGuinness in 2007.

THE NEW MILLENNIUM

Honda shifted focus once more as the Noughties got into their swing. While Yamaha and Suzuki used the prodigious talents of David Jefferies to take wins, Honda's sights were on the 500cc Grand Prix and later MotoGP crowns – as well as World Superbikes with the SP1 and SP2 V-twin four-strokes. The company would take the title in 2000 and 2002 with Colin Edwards, while Valentino Rossi was supreme in the GP class, winning in 2001, 2002 and 2003.

In the UK, Honda Racing with HRC and Michelin support would make an all-out assault on the British Superbike title, which they would eventually win with Ryuichi Kiyonari in 2006. That same year Honda came back with a bang into TT racing complete with HM Plant backing. They had linked up with John McGuinness who'd won three big-bike races for Yamaha in 2004-05. Honda's last large capacity win at the TT had been Joey Dunlop's F1 on the SP1 in 2000, so the time was ripe for revenge… It would be the start of a fruitful relationship between Honda and McGuinness.

John took a start to finish victory and outright lap record in the Superbike Race and success continued with another win and lap record in the Supersport Race. The Morecambe Missile duly completed his hat-trick in the Senior Race, bettering his six-day old outright lap record with a new mark of 129.451mph.

For the 2007 Centenary TT, the team expanded to two solo riders with Ian Hutchinson joining McGuinness, while Dave Molyneux became a 'proper' Honda Racing team member in the Sidecar class as Honda looked to dominate the 2007 event.

Domination was just what happened, with McGuinness taking record-breaking wins in the Superbike and Senior Races, setting the first ever 130mph lap in the Senior event. Hutchinson backed him up with two 3rd place finishes but beating McGuinness in the Supersport Race as he claimed his maiden TT victory. McGuinness was not far behind in 2nd. Bruce Anstey's Suzuki stopped a clean sweep with victory in the Superstock, with McGuinness 2nd and Hutchinson in 3rd. Moly and Rick Long took both sidecar race wins.

Padgett's Racing would take the reins of the Honda effort for 2008, with McGuinness taking the Senior, Nick Crowe and Mark Cox taking Honda-powered LCRs to both Sidecar wins, and Chris Palmer winning the 125cc race. 2009 saw Honda Racing return with Steve Plater now alongside McGuinness in the HM Plant set-up: both would contest the Superbike, Senior and Supersport Races. John took another Superbike win ahead of Plater but a broken chain would ruin McGuinness' Senior, leaving Plater to take a well-earned win.

Honda and Ian Hutchinson would have a special year in 2010. 'Hutchy' would take a five-win streak across all the solo classes on his Padgett's Racing Hondas while Klaus Klaffenbock and Dan Sayle would do the sidecar double thanks to Honda power… The following year the 'official' team, now called the 'Honda TT Legends' team, returned but only to contest the Superbike and Senior races. John McGuinness would take the double win.

McGuinness took his fifth superbike race win for Honda in 2012, while in 2013 he was joined by Michaels Dunlop and Rutter, with the team as a whole still concentrating on the two 'big bike' races. The results were brilliant – with Dunlop and McGuinness taking 1st and 3rd in the Superbike Race, where the latter upped his outright lap record to 131.671mph. John also took the win in the Senior though where Dunlop took 2nd: Rutter would take two 6ths in the big bike classes.

Now named 'Honda Racing' for 2014, a wrist injury would mean McGuinness would sit this one out, while

HONDA

2000s
2010s

Conor Cummins would secure 3rd in the Superbike and 2nd in the Senior. McGuinness would come back with a vengeance in 2015, taking the Senior win (his fifth for Honda) and take the outright lap record to 132.701mph.

Amazingly, that's the last Honda 'big-bike' win. Sure, sidecars powered by Honda engines have continued to win in the capable hands of John Holden/Andrew Winkle and the Birchall brothers – and Michael Dunlop even nicked a Supersport win in 2018, but that's pretty much been it… BMW has loomed large and dominated the main classes, with even Triumph having a Supersport win in the meantime.

Issues with the new Honda CBR1000RR Fireblade for 2017 would see McGuinness suffering a big crash at the North West 200, leaving him with serious injuries which would keep him out of racing for 18 months. His team-mate Guy Martin would also suffer a crash at that year's TT, leading him and the team to pull out of the event. Even bringing Ian Hutchinson into the team for 2018 couldn't bring back the spark to ignite a victory. The only high spot has been David Johnson's 3rd place in the 2019 Superstock race.

Which brings us neatly on… 2020 and 2021 were COVID-induced washouts, but looking ahead, 2022 could be good for Honda. It would be a fairy-tale for John McGuinness – the old battler himself – to take a win, wouldn't it? And who knows what talented newcomer Glenn Irwin can do?

Whatever happens, Honda in its various guises of the official factory team from Japan, through Honda Britain, Honda UK, Honda TT Legends and Honda Racing UK has a long and proud legacy on the Island and it's not looking likely to be overtaken anytime soon!

LEFT: Honda and John would break records together…

BELOW LEFT TO RIGHT:
Steve Plater was in it to win it at the 2009 Senior.

Hutchy made it big with FIVE wins in 2010.

Hutchinson on the CBR600 in the first Supersport race of 2010.

Michael would also ride Honda, just like dad Robert and uncle Joey.

KTM ADVERTORIAL

The GREATEST road test in the WORLD

Island Racer's sister title *Fast Bikes* has teamed up with TT legend Michael Rutter for a world exclusive feature, and they need your help.

Seven-time TT race winner Rutter, whose personal best lap of the TT course is an average of 131.709mph, has agreed to help *Fast Bikes* answer a question that has been niggling them for some time – just how fast could a super-naked bike lap the TT course?

Subject to weather and delays, Rutter and *Fast Bikes* have been granted the holy grail of motorcycling: full access to the closed TT course before it re-opens at the end of each evening session during practice week.

Over recent years, the super-naked class of machine has become more powerful, more loaded with tech and crucially more popular in the showrooms. So, it seems natural to try and discover just how well this genre of bike could perform in the most extreme road test in the world.

The Isle of Man TT course needs no introduction, but it is worth reminding ourselves just what the bike will be subjected to for around 20 minutes in Rutter's hands. Bumps and compressions big enough to rip sumps clean off the engine, jumps taken in sixth-gear, an elevation gain of around 2000ft, and parts of the course where bikes are held flat out in top gear for three miles. It is brutal, and every single aspect of the bike will be tested to the absolute limit. If there is a faster, more extreme test of a motorcycle on the planet, we have yet to hear of it.

Representing the super-naked is the original bad-boy, the KTM 1290 Super Duke R Evo, also known as 'The Beast'. It has been updated for 2022 with the addition of new semi-active WP suspension that KTM claim adapts to road conditions and rider inputs, so it should be ideal for a pounding around the TT course.

Other than reversing the gearshift to race pattern for Rutter, the KTM will be lapped in 100 per cent standard trim, right down to the number-plate and mirrors which will remain on the bike. It will be exactly as it comes out of the showroom apart from its tyres. *Fast Bikes* have teamed up with Metzeler to fit the KTM with their latest Sportec M9 RR road tyre which will be run at road pressures and won't be pre-heated before the lap, thus replicating the exact same conditions every road rider does as they set off for a ride.

Fast Bikes have got the course, they've got the rider, they've got the bike and they've got the tyres all set and ready to go, but they also need your help.

If you are going to be trackside at the TT during practice week, *Fast Bikes* need you to be ready for Rutter and the KTM at the end of each practice session because they will need photos of him to use in the subsequent magazine feature.

Your photo could be our main front cover image!

■ If you get a sharp picture of Rutter on the KTM, get in touch with John McAvoy who will be on the Isle of Man, based at Rutter's Bathams Racing truck in the paddock, or via editor Bruce Wilson at: bwilson@mortons.co.uk or the mag itself on: Twitter @fastbikesmag or Facebook @ FastBikesMagazine

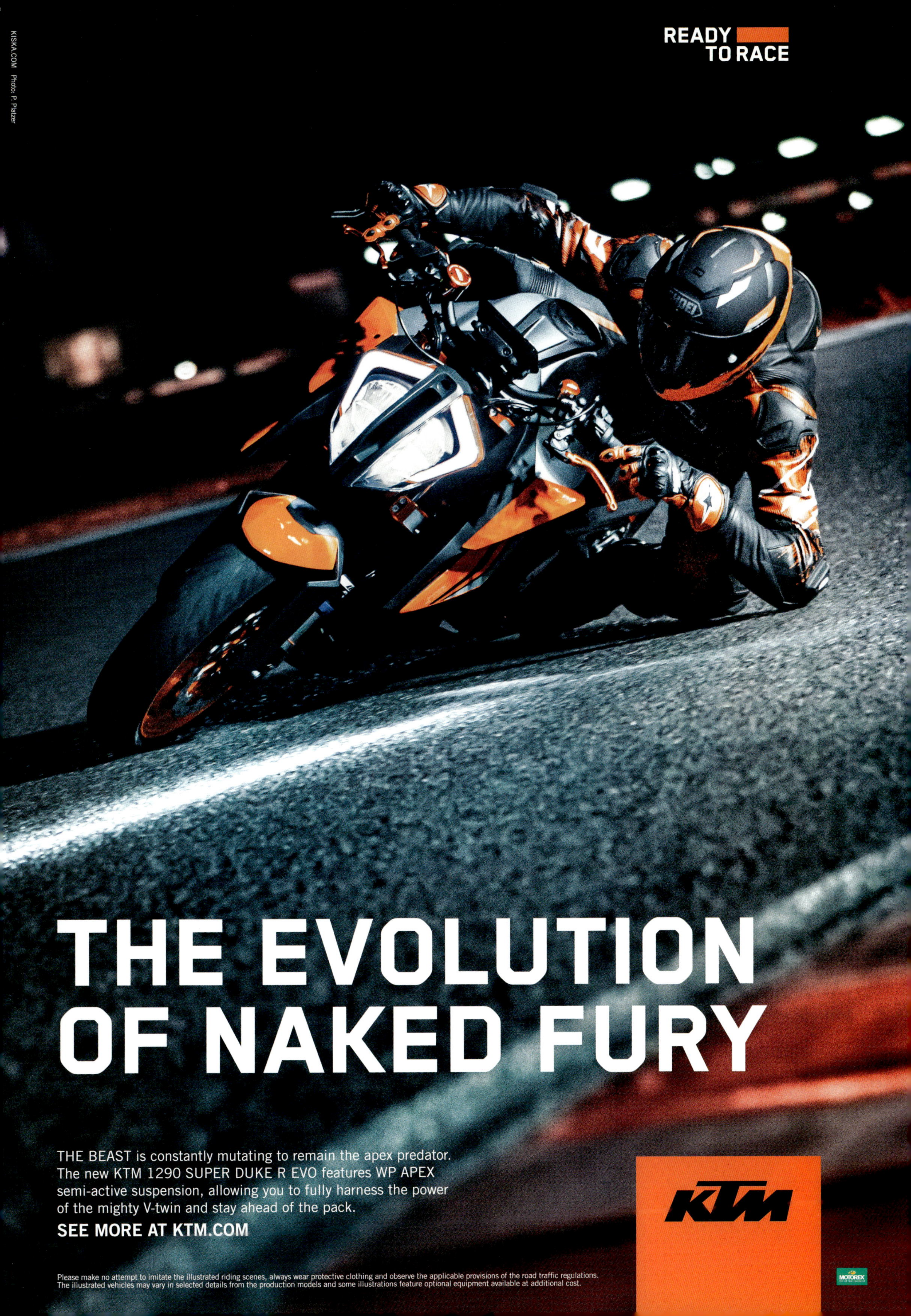

READY TO RACE

THE EVOLUTION OF NAKED FURY

THE BEAST is constantly mutating to remain the apex predator. The new KTM 1290 SUPER DUKE R EVO features WP APEX semi-active suspension, allowing you to fully harness the power of the mighty V-twin and stay ahead of the pack.

SEE MORE AT KTM.COM

Please make no attempt to imitate the illustrated riding scenes, always wear protective clothing and observe the applicable provisions of the road traffic regulations. The illustrated vehicles may vary in selected details from the production models and some illustrations feature optional equipment available at additional cost.

ORDER NOW

MIKE HAILWOOD IN 100 OBJECTS

AN INTIMATE INSIGHT INTO A RACING LIFE

JAMES ROBINSON

ONLY £30

OFFICIAL HAILWOOD PRODUCT

Stanley Michael Bailey Hailwood, known to all as Mike and to race fans as Mike the Bike, was arguably the greatest motorcycle racer of all time.

He raced to two-wheeled world championship after world championship on MV Agustas and Hondas, as well as campaigning cars, finishing on the podium at Le Mans in a GT40 Ford, competing in 50 F1 GPs and clinched the Formula 2 world championship in 1972. Tragically, his life was ended prematurely, at just 40 years old.

Throughout his childhood and career, Mike kept things – albeit not necessarily the things one might expect. The things he retained were more personal – wallets, diaries, tie pins, rings, paperwork, a whole host of items. And now, Mike's son David is custodian of this treasure trove, which he has opened up and allowed exclusive access to. This forms the basis of the book Mike Hailwood in 100 Objects.

Here's a sneak peak of some of Hailwood's personal artefacts:

ORDER YOUR COPY TODAY!

From **www.mortonsbooks.co.uk** or call **01507 529529**

Subscribe to MOTORCYCLE
FOR THE LOVE OF THE RIDE — SPORT & LEISURE

SPECIAL OFFER! Expires 31/12/22

£20 for 6 issues

Motorcycle Sport & Leisure magazine has all the latest news, test rides and interviews with the top figures from the world of two wheels every month.

There are touring tales from every corner of the globe, and strong views from our expert columnists. It doesn't matter what type of bike you've got, how you like to ride it or how experienced you are, *MSL* is the grown-up's magazine written for sheer motorcycling pleasure.

Get your FREE digital copy!

SUBSCRIBE TODAY

Visit: www.classicmagazines.co.uk/MSLIR22
Call: 01507 529529 and quote **MSLIR22**

Download your FREE digital copy of Motorcycle Sport & Leisure! Visit: www.mslmagazine.co.uk/islandracer

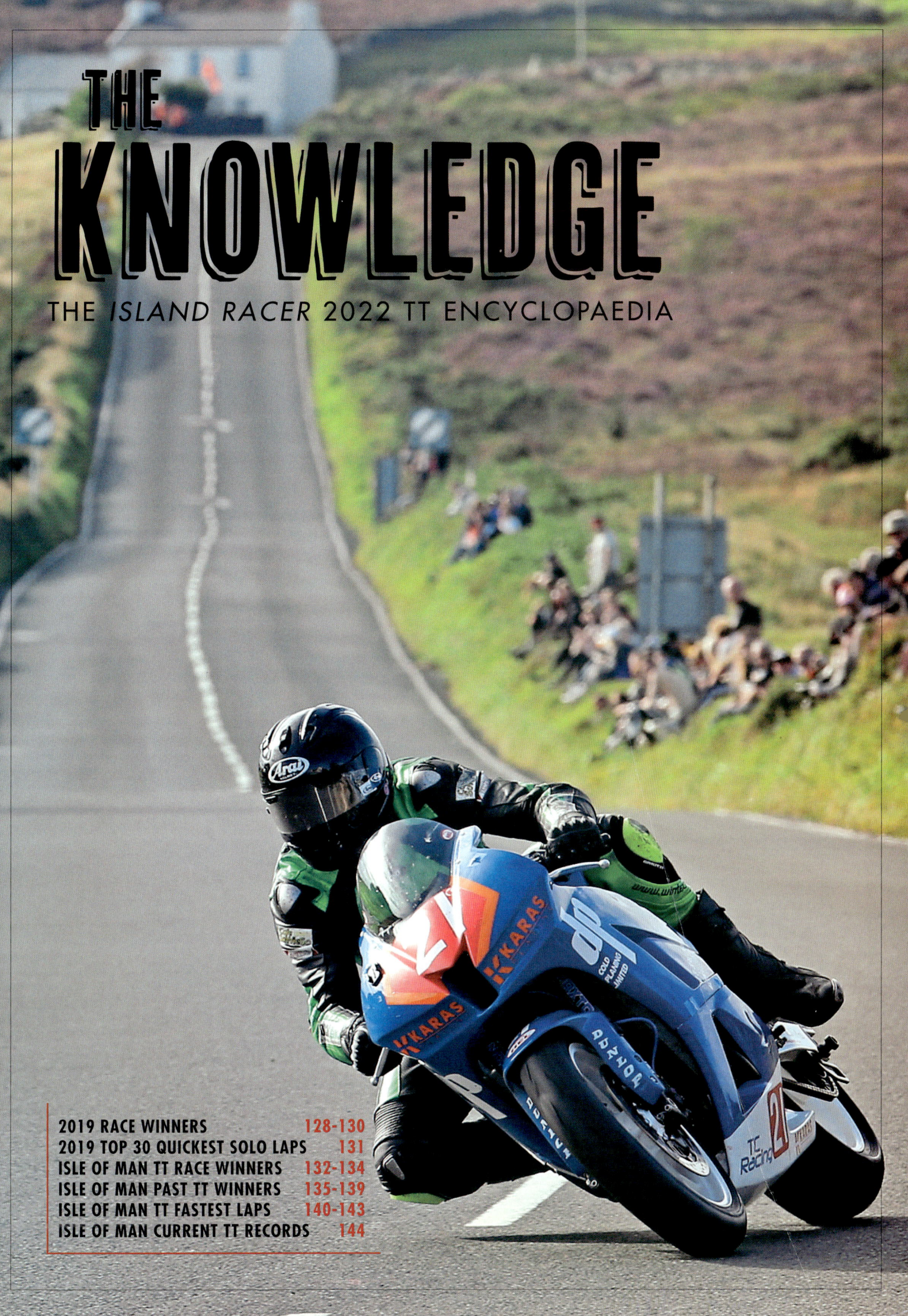

THE KNOWLEDGE
THE *ISLAND RACER* 2022 TT ENCYCLOPAEDIA

2019 RACE WINNERS	128-130
2019 TOP 30 QUICKEST SOLO LAPS	131
ISLE OF MAN TT RACE WINNERS	132-134
ISLE OF MAN PAST TT WINNERS	135-139
ISLE OF MAN TT FASTEST LAPS	140-143
ISLE OF MAN CURRENT TT RECORDS	144

ENCYCLOPAEDIA

TT 2019 RST SUPERBIKE TT RESULTS (TOP 15 FINISHERS)

POSN	NO	COMPETITOR	MACHINE	TIME	SPEED	
1	10	Peter Hickman	BMW	34:08.008	132.644	Silver
2	2	Dean Harrison	Kawasaki	34:09.790	132.529	Silver
3	1	Conor Cummins	Honda	34:17.353	132.042	Silver
4	5	James Hillier	Kawasaki	34:49.727	129.996	Silver
5	8	Michael Rutter	Honda	35:02.618	129.199	Silver
6	6	Michael Dunlop	BMW	35:05.324	129.033	Silver
7	9	David Johnson	Honda	35:18.153	128.251	Silver
8	15	James Coward	Yamaha	35:19.189	128.189	Silver
9	7	Gary Johnson	Kawasaki	35:25.653	127.799	Silver
10	18	Davey Todd	BMW	35:34.642	127.261	Silver
11	22	Brian McCormack	BMW	35:34.991	127.24	Silver
12	13	Sam West	BMW	35:36.826	127.131	Silver
13	4	Ian Hutchinson	Honda	35:47.078	126.524	Silver
14	14	Philip Crowe	BMW	35:58.345	125.863	Bronze
15	11	Lee Johnston	BMW	36:00.526	125.736	Bronze

TT 2019 DUNLOP SENIOR TT RESULTS (TOP 15 FINISHERS)

POSN	NO	COMPETITOR	MACHINE	TIME	SPEED	
1	2	Dean Harrison	Kawasaki	01:43:49.521	130.824	Silver
2	10	Peter Hickman	BMW	01:44:42.583	129.719	Silver
3	1	Conor Cummins	Honda	01:44:48.400	129.599	Silver
4	6	Michael Dunlop	BMW	01:45:16.230	129.028	Silver
5	5	James Hillier	Kawasaki	01:46:19.873	127.74	Silver
6	18	Davey Todd	BMW	01:46:22.441	127.689	Silver
7	8	Michael Rutter	Honda	01:46:53.092	127.079	Silver
8	15	James Coward	Yamaha	01:47:03.082	126.881	Silver
9	22	Brian McCormack	BMW	01:47:39.492	126.166	Silver
10	20	Dominic Herbertson	Kawasaki	01:47:58.783	125.79	Silver
11	7	Gary Johnson	Kawasaki	01:48:31.186	125.164	Silver
12	17	Shaun Anderson	BMW	01:49:48.261	123.7	Bronze
13	16	Derek Sheils	Suzuki	01:49:57.265	123.531	Bronze
14	31	Mike Booth	Kawasaki	01:50:44.891	122.646	Bronze
15	25	Michael Sweeney	BMW	01:51:03.728	122.299	Bronze

TT 2019 MONSTER ENERGY SUPERSPORT TT 1 RESULTS (TOP 15 FINISHERS)

POSN	NO	COMPETITOR	MACHINE	TIME	SPEED	
1	11	Lee Johnston	Yamaha	35:48.337	126.449	Silver
2	5	James Hillier	Kawasaki	35:51.978	126.235	Silver
3	10	Peter Hickman	Triumph	35:53.304	126.158	Silver
4	2	Dean Harrison	Kawasaki	36:06.308	125.4	Silver
5	6	Michael Dunlop	Honda	36:09.462	125.218	Silver
6	1	Conor Cummins	Honda	36:15.922	124.846	Silver
7	7	Gary Johnson	Triumph	36:17.425	124.76	Silver
8	15	James Coward	Yamaha	36:25.255	124.313	Silver
9	8	Davey Todd	Honda	36:47.028	123.087	Silver
10	4	Ian Hutchinson	Honda	36:55.133	122.636	Silver
11	28	Derek Sheils	Yamaha	37:04.448	122.123	Silver
12	17	Paul Jordan	Kawasaki	37:21.557	121.191	Silver
13	20	Dominic Herbertson	Kawasaki	37:23.807	121.069	Silver
14	9	David Johnson	Honda	37:25.784	120.963	Silver
15	18	Michael Sweeney	Yamaha	37:37.017	120.361	Bronze

TT 2019 MONSTER ENERGY SUPERSPORT TT 2 RESULTS (TOP 15 FINISHERS)

POSN	NO	COMPETITOR	MACHINE	TIME	SPEED	
1	10	Peter Hickman	Triumph	35:27.780	127.671	Silver
2	2	Dean Harrison	Kawasaki	35:31.082	127.473	Silver
3	5	James Hillier	Kawasaki	35:35.636	127.201	Silver
4	1	Conor Cummins	Honda	35:44.231	126.692	Silver
5	15	James Coward	Yamaha	35:48.778	126.423	Silver
6	6	Michael Dunlop	Honda	36:10.408	125.164	Silver
7	8	Davey Todd	Honda	36:10.903	125.135	Silver
8	7	Gary Johnson	Triumph	36:12.192	125.061	Silver
9	11	Lee Johnston	Yamaha	36:14.796	124.911	Silver
10	9	David Johnson	Honda	36:35.130	123.754	Silver
11	17	Paul Jordan	Kawasaki	36:44.426	123.232	Silver
12	28	Derek Sheils	Yamaha	36:48.343	123.013	Silver
13	13	Sam West	Yamaha	36:53.887	122.705	Silver
14	20	Dominic Herbertson	Kawasaki	36:58.057	122.475	Silver
15	3	John McGuinness	Honda	37:03.838	122.156	Silver

Press conferences are always good for a giggle…

ENCYCLOPAEDIA

TT 2019 RL360 SUPERSTOCK TT 2 RESULTS (TOP 15 FINISHERS)

POSN	NO	COMPETITOR	MACHINE	TIME	SPEED	
1	10	Peter Hickman	BMW	52:02.761	130.488	Silver
2	2	Dean Harrison	Kawasaki	52:28.806	129.409	Silver
3	9	David Johnson	Honda	52:42.648	128.843	Silver
4	6	Michael Dunlop	BMW	52:42.856	128.834	Silver
5	1	Conor Cummins	Honda	52:52.004	128.463	Silver
6	8	Michael Rutter	BMW	52:58.855	128.186	Silver
7	5	James Hillier	Kawasaki	53:17.624	127.433	Silver
8	18	Davey Todd	BMW	53:39.409	126.571	Silver
9	15	James Coward	Yamaha	53:42.541	126.448	Silver
10	7	Gary Johnson	Kawasaki	53:45.811	126.32	Silver
11	22	Brian McCormack	BMW	54:12.194	125.295	Silver
12	11	Lee Johnston	BMW	54:20.263	124.985	Silver
13	13	Sam West	BMW	54:25.426	124.787	Silver
14	46	Paul Jordan	Kawasaki	54:48.665	123.906	Bronze
15	23	Stefano Bonetti	BMW	54:58.161	123.549	Bronze

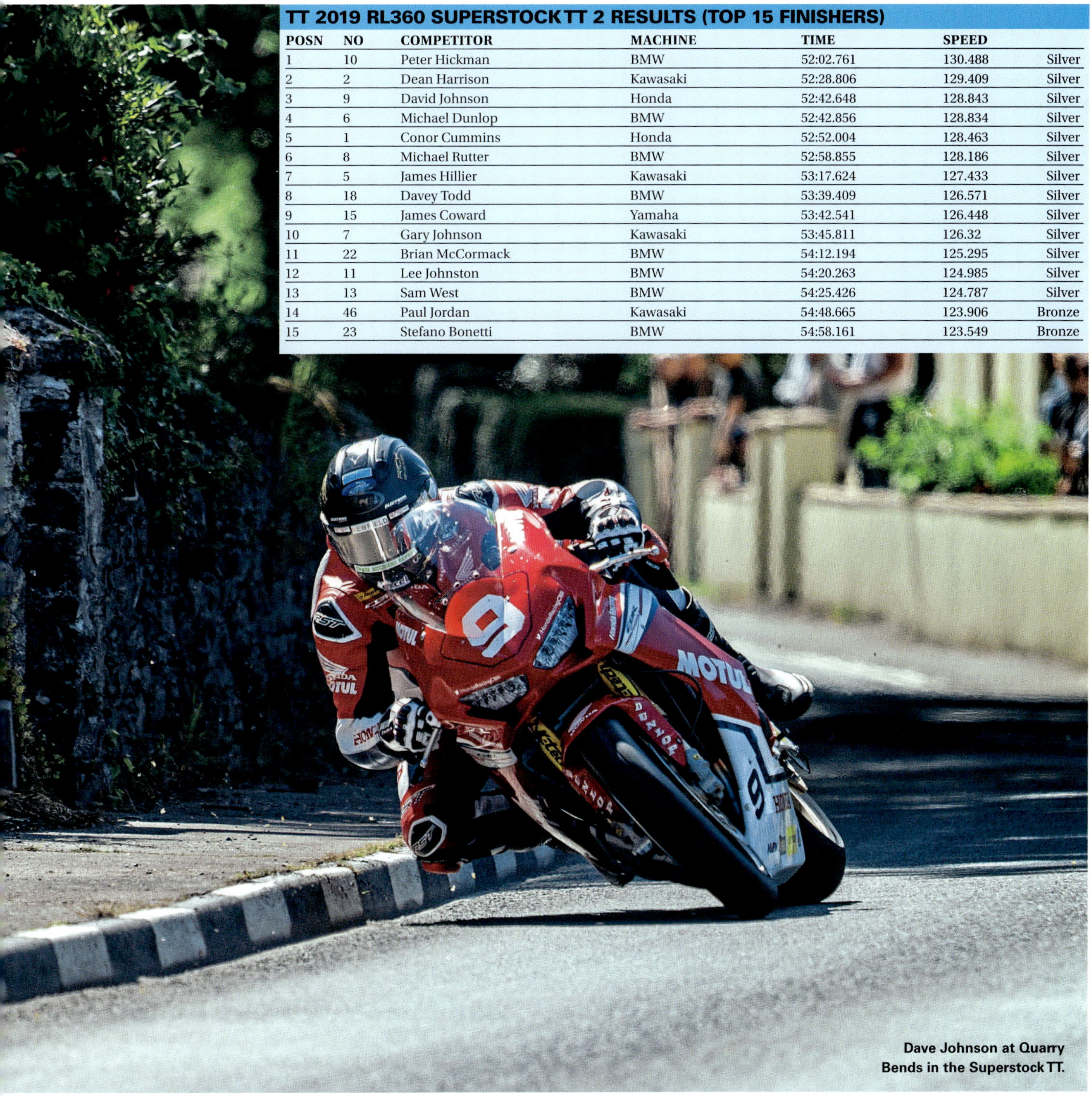

Dave Johnson at Quarry Bends in the Superstock TT.

TT 2019 BENNETTS LIGHTWEIGHT TT RESULTS (TOP 15 FINISHERS)

POSN	NO	COMPETITOR	MACHINE	TIME	SPEED	
1	6	Michael Dunlop	Paton	37:13.161	121.646	Silver
2	15	James Coward	Kawasaki	37:14.460	121.576	Silver
3	9	Lee Johnston	Kawasaki	37:37.151	120.353	Silver
4	12	Paul Jordan	Kawasaki	37:42.426	120.073	Silver
5	8	Michael Rutter	Kawasaki	37:47.367	119.811	Silver
6	4	Stefano Bonetti	Paton	37:50.371	119.653	Silver
7	7	Gary Johnson	Kawasaki	37:57.315	119.288	Silver
8	10	Peter Hickman	Norton	38:02.743	119.004	Silver
9	20	Dominic Herbertson	Kawasaki	38:36.735	117.258	Silver
10	14	Horst Saiger	Paton	38:49.385	116.621	Silver
11	18	James Chawke	Paton	39:03.074	115.94	Silver
12	11	Ian Lougher	Paton	39:19.577	115.129	Bronze
13	17	John Barton	Kawasaki	39:41.670	114.061	Bronze
14	25	Jonathan Perry	Kawasaki	39:45.615	113.873	Bronze
15	26	Michal Dokoupil	Kawasaki	39:51.974	113.57	Bronze

ENCYCLOPAEDIA

ABOVE: 2019's TT Zero podium was Ian Lougher, Michael Rutter and John McGuinness. The old boys on the new tech bikes!

TT 2019 SES TT ZERO RESULTS (ALL FINISHERS)

POSN	NO	COMPETITOR	MACHINE	TIME	SPEED	
1	1	Michael Rutter	MUGEN	18:34.172	121.909	Silver
2	3	John McGuinness	MUGEN	18:42.738	120.979	Silver
3	6	Ian Lougher	IDATEN X	22:02.697	102.69	Silver
4	5	Matthew Rees	University of Bath	23:52.100	94.845	Bronze
5	4	Allann Venter	Brunel	24:44.815	91.478	Bronze
6	7	Mike Norbury	Duffy Motorsport SR	27:10.800	83.289	Bronze
7	8	Shaun Anderson	Duffy Motorsport	31:25.831	72.026	Bronze

TT 2019 LOCATE.IM SIDECAR TT 1 RESULTS (TOP 10 FINISHERS)

POSN	NO	COMPETITOR	MACHINE	TIME	SPEED	
1	1	Ben Birchall & Tom Birchall	LCR	57:24.005	118.317	Silver
2	2	John Holden & Lee Cain	Honda	58:12.121	116.687	Silver
3	4	Alan Founds & Jake Lowther	Yamaha	58:40.747	115.738	Silver
4	5	Pete Founds & Jevan Walmsley	Suzuki	58:46.319	115.555	Silver
5	44	Ryan Crowe & Callum Crowe	Triumph	01:00:01.526	113.142	Silver
6	6	Lewis Blackstock & Patrick Rosney	Honda	01:00:31.493	112.208	Bronze
7	10	Gary Bryan & Philip Hyde	Baker	01:00:44.565	111.806	Bronze
8	8	Conrad Harrison & Andrew Winkle	Honda	01:01:05.904	111.155	Bronze
9	21	Allan Schofield & Steve Thomas	DDM	01:01:59.376	109.557	Bronze
10	17	Gary Gibson & Daryl Gibson	Suzuki	01:02:38.874	108.406	Bronze

TT 2019 LOCATE.IM SIDECAR TT 2 RESULTS (TOP 10 FINISHERS)

POSN	NO	COMPETITOR	MACHINE	TIME	SPEED	
1	1	Ben Birchall & Tom Birchall	LCR	38:12.563	118.494	Silver
2	2	John Holden & Lee Cain	Honda	38:33.074	117.444	Silver
3	5	Pete Founds & Jevan Walmsley	Suzuki	39:07.457	115.724	Silver
4	3	Tim Reeves & Mark Wilkes	Yamaha	40:16.265	112.428	Bronze
5	10	Gary Brian & Phil Hyde	Baker	40:18.805	112.310	Bronze
6	11	Estelle Leblond & Frank Claeys	Suzuki	41:15.009	109.760	Bronze
7	6	Lewis Blackstock & Patrick Rosney	Honda	41:36.415	108.818	Bronze
8	21	Allan Schofield & Steve Thomas	DDM	41:37.731	108.761	Bronze
9	19	John Lowther & Scott Hardie	Honda	41:42.336	108.561	Bronze
10	7	Dave Molyneux & Harry Payne	Yamaha	41:43.136	108.526	Bronze

ABOVE: Lee Johnston leaps Ballaugh Bridge in the Lightweight TT.

ENCYCLOPAEDIA

TT 2019 TOP 30 QUICKEST SOLO LAPS

#	Rider	Speed	#	Rider	Speed	#	Rider	Speed
1	Peter Hickman	134.284mph	11	Gary Johnson	128.863mph	21	Mike Booth	125.917mph
2	Dean Harrison	133.992mph	12	Brian McCormack	128.812mph	22	Paul Jordan	125.385mph
3	Conor Cummins	132.61mph	13	Sam West	128.365mph	23	Stefano Bonetti	125.166mph
4	Michael Dunlop	132.024mph	14	Ian Hutchinson	127.668mph	24	Jay Lawrence	125.034mph
5	James Hillier	131.597mph	15	Derek Sheils	127.564mph	25	Michael Sweeney	124.998mph
6	Davey Todd	131.491mph	16	Shaun Anderson	127.547mph	26	Forest Dunn	124.773mph
7	David Johnson	130.983mph	17	Phil Crowe	127.125mph	27	Frank Gallagher	124.468mph
8	Michael Rutter	130.402mph	18	Lee Johnston	127.113mph	28	John McGuinness	124.422mph
9	Jamie Coward	130.317mph	19	Daley Mathison	127.08mph	29	Rob Hodson	124.28mph
10	Dominic Herbertson	129.587mph	20	Horst Saiger	125.966mph	30	Julian Trummer	124.258mph

Conor Cummins would leave TT 2019 with the third quickest lap.

Island**Racer** 131

ENCYCLOPAEDIA

ISLE OF MAN TT
RACE WINNERS

www.dukevideo.com

Still a legend – Mike Hailwood on 14 wins.

ISLE OF MAN TT RACE WINNERS

	RIDER	WINS
1	DUNLOP, Joey	26
2	MCGUINNESS, John	23
3	DUNLOP, Michael	19
4	MOLYNEUX, Dave	17
5	HUTCHINSON, Ian	16
6	HAILWOOD, Mike	14
7	ANSTEY, Bruce	12
7	LOUGHER, Ian	12
8	HISLOP, Steve	11
8	MCCALLEN, Phillip	11
9	AGOSTINI, Giacomo	10
9	BIRCHALL, Ben	10
9	BIRCHALL, Tom	10
9	FISHER, Rob	10
9	WOODS, Stanley	10
10	BODDICE, Mick	9
10	JEFFERIES, David	9
10	SCHAUZU, Siegfried	9
11	LONG, Rick	8
11	MOODIE, Jim	8
11	MORTIMER, Chas	8
11	READ, Phil	8
11	SAYLE, Dan	8
11	WILLIAMS, Charlie	8
12	GRANT, Mick	7
12	KALAUCH, Wolfgang	7
12	RUTTER, Michael	7
12	RUTTER, Tony	7
13	BIRKS, Chas	6
13	DUKE, Geoff	6
13	GUTHRIE, Jimmy	6
13	REDMAN, Jim	6
13	SURTEES, John	6
13	UBBIALI, Carlo	6
14	BENNETT, Alec	5
14	CROWE, Nick	5
14	DUNLOP, Robert	5
14	HICKMAN, Peter	5
14	REID, Brian	5
15	ENDERS, Klaus	4
15	FRITH, Freddie	4
15	HANDLEY, Wal	4
15	IRESON, Trevor	4
15	JOHANNSON, Benga	4
15	LEACH, Dave	4
15	PALMER, Chris	4
15	PICKRELL, Ray	4
15	PROVINI, Tarquinio	4
15	SCHNEIDER, Horst	4
15	SMITH, Barry	4
15	SMITH, Bill	4
15	TAYLOR, Jock	4
15	WILLIAMS, John G.	4
16	AMM, Ray	3
16	ARCHIBALD, Adrian	3
16	CROSBY, Graeme	3
16	DANIELL, Harold	3
16	DEUBEL, Max	3
16	ENGELHARDT, Ralf	3
16	FARQUHAR, Ryan	3
16	FARRANCE, Patrick	3
16	FOGARTY, Carl	3
16	GEORGE, Alex	3
16	HARRISON, Dean	3
16	HERRON, Tom	3
16	HOPE, Darren	3
16	HORNER, Emil	3
16	JACKSON, Alan	3
16	JEFFERIES, Tony	3
16	JOHNSON, Geoff	3
16	KLAFFENBOCK, Klaus	3
16	MCELNEA, Rob	3
16	MCINTYRE, Bob	3
16	MELLOR, Phil	3
16	MORRIS, Dave	3
16	POLLINGTON, Clive	3
16	SCHNEIDER, Walter	3
16	SIMPSON, Ian	3
16	STEINHAUSEN, Rolf	3
16	STRAUSS, Hans	3
16	TAVERI, Luigi	3
16	WOODLAND, Barry	3
17	ANDERSON, Fergus	2
17	ANDERSON, Hugh	2
17	BARRINGTON, Manliff	2
17	BELL, Artie	2
17	BELL, Geoff	2

132 **Island**Racer

ENCYCLOPAEDIA

ISLE OF MAN TT RACE WINNERS

17	BURTON, Lowry	2	18	ARMSTRONG, Reg	1						
17	CARRUTHERS, Kel	2	18	ARTHUR, Kenny	1						
17	CODD, Bernard	2	18	ATKINSON, Stewart	1						
17	COLLIER, Charlie	2	18	AUERBACHER, Georg	1						
17	CORNBILL, Keith	2	18	AYLOTT, Mike	1						
17	COX, Mark	2	18	BALDWIN, Mark	1						
17	CULL, Steve	2	18	BARBER, Rob	1						
17	CUSHNAHAN, Pat	2	18	BASHALL, Harry	1						
17	DAVIES, Howard	2	18	BELL, Ian	1						
17	DIXON, Freddie	2	18	BIGGS, Phillip	1						
17	DODSON, Charlie	2	18	BLISS, Eric	1						
17	DONALD, Cameron	2	18	BRAUN, Dieter	1						
17	DUFFUS, Iain	2	18	BRIGGS, Eric	1						
17	ELLISON, Karl	2	18	BROWN, Norman	1						
17	FOSTER, Bob	2	18	BRYANS, Ralph	1						
17	GREASLEY, Dick	2	18	BUCHAN, Jimmy	1						
17	GRUNWALD, Manfred	2	18	BURGESS, Trevor	1						
17	HAHN, Hermann	2	18	BURNETT, Roger	1						
17	HALLAM, Craig	2	18	BURNS, Mick	1						
17	HARRIS, Shaun	2	18	CAMATHIAS, Florian	1						
17	HARTLE, John	2	18	CANN, Maurice	1						
17	HILL, Peter	2	18	CARPENTER, Neil	1						
17	HILLEBRAND, Fritz	2	18	CARPENTER, Phil	1						
17	HOBSON, Mac	2	18	CARTER, Phil	1	18	HAZLEHURST, Ronnie	1	18	MELLORS, Ted	1
17	HOCKING, Gary	2	18	CLARK, Harold	1	18	HEATH, Chris	1	18	MILLER, Mark	1
17	HOLDEN, John	2	18	COLEMAN, Rod	1	18	HERZIG, Alfred	1	18	MINTER, Derek	1
17	HUBER, Josef	2	18	COLLIER, Harry	1	18	HICKS, Freddie	1	18	MORRISON, Brian	1
17	HUNT, Tim	2	18	COLLINS, Stuart	1	18	HILLIER, James	1	18	NUTT, Les	1
17	HUTCHINSON, Boyd	2	18	CRABTREE, Syd	1	18	HOLDEN, Robert	1	18	O'DELL, George	1
17	IVY, Bill	2	18	CROXFORD, Dave	1	18	HOLLAUS, Rupert	1	18	OLIVER, Eric	1
17	JOHNSON, Gary	2	18	DANIELS, Jack	1	18	HORSTMAN, K.J.	1	18	OXLEY, Mat	1
17	KING, Alistair	2	18	DAVENPORT, Leo	1	18	HORTON, Clive	1	18	PALMER, Phil	1
17	LAW, Con	2	18	DAVISON, Geoff	1	18	HOUSELEY, Eric	1	18	PARKER, Len	1
17	LAYCOCK, Eddie	2	18	DE LA HAY, Tommy	1	18	IRELAND, Denis	1	18	PARKINSON, Denis	1
17	LINTIN, Ivan	2	18	DEGNER, Ernst	1	18	ITOH, Mitsui	1	18	PENNY, Graham	1
17	LOMAS, Bill	2	18	DENNY, Walter	1	18	JACKSON, Brian	1	18	PHILLIP, Alex	1
17	MCGREGOR, Graeme	2	18	DOUGLASS, George	1	18	JEFFERIES, Nick	1	18	POWELL, Derek	1
17	NATION, Trevor	2	18	DOW, Eddie	1	18	JEWELL, Doug	1	18	PULLIN, Cyril	1
17	PADGETT, Gary	2	18	EVANS, Percy	1	18	JOHNSTON, Lee	1	18	PURSLOW, Brian	1
17	PLATER, Steve	2	18	FATH, Helmut	1	18	JOHNSTON, Paddy	1	18	QUAYLE, Richard	1
17	PORTER, Jock	2	18	FINDLAY, Jack	1	18	KAVANAGH, Ken	1	18	REA, Johnny	1
17	ROCHE, Nick	2	18	FLAXMAN, John	1	18	KEELER, Bob	1	18	REED, Harry	1
17	SANDFORD, Cecil	2	18	FLETCHER, Frank	1	18	KELLY, T. Neil	1	18	REEVES, Tim	1
17	SAVILLE, Dave	2	18	FOWLER, Rem	1	18	KIDSON, John	1	18	RICHMOND, Brett	1
17	SHEARD, Thomas Mylchreest	2	18	GIBBARD, John	1	18	KLUGE, Ewald	1	18	ROBB, Tommy	1
17	TWEMLOW, Eddie	2	18	GLEAVE, Sid	1	18	KNIGHT, Ray	1	18	ROBINSON, John	1
17	UPHILL, Malcolm	2	18	GODFREY, Oliver	1	18	LASHMAR, Dennis	1	18	ROGERS, Mike	1
17	WELLS, Dave	2	18	GRAHAM, Les	1	18	LOCKWOOD, Monty	1	18	ROLLASON, Nigel	1
17	WILLIAMS, Don	2	18	GRAHAM, Stuart	1	18	LONGMAN, Frank	1	18	ROPER, Dave	1
17	WILLIAMS, Eric	2	18	HAAS, Werner	1	18	LUTHRINGSHAUSER, Heinz	1	18	RUSSELL, Gordon	1
17	WINKLE, Andy	2	18	HALLAM, Dave	1	18	MARSHALL, Jack	1	18	SCHEIDEGGER, Fritz	1
17	WYNN, Mike	2	18	HANKS, Roy	1	18	MARTIN, Keith	1	18	SHARPE, Martin	1
18	ABBOTT, Steve	1	18	HARDMAN, Colin	1	18	MASON, Hugh	1	18	SIMMONDS, Dave	1
18	AMBROSINI, Dario	1	18	HARGREAVES, Bernard	1	18	MCCANDLESS, Cromie	1	18	SIMPSON, Bill	1
18	APPLEBEE, Frank A.	1	18	HARRISON, Conrad	1	18	MCVEIGH, Bill	1	18	SIMPSON, Jimmie	1
18	ARBER, Ivor	1	18	HASLAM, Ron	1	18	MEIER, Georg	1	18	SMITH, Shaun	1
									18	SMITH, Tyrell	1
									18	TAFT, Cyril	1
									18	TENNI, Omobono	1
									18	TONKIN, Steve	1
									18	TUCKER, George	1
									18	TWEMLOW, Kenneth	1
									18	VINCENT, Chris	1
									18	VINICOMBE, Terry	1
									18	WALKER, Graham	1
									18	WHITEWAY, Frank	1
									18	WIILIAMS, Donny	1
									18	WILLIAMS, Cyril	1
									18	WILLIAMS, Paul	1
									18	WILLIAMS, Peter	1
									18	WOHLGEMUTH, Alfred	1
									18	WOOD, Tim	1
									18	WOOD, Tommy	1
									18	WOODS, Stan	1

The late, great Tony and son Michael are tied on seven wins apiece.

Half a clutch of riders ready for the off...

ISLE OF MAN TT
PAST WINNERS

ST JOHN'S COURSE

	RIDER	MACHINE	LAPS	AVG
1907	C R Collier	Matchless	10	38.22
1907	H R Fowler	Norton	10	36.22
1908	J Marshall	Triumph	10	40.40
1908	H Reed	DOT	10	38.50
1909	H A Collier	Matchless	10	49.01
1910	C R Collier	Matchless	10	50.63

THE MOUNTAIN AND CLYPSE COURSES
*Races marked with an asterisk were run on the Clypse Course.

WINNERS, ULTRA-LIGHTWEIGHT (125CC)

	Rider	Machine	Laps	Avg
1924	J A Porter	New Gerrard	3	51.20
1925	W L Handley	Rex-Acme	4	53.45
1951	W C McCandless	Mondial	2	74.85
1952	C C Sandford	MV	2	75.54
1953	R L Graham	MV	3	77.79
1954*	R Hollaus	NSU	10	69.57
1955*	C Ubbiali	MV	9	69.67
1956*	C Ubbiali	MV	9	69.13
1957*	T Provini	Mondial	10	73.69
1958*	C Ubbiali	MV	10	72.86
1959*	T Provini	MV	10	74.06
1960	C Ubbiali	MV	3	85.60
1961	M Hailwood	Honda	3	88.23
1962	L Taveri	Honda	3	89.88
1963	H R Anderson	Suzuki	3	89.27
1964	L Taveri	Honda	3	92.14
1965	P W Read	Yamaha	3	94.28
1966	W Ivy	Yamaha	3	97.66
1967	P W Read	Yamaha	3	97.48
1968	P W Read	Yamaha	3	99.12
1969	D A Simmonds	Kawasaki	3	91.08
1970	D Braun	Suzuki	3	89.27
1971	C Mortimer	Yamaha	3	83.96
1972	C Mortimer	Yamaha	3	87.49
1973	T H Robb	Yamaha	3	88.90
1974	C Horton	Yamaha	3	88.44
1989	R Dunlop	Honda	2	102.56
1990	R Dunlop	Honda	3	103.41
1991	R Dunlop	Honda	4	103.68
1992	J Dunlop	Honda	4	106.49
1993	J Dunlop	Honda	4	107.26
1994	J Dunlop	Honda	4	105.74
1995	M Baldwin	Honda	4	107.14
1996	J Dunlop	Honda	2	106.33
1997	I Lougher	Honda	4	107.89
1998	R Dunlop	Honda	3	106.38
1999	I Lougher	Honda	4	107.43
2000	J Dunlop	Honda	4	107.14
2002	I Lougher	Honda	4	108.65
2003	C Palmer	Honda	4	108.65
2004	C Palmer	Honda	4	108.93
2008	C Palmer	Honda (Billown)	12	94.042
2009	I Lougher	Honda (Billown)	12	94.911
2009	C Palmer	Honda (Billown)	12	93.575

MOST WINS, MANUFACTURERS

Honda	11
Yamaha	8
MV Agusta	7
Mondial	2
Suzuki	2

MOST WINS, RIDERS

J Dunlop	5
C Ubbiali	4
R Dunlop	4
I Lougher	4
P Read	3

MOST CONSECUTIVE WINS, MANUFACTURER

Honda	19, 1989-2008

MOST CONSECUTIVE WINS, RIDER

C Palmer	4, 2003-2009

WINNERS, LIGHTWEIGHT (250CC)

	Rider	Machine	Laps	Avg
1922	G S Davison	Levis	5	49.89
1923	J A Porter	New Gerrard	6	51.93
1924	E Twemlow	New Imperial	6	55.44
1925	E Twemlow	New Imperial	6	57.74
1926	C W Johnson	Cotton	7	63.20
1927	W L Handley	Rex-Acme	7	60.30
1928	F A Longman	OK Supreme	7	62.90
1929	S A Crabtree	Excelsior	7	63.87
1930	J Guthrie	AJS	7	64.71
1931	G W Walker	Rudge	7	68.98
1932	L H Davenport	New Imperial	7	70.48
1933	S Gleave	Excelsior	7	71.59
1934	J H Simpson	Rudge	7	70.81
1935	S Woods	Moto Guzzi	7	71.56
1936	A R Foster	New Imperial	7	74.28
1937	O Tenni	Moto Guzzi	7	74.72
1938	E Kluge	DKW	7	78.48
1939	EA Mellors	Benelli	7	74.25
1947	M Barrington	Moto Guzzi	7	73.22
1948	M Cann	Moto Guzzi	7	75.18
1949	M Barrington	Moto Guzzi	7	77.96
1950	D Ambrosini	Benelli	7	78.08
1951	T L Wood	Moto Guzzi	4	81.39
1952	F Anderson	Moto Guzzi	4	83.82
1953	F Anderson	Moto Guzzi	4	84.73
1954	W Haas	NSU	3	90.88
1955*	W A Lomas	MV	9	71.37
1956*	C Ubbiali	MV	9	67.05
1957*	CC Sandford	Mondial	10	75.80
1958*	T Provini	MV	10	76.89
1959*	T Provini	MV	10	77.77
1960	G Hocking	MV	5	93.64
1961	M Hailwood	Honda	5	98.38
1962	DW Minter	Honda	6	96.68
1963	J Redman	Honda	6	94.85
1964	J Redman	Honda	6	97.45
1965	J Redman	Honda	6	97.19
1966	M Hailwood	Honda	6	101.79
1967	M Hailwood	Honda	6	103.07
1968	W D Ivy	Yamaha	6	99.58
1969	K Carruthers	Benelli	6	95.95
1970	K Carruthers	Yamaha	6	96.13
1971	P Read	Yamaha	4	98.02
1972	P Read	Yamaha	4	99.68
1973	C Williams	Yamaha	4	100.05
1974	C Williams	Yamaha	4	94.16
1975	C Mortimer	Yamaha	4	101.78
1976	T Herron	Yamaha	4	103.55
1995	J Dunlop	Honda	4	115.68
1996	J Dunlop	Honda	4	115.31
1997	J Dunlop	Honda	4	115.59
1998	J Dunlop	Honda	2	96.61
1999	J McGuinness	Honda	2	116.79
2000	J Dunlop	Honda	3	116.01
2002	B Anstey	Yamaha	4	115.32
2008	I Lougher	Honda (Billown)	12	100.741
2009	I Lougher	Honda (Billown)	12	101.168
2009	I Lougher	Honda (Billown)	12	100.273

WINNERS, JUNIOR (250CC)

	Rider	Machine	Laps	Avg
1977	C Williams	Yamaha	3	99.62
1978	C Mortimer	Yamaha	6	100.70
1979	C Williams	Yamaha	6	105.13
1980	C Williams	Yamaha	4	102.22
1981	S Tonkin	Armstrong CCM	6	106.21
1982	C Law	Waddon Ehrlich	6	105.32
1983	C Law	EMC	6	108.09
1984	G McGregor	EMC	6	109.57
1985	J Dunlop	Honda	6	109.91
1986	S Cull	Honda	6	109.62

MOST WINS, MANUFACTURERS (ALL 250CC)

Honda	18
Yamaha	13
Moto Guzzi	8
MV Agusta	5
New Imperial	4

MOST WINS, RIDERS (ALL 250CC)

J Dunlop	6
C Williams	5
M Hailwood	3
I Lougher	3
J Redman	3

MOST CONSECUTIVE WINS, MANUFACTURER (ALL 250CC)

Yamaha	11, 1970-1980

MOST CONSECUTIVE WINS, RIDER (ALL 250CC)

J Dunlop	4, 1995-1998

ENCYCLOPAEDIA

WINNERS, JUNIOR (350CC)

Year	Rider	Machine	Laps	Speed
1911	P J Evans	Humber	4	41.45
1912	W H Bashall	Douglas	4	39.65
1913	H Mason	NUT	6	43.75
1914	E Williams	AJS	5	45.58
1920	C Williams	AJS	5	40.74
1921	E Williams	AJS	5	52.11
1922	T M Sheard	AJS	5	54.75
1923	S Woods	Cotton	6	55.73
1924	K Twemlow	New Imperial	6	55.67
1925	W L Handley	Rex-Acme	6	65.02
1926	A Bennett	Velocette	7	66.70
1927	F W Dixon	HRD	7	67.19
1928	A Bennett	Velocette	7	68.65
1929	F G Hicks	Velocette	7	69.71
1930	H G Tyrell Smith	Rudge Whitworth	7	71.08
1931	P Hunt	Norton	7	73.94
1932	S Woods	Norton	7	77.16
1933	S Woods	Norton	7	78.08
1934	J Guthrie	Norton	7	79.16
1935	J Guthrie	Norton	7	79.14
1936	FL Frith	Norton	7	80.14
1937	J Guthrie	Norton	7	84.43
1938	S Woods	Velocette	7	84.08
1939	S Woods	Velocette	7	83.19
1947	AR Foster	Velocette	7	80.31
1948	F L Frith	Velocette	7	81.45
1949	F L Frith	Velocette	7	83.15
1950	A J Bell	Norton	7	86.33
1951	G E Duke	Norton	7	89.90
1952	G E Duke	Norton	7	90.29
1953	W R Amm	Norton	7	90.52
1954	R W Coleman	AJS	5	91.51
1955	W A Lomas	Moto Guzzi	7	92.33
1956	T K Kavanagh	Moto Guzzi	7	89.29
1957	R McIntyre	Gilera	7	94.99
1958	J Surtees	MV	7	93.97
1959	J Surtees	MV	7	95.38
1960	J Hartle	MV	6	96.70
1961	P W Read	Norton	6	95.10
1962	M Hailwood	MV	6	99.59
1963	J Redman	Honda	6	94.91
1964	J Redman	Honda	6	98.50
1965	J Redman	Honda	6	100.72
1966	G Agostini	MV	6	100.87
1967	M Hailwood	Honda	6	104.68
1968	G Agostini	MV	6	104.78
1969	G Agostini	MV	6	101.81
1970	G Agostini	MV	6	101.77
1971	A Jefferies	Yamsel	5	89.98
1972	G Agostini	MV	5	102.03
1973	T Rutter	Yamaha	5	101.99
1974	T Rutter	Yamaha	5	104.44
1975	C Williams	Yamaha	5	104.38
1976	C Mortimer	Yamaha	5	106.78
1982	T Rutter	Yamaha	6	108.58
1983	P Mellor	Spondon Yamaha	6	107.44
1986	D Leach	Yamaha	6	110.63
1987	E Laycock	EMC	6	108.52
1988	J Dunlop	Honda	4	111.87
1989	J Rea	Yamaha	4	112.12
1990	I Lougher	Yamaha	4	115.16
1991	R Dunlop	Yamaha	4	114.89
1992	B Reid	Yamaha	4	115.13
1993	B Reid	Yamaha	4	115.14
1994	J Dunlop	Honda	4	114.67

WINNERS, JUNIOR/SUPERSPORT (600CC)

Year	Rider	Machine	Laps	Speed
1995	L Duffus	Honda	4	116.58
1996	P McCallen	Honda	3	117.65
1997	L Simpson	Honda	4	118.41
1998	M Rutter	Honda	3	114.37
1999	J Moodie	Honda	4	118.11
2000	D Jefferies	Yamaha	4	119.33
2002	J Moodie	Yamaha	4	119.92
2003	B Anstey	Triumph	4	120.36
2004	J McGuinness	Yamaha	4	120.57
2005	I Lougher	Honda	4	120.928
2005	R Farquhar	Kawasaki	4	120.697
2006	J McGuinness	Honda	6	122.264
2007	I Hutchinson	Honda	4	123.225
2008	S Plater	Yamaha	4	122.34
2008	B Anstey	Suzuki	4	123.04
2009	I Hutchinson	Honda	4	124.141
2009	M Dunlop	Yamaha	4	121.416
2010	I Hutchinson	Honda	4	124.677
2010	I Hutchinson	Honda	4	125.161
2011	B Anstey	Honda	4	124.232
2011	G Johnson	Honda	4	123.819
2012	B Anstey	Honda	4	124.160
2012	M Dunlop	Yamaha	4	123.543
2013	M Dunlop	Honda	4	125.182
2013	M Dunlop	Honda	4	125.997
2014	G Johnson	Triumph	4	124.526
2014	M Dunlop	Honda	4	125.078
2015	I Hutchinson	Yamaha	4	125.451
2015	I Hutchinson	Yamaha	4	125.803
2016	I Hutchinson	Yamaha	4	126.445
2016	I Hutchinson	Yamaha	4	125.905
2017	M Dunlop	Yamaha	4	124.368
2018	M Dunlop	Honda	4	126.027
2018	D Harrison	Kawasaki	4	126.703
2019	L Johnston	Yamaha	4	126.449
2019	P Hickman	Triumph	4	127.671

MOST WINS, MANUFACTURERS (ALL JUNIOR)

Yamaha	23
Honda	22
Norton	11
MV Agusta	9

MOST WINS, RIDERS (ALL JUNIOR)

I Hutchinson	8
M Dunlop	7
G Agostini	5
B Anstey	4
S Woods	4

MOST CONSECUTIVE WINS, MANUFACTURER (ALL JUNIOR)

Norton	7, 1931-1937
Yamaha	7, 1973-1986
Honda	7, 1994-1999

MOST CONSECUTIVE WINS, RIDER (ALL JUNIOR)

J Redman	3, 1963-1965
G Agostini	3, 1968-1970

WINNERS, SENIOR (500CC)

Year	Rider	Machine	Laps	Speed
1911	O C Godfrey	Indian	5	47.63
1912	F A Applebee	Scott	5	48.69
1913	H O Wood	Scott	7	48.27
1914	C G Pullin	Rudge	6	49.49
1920	T C de la Hay	Sunbeam	6	51.48
1921	H R Davies	AJS	6	54.49
1922	A Bennett	Sunbeam	6	58.31
1923	T M Sheard	Douglas	6	55.55
1924	A Bennett	Norton	6	61.64
1925	H R Davies	HRD	6	66.13
1926	S Woods	Norton	7	67.54
1927	A Bennett	Norton	7	68.41
1928	C J P Dodson	Sunbeam	7	62.98
1929	C J P Dodson	Sunbeam	7	72.05
1930	W L Handley	Rudge Whitworth	7	74.24
1931	P Hunt	Norton	7	77.90
1932	S Woods	Norton	7	79.83
1933	S Woods	Norton	7	81.04
1934	J Guthrie	Norton	7	78.01
1935	S Woods	Moto Guzzi	7	84.68
1936	J Guthrie	Norton	7	85.80
1937	F L Frith	Norton	7	88.21

ENCYCLOPAEDIA

Year	Rider	Bike	Laps	Speed
1938	H L Daniell	Norton	7	89.11
1939	G Meier	BMW	7	89.38
1947	H L Daniell	Norton	7	82.81
1948	A J Bell	Norton	7	84.97
1949	H L Daniell	Norton	7	86.93
1950	G E Duke	Norton	7	92.27
1951	G E Duke	Norton	7	93.83
1952	H R Armstrong	Norton	7	92.97
1953	W R Amm	Norton	7	93.85
1954	W R Amm	Norton	4	88.12
1955	G E Duke	Gilera	7	97.93
1956	J Surtees	MV	7	96.57
1957	R McIntyre	Gilera	8	98.99
1958	J Surtees	MV	7	98.63
1959	J Surtees	MV	7	87.94
1960	J Surtees	MV	6	102.44
1961	M Hailwood	Norton	6	100.60
1962	G Hocking	MV	6	103.51
1963	M Hailwood	MV	6	104.64
1964	M Hailwood	MV	6	100.95
1965	M Hailwood	MV	6	91.69
1966	M Hailwood	Honda	6	103.11
1967	M Hailwood	Honda	6	105.62
1968	G Agostini	MV	6	101.63
1969	G Agostini	MV	6	104.75
1970	G Agostini	MV	6	101.52
1971	G Agostini	MV	6	102.59
1972	G Agostini	MV	6	104.02
1973	J Findlay	Suzuki	6	101.55
1974	P Carpenter	Yamaha	6	96.99
1975	M Grant	Kawasaki	6	100.27
1976	T Herron	Yamaha	6	105.15
1977	P Read	Suzuki	5	106.97
1978	T Herron	Suzuki	6	111.74
1979	M Hailwood	Suzuki	6	111.75
1980	G Crosby	Suzuki	6	109.65
1981	M Grant	Suzuki	6	106.14
1982	N Brown	Suzuki	6	110.98
1983	R McElnea	Suzuki	6	114.81
1984	R McElnea	Suzuki	6	115.66

WINNERS, SENIOR (1000CC)

Year	Rider	Bike	Laps	Speed
1985	J Dunlop	Honda	6	113.69
1986	R Burnett	Honda	6	113.98
1987	J Dunlop	Honda	4	99.85
1988	J Dunlop	Honda	6	117.38
1989	S Hislop	Honda	6	118.23
1990	C Fogarty	Honda	6	110.95
1991	S Hislop	Honda	6	121.09
1992	S Hislop	Norton	6	121.28
1993	P McCallen	Honda	6	118.32
1994	S Hislop	Honda	6	119.25
1995	J Dunlop	Honda	6	119.11
1996	P McCallen	Honda	6	119.76
1997	P McCallen	Honda	6	119.55
1998	I Simpson	Honda	6	119.79
1999	D Jefferies	Yamaha	6	121.27
2000	D Jefferies	Yamaha	6	121.95
2002	D Jefferies	Suzuki	6	124.74
2003	A Archibald	Suzuki	4	124.53
2004	A Archibald	Suzuki	4	123.81
2005	J McGuinness	Yamaha	6	124.324
2006	J McGuinness	Honda	6	126.178
2007	J McGuinness	Honda	6	127.255
2008	J McGuinness	Honda	6	127.19
2009	S Plater	Honda	6	128.278
2010	I Hutchinson	Honda	4	128.607
2011	J McGuinness	Honda	6	128.426
2013	J McGuinness	Honda	6	128.943
2014	M Dunlop	BMW	6	128.68
2015	J McGuinness	Honda	4	130.481
2016	J McGuinness	BMW	6	130.481
2017	M Dunlop	Suzuki/Bennetts	6	130.456
2018	P Hickman	BMW	6	131.70
2019	D Harrison	Kawasaki	6	130.824

MOST WINS, MANUFACTURERS (ALL SENIOR)

Manufacturer	Wins
Honda	22
Norton	19
MV Agusta	13
Suzuki	12

MOST WINS, RIDERS (ALL SENIOR)

Rider	Wins
J McGuinness	7
M Hailwood	7
G Agostini	5
J Dunlop	4
J Surtees	4
S Woods	4

MOST CONSECUTIVE WINS, MANUFACTURER (ALL SENIOR)

Manufacturer	Wins
Norton	7, 1947-1954
Suzuki	7, 1977-1984

MOST CONSECUTIVE WINS, RIDER (ALL SENIOR)

G Agostini	5, 1968-1972
M Hailwood	5, 1963-1967

WINNER, PREMIER CLASSIC

Year	Rider	Bike	Laps	Speed
1984	R McElnea	Suzuki	6	116.12

WINNERS, SIDECAR (500CC)

Year	Rider	Bike	Laps	Speed
1923	F W Dixon/W Perry	Douglas	3	53.15
1924	G H Tucker	Norton	4	51.31
1925	L Parker	Douglas	4	55.22
1954*	E S Oliver/L Nutt	Norton	10	68.87
1955*	W Schneider/H Strauss	BMW	9	70.01
1956*	F Hillebrand/M Grunwald	BMW	9	70.03
1957*	F Hillebrand/M Grunwald	BMW	10	71.89
1958*	W Schneider/H Strauss	BMW	10	73.01
1959*	W Schneider/H Strauss	BMW	10	72.69
1960	H Fath/A Wohlgemuth	BMW	3	84.10
1961	M Deubel/E Horner	BMW	3	87.65
1962	C Vincent/E Bliss	BSA	3	83.57
1963	F Camathias/A Herzig	BMW	3	88.38
1964	M Deubel/E Horner	BMW	3	89.12
1965	M Deubel/E Horner	BMW	3	90.57
1966	F Scheidegger/J Robinson	BMW	3	90.76
1967	S Schauzu/H Schneider	BMW	3	90.96
1968	S Schauzu/H Schneider	BMW	3	91.09
1969	K Enders/R Englehardt	BMW	3	92.48
1970	K Enders/W Kalauch	BMW	3	92.93
1971	S Schauzu/W Kalauch	BMW	3	86.21
1972	S Schauzu/W Kalauch	BMW	3	91.85
1973	K Enders/R Englehardt	BMW	3	94.93
1974	H Luthringshauser/H Hahn	BMW	3	92.97
1975	R Steinhausen/J Huber	Konig	3	95.94
1976	R Steinhausen/J Huber	Konig	3	96.42

WINNERS, SIDECAR (750CC)

Year	Rider	Bike	Laps	Speed
1968	T Vinicome/J Flaxman	BSA	3	85.85
1969	S Schauzu/H Schneider	BMW	3	89.83
1970	S Schauzu/H Schneider	BMW	3	90.20
1971	G Auerbacher/H Hahn	BMW	3	86.86
1972	S Schauzu/W Kalauch	BMW	3	90.97
1973	K Enders/R Englehardt	BMW	3	93.01
1974	S Schauzu/W Kalauch	BMW	3	96.59

ENCYCLOPAEDIA

WINNERS, SIDECAR (1000CC)

Year		Riders	Make	Laps	Speed
1975		S Schauzu/W Kalauch	BMW	3	97.55
1976		M Hobson/M Burns	Yamaha	3	97.77
1977	'A'	G O'Dell/K Arthur	Yamaha	4	100.03
1977	'B'	M Hobson/S Collins	Yamaha	4	99.74
1978	'A'	D Greasley/G Russell	Yamaha	3	101.75
1978	'B'	R Steinhausen/W Kalauch	Yamaha	3	93.67
1979	'A'	T Ireson/C Pollington	Yamaha	3	102.14
1979	'B'	T Ireson/C Pollington	Yamaha	3	98.13
1980	'A'	T Ireson/C Pollington	Yamaha	3	98.13
1980	'B'	J Taylor/B Johannson	Yamaha	3	103.55
1981	'A'	J Taylor/B Johannson	Yamaha	3	107.02
1981	'B'	J Taylor/B Johannson	Yamaha	3	104.55
1982	'A'	T Ireson/D Williams	Yamaha	3	106.29
1982	'B'	J Taylor/B Johannson	Yamaha	3	106.09
1983	'A'	D Greasley/S Atkinson	Yamaha	3	104.25
1983	'B'	M Boddice/C Birks	Yamaha	3	105.11
1984	'A'	M Boddice/C Birks	Yamaha	3	103.97
1984	'B'	S Abbott/S Smith	Yamaha	3	105.29
1985	'A'	D Hallam/J Gibbard	Yamaha	3	104.45
1985	'B'	M Boddice/C Birks	Yamaha	3	105.26
1986	'A'	L Burton/P Cushnahan	Yamaha	3	104.53
1986	'B'	N Rollason/D Williams	Barton Phoenix	3	103.81
1987	'A'	M Boddice/D Williams	Yamaha	3	104.76
1987	'B'	L Burton/P Cushnahan	Yamaha	3	105.53
1988	'A'	M Boddice/C Birks	Yamaha	3	106.27
1988	'B'	M Boddice/C Birks	Yamaha	3	106.46
1989	'A'	D Molyneux/C Hardman	Yamaha	3	104.56
1989	'B'	M Boddice/C Birks	Yamaha	3	107.17

SIDECAR (F2)

Year		Riders	Make	Laps	Speed
1984	'A'	C Pritchard/K Morgan	Yamaha	3	83.19
1984	'B'	B Hodgkins/J Parkins	Yamaha	3	85.24
1985	'A'	D Saville/D Hall	Derbyshire	3	93.08
1985	'B'	B Hodgkins/J Parkins	Yamaha	3	92.08
1986	'A'	D Saville/D Hall	Windle	3	95.77
1986	'B'	C Hopper/N Burgess	Armstrong	3	92.77
1987	'A'	D Saville/D Hall	Sabre	3	96.49
1987	'B'	D Saville/D Hall	Sabre	3	95.07
1988	'A'	M Hamblin/R Smith	Yamaha	3	94.86
1988	'B'	D Saville/D Hall	Sabre	3	96.46
1989	'A'	D Saville/R Crossley	Sabre	3	98.15
1989	'B'	D Saville/R Crossley	Sabre	3	98.56
1990	'A'	D Saville/N Roche	Sabre	3	100.72
1990	'B'	D Saville/N Roche	Sabre	2	100.17
1991	'A'	M Boddice/D Wells	Honda	3	99.26
1991	'B'	M Boddice/D Wells	Honda	3	99.27
1992	'A'	G Bell/K Cornbill	Yamaha	3	101.50
1992	'B'	G Bell/K Cornbill	Yamaha	3	101.49
1993	'A'	D Molyneux/K Ellison	Yamaha	3	103.33
1993	'B'	D Molyneux/K Ellison	Yamaha	3	103.16
1994	'A'	R Fisher/M Wynn	Yamaha	3	105.71
1994	'B'	R Fisher/M Wynn	Yamaha	3	103.39
1995	'A'	R Fisher/B Hutchinson	Yamaha	3	106.47
1995	'B'	R Fisher/B Hutchinson	Yamaha	3	107.58
1996	'A'	D Molyneux/P Hill	DMR	3	109.81
1996	'B'	D Molyneux/P Hill	DMR	3	110.28
1997	'A'	R Hanks/P Biggs	NRH Ireson	3	106.95
1997	'B'	R Fisher/R Long	Yamaha	3	109.89
1998	'A'	Race cancelled			
1998	'B'	D Molyneux/D Jewell	Honda	3	106.52
1999	'A'	D Molyneux/C Hallam	Honda	3	111.90
1999	'B'	R Fisher/R Long	Honda	3	108.76
2000	'A'	R Fisher/R Long	Honda	3	109.94
2000	'B'	R Fisher/R Long	Honda	3	108.02
2002	'A'	R Fisher/R Long	Yamaha	3	110.55
2002	'B'	R Fisher/R Long	Yamaha	3	110.75
2003	'A'	I Bell/N Carpenter	DMR Yamaha	3	110.16
2003	'B'	D Molyneux/C Hallam	DMR Honda	3	105.42
2004	'A'	D Molyneux/D Sayle	DMR Honda	3	111.33
2004	'B'	D Molyneux/D Sayle	DMR Honda	3	111.20
2005	'A'	N Crowe/D Hope	DMR Honda	3	109.85
2005	'B'	D Molyneux/D Sayle	DMR Honda	3	114.901
2006	'A'	N Crowe/D Hope	DMR Honda	3	112.342
2006	'B'	N Crowe/D Hope	DMR Honda	3	111.467
2007	'A'	D Molyneux/R Long	DMR Honda	3	111.668
2007	'B'	D Molyneux/R Long	DMR Honda	3	113.851
2008	'A'	N Crowe/M Cox	LCR Honda	3	114.37
2008	'B'	N Crowe/M Cox	LCR Honda	3	113.99
2009	'A'	D Molyneux/D Sayle	DMR Suzuki		115.132
2010	'A'	K Klaffenbock/D Sayle	LCR Honda		114.410
2010	'B'	K Klaffenbock/D Sayle	LCR Honda		113.430
2011	'A'	K Klaffenbock/D Sayle	Honda		114.262
2011	'B'	J Holden/A Winkle	LCR Honda		113.469
2012	'A'	D Molyneux/P Farrance	DMR/DMR		113.055
2012	'B'	D Molyneux/P Farrance	DMR/DMR		113.071
2013	'A'	T Reeves/D Sayle	SMT/Haith LCR		113.728
2013	'B'	B Birchall/T Birchall	LCR Hanni		114.387
2014	'A'	C Harrison/M Aylott	Honda	4	113.987
2014	'B'	D Molyneux/P Farrance	Kawasaki	4	113.147
2015	'A'	B Birchall/T Birchall	LCR		115.77
2015	'B'	B Birchall/T Birchall	LCR		116.259
2016	'A'	J Holden/A Winkle	LCR	3	114.282
2016	'B'	B Birchall/T Birchall	LCR	2	115.658
2017		B Birchall/T Birchall	LCR/IEG	1	115.760
2018	'A'	B Birchall/T Birchall	LCR	3	117.987
2018	'B'	B Birchall/T Birchall	LCR	3	118.281
2019	'A'	B Birchall/T Birchall	LCR	3	118.317
2019	'B'	B Birchall/T Birchall	LCR	2	118.494

WINNERS, 50CC

Year	Rider	Make	Laps	Speed
1962	E Degner	Suzuki	3	75.12
1963	M Itoh	Suzuki	3	78.81
1964	HR Anderson	Suzuki	3	80.64
1965	L Taveri	Honda	3	79.66
1966	R Bryans	Honda	3	85.56
1967	S Graham	Suzuki	3	82.89
1968	B Smith	Derbi	3	72.90

WINNERS, PRODUCTION

Year	Rider	Make	Laps	Speed
1967	W A Smith	250 Bultaco	3	88.63
1967	N Kelly	500 Velocette	3	89.89
1967	J Hartle	750 Triumph	3	97.10
1968	T E Burgess	250 Ossa	3	87.21
1968	R Knight	500 Triumph	3	90.09
1968	R Pickrell	750 Dunstall	3	98.13
1969	A M Rogers	250 Ducati	3	83.79
1969	W G Penny	500 Honda	3	88.18
1969	M Uphill	750 Triumph	3	99.99
1970	C Mortimer	250 Ducati	5	84.87
1970	F Whiteway	500 Suzuki	5	89.94
1970	M Uphill	750 Triumph	5	97.71
1971	B Smith	250 Honda	4	84.14
1971	J Williams	500 Honda	4	91.04
1971	R Pickrell	750 Triumph	4	100.07
1972	J Williams	250 Honda	4	85.32
1972	S Woods	500 Suzuki	4	92.20
1972	R Pickrell	750 Triumph	4	100.00
1973	C Williams	250 Yamaha	4	81.76
1973	WA Smith	500 Honda	4	88.10
1973	A Jefferies	750 Triumph	4	95.62
1974	M Sharpe	247 Yamaha	4	86.95
1974	K Martin	492 Kawasaki	4	93.85
1974	M Grant	741 Triumph	4	99.72
1975	D Croxford/A George	748 Triumph	10	99.60
1976	B Simpson/C Mortimer	250 Yamaha	10	87.00
1984	P Mellor	250 Yamaha	3	92.58
1984	T Nation	750 Honda	3	102.24
1984	G Johnson	900 Kawasaki	3	105.28
1985	M Oxley	250 Honda	3	94.84
1985	M Grant	750 Suzuki	3	104.36
1985	G Johnson	998 Honda	3	105.12
1986	B Woodland	400 Suzuki	3	99.82
1986	P Mellor	750 Suzuki	3	109.23
1986	T Nation	1100 Suzuki	3	111.99
1986	G Padgett	400 Suzuki	3	102.98
1987	B Woodland	400 Yamaha	3	102.98
1987	G Johnson	750 Yamaha	3	109.98
1988	B Woodland	400 Yamaha	4	102.21
1988	B Morrison	600 Honda	4	108.42
1988	S Hislop	750 Honda	4	112.29
1988	D Leach	1000 Yamaha	4	114.32
1989	C Fogarty	750 Honda	4	114.68
1989	D Leach	1000 Yamaha	4	115.61
1996	P McCallen	900 Honda	3	117.32
1997	P McCallen	900 Honda	2	117.12
1998	J Moodie	900 Honda	3	119.19
1999	D Jefferies	1000 Yamaha	3	119.50
2000	D Jefferies	1000 Yamaha	2	98.58
2002	D Jefferies	1000 Suzuki	3	122.64
2002	I Lougher	600 Suzuki	3	118.85
2003	S Harris	1000 Suzuki	3	123.55
2003	S Harris	600 Suzuki	2	119.68
2004	B Anstey	1000 Suzuki	3	123.72
2004	R Farquhar	600 Kawasaki	3	117.54

WINNERS, SUPERSTOCK

Year	Rider	Make	Laps	Speed
2005	B Anstey	Suzuki	3	124.242
2006	B Anstey	Suzuki	4	124.147
2007	B Anstey	Suzuki	4	125.875
2008	C Donald	Suzuki	4	125.76
2009	I Hutchinson	Honda	4	127.612
2010	I Hutchinson	Honda	4	128.000
2011	M Dunlop	Kawasaki	4	127.129
2012	J McGuinness	Honda	4	126.657
2013	M Dunlop	Honda	4	128.218

ENCYCLOPAEDIA

2014	M Dunlop	BMW	4	127.216
2015	I Hutchinson	Yamaha	4	125.803
2016	M Dunlop	BMW	4	129.274
2017	I Hutchinson	BMW/Tyco BMW		129.383
2018	P Hickman	BMW	4	131.553
2019	P Hickman	BMW	4	130.488

WINNERS, FORMULA 750

1971	A Jefferies	Triumph	3	102.85
1972	R Pickrell	Triumph	5	104.23
1973	P Williams	Norton	5	105.47
1974	C Mortimer	Yamaha	6	100.52

WINNERS, CLASSIC 1000CC

1975	J Williams	Yamaha	6	105.33
1976	J Williams	Suzuki	6	108.18
1977	M Grant	Kawasaki	6	110.76
1978	M Grant	Kawasaki	6	112.40
1979	A George	Honda	6	113.08
1980	J Dunlop	Yamaha	6	112.72
1981	G Crosby	Suzuki	6	113.58
1982	D Ireland	Suzuki	6	109.21

WINNERS, TTF1

1977	P Read	Honda	4	97.02
1978	M Hailwood	Ducati	6	108.51
1979	A George	Honda	6	110.57
1980	M Grant	Honda	6	105.29
1981	G Crosby	Suzuki	6	111.81
1982	R Haslam	Honda	6	113.33
1983	J Dunlop	Honda	6	114.03
1984	J Dunlop	Honda	6	111.68
1985	J Dunlop	Honda	6	113.95
1986	J Dunlop	Honda	6	112.96
1987	J Dunlop	Honda	6	115.03
1988	J Dunlop	Honda	6	116.25
1989	S Hislop	Honda	6	119.36
1990	C Fogarty	Honda	6	118.35
1991	S Hislop	Honda	6	121.00
1992	P McCallen	Honda	6	119.80
1993	N Jefferies	Honda	6	118.15
1994	S Hislop	Honda	6	119.54
1995	P McCallen	Honda	6	117.84
1996	P McCallen	Honda	6	116.18
1997	P McCallen	Honda	6	119.90
1998	I Simpson	Honda	4	118.74
1999	D Jefferies	Yamaha	4	121.35
2000	J Dunlop	Honda	6	120.99
2002	D Jefferies	Suzuki	6	123.38
2003	A Archibald	Suzuki	6	123.18
2004	J McGuinness	Yamaha	4	125.38

WINNERS, TTF2

1977	A Jackson	Honda	4	99.36
1978	A Jackson	Honda	4	99.35
1979	A Jackson	Honda	4	101.55
1980	C Williams	Yamaha	4	96.24
1981	A Rutter	Ducati	4	101.91
1982	A Rutter	Ducati	4	108.05
1983	A Rutter	Ducati	4	108.20
1984	G McGregor	Yamaha	4	108.78
1985	A Rutter	Ducati	6	107.79
1986	B Reid	Yamaha	4	109.72
1987	S Hislop	Yamaha	6	110.40

WINNERS, TTF3

1977	J Kidson	Honda	4	93.28
1978	WA Smith	Honda	4	94.47
1979	B Smith	Yamaha	4	97.82
1980	B Smith	Yamaha	4	91.98
1981	B Smith	Yamaha	4	99.66
1982	G Padgett	Yamaha	4	96.17

WINNERS, SUPERBIKE

2005	J McGuinness	Yamaha	6	124.124
2006	J McGuinness	Honda	6	124.764
2007	J McGuinness	Honda	6	125.550
2008	C Donald	Suzuki	6	126.826
2009	J McGuinness	Honda	6	127.996
2010	I Hutchinson	Honda	6	127.502
2011	J McGuinness	Honda	6	127.870
2012	J McGuinness	Honda	6	128.078
2013	M Dunlop	Honda	6	128.747
2014	M Dunlop	BMW	6	128.680
2015	B Anstey	Honda	6	128.749
2016	M Dunlop	BMW	6	130.306
2017	I Hutchinson	BMW/Tyco BMW	4	128.170
2018	M Dunlop	BMW	4	130.324
2019	P Hickman	BMW	4	132.644

WINNER, JUBILEE RACE

1977	J Dunlop	Yamaha	4	108.86

WINNERS, HISTORIC TT

1984	S Cull	350 Aermacchi	3	94.26
1984	D Roper	500 Matchless	3	96.11

WINNERS, SUPERSPORT (400CC)

1989	E Laycock	Suzuki	4	105.27
1990	D Leach	Yamaha	3	107.73
1991	D Leach	Yamaha	4	105.49
1992	B Reid	Yamaha	4	110.50
1993	J Moodie	Yamaha	4	111.43
1994	J Moodie	Yamaha	4	108.20
1995	D Leach	Yamaha	4	107.98
1996	N Piercy	Yamaha	4	106.29
1997	N Piercy	Yamaha	4	105.70
1998	P Williams	Honda	2	89.71
1999	P Williams	Honda	4	109.01
2000	B Richmond	Honda	3	104.13
2002	R Quayle	Honda	4	109.27
2003	J McGuinness	Honda	4	109.52
2004	J McGuinness	Honda	4	110.28

WINNERS, SUPERSPORT (600CC)

1989	S Hislop	Honda	4	112.58
1990	B Reid	Yamaha	4	111.98
1991	S Hislop	Honda	4	114.28
1992	P McCallen	Honda	4	115.04
1993	J Moodie	Honda	4	115.06
1994	I Duffus	Yamaha	4	115.30

WINNERS, SINGLES TT

1994	J Moodie	Yamaha	4	111.29
1995	R Holden	Ducati	4	110.78
1996	J Moodie	Yamaha	2	108.19
1997	D Morris	BMW	4	110.46
1998	D Morris	BMW	3	107.48
1999	D Morris	BMW	4	110.56
2000	J McGuinness	AMDM Chrysalis	4	109.63

WINNERS, LIGHTWEIGHT CLUBMANS

1947	W McVeigh	Triumph	3	65.30
1948	M V Lockwood	Excelsior	3	64.93
1949	CV Taft	Excelsior	2	68.10
1950	F Fletcher	Excelsior	3	66.89

WINNERS, JUNIOR CLUBMANS

1947	D Parkinson	Norton	4	70.74
1948	R J Hazlehurst	Velocette	4	70.33
1949	H Clarke	BSA	3	75.81
1950	B A Jackson	BSA	4	74.25
1951	B G Purslow	BSA	4	75.36
1952	E Housely	BSA	4	78.92
1953	DT Powell	BSA	4	80.17
1954	P Palmer	BSA	4	81.83
1955*	J Buchan	BSA	9	68.23
1956	B D Codd	BSA	3	82.02

WINNERS, SENIOR CLUBMANS

1947	E E Briggs	Norton	4	78.67
1948	J D Daniels	Vincent HRD	4	80.51
1949	G E Duke	Norton	3	82.97
1950	P H Carter	Norton	4	75.60
1951	I K Arber	Norton	4	79.70
1952	B J Hargreaves	Triumph	4	82.45
1953	R D Keeler	Norton	3	84.14
1954	A King	BSA	4	85.76
1955*	W E Dow	BSA	9	70.73
1956	B D Codd	BSA	3	86.33

WINNERS, 1000CC CLUBMANS

1949	D G Lashmar	Vincent HRD	3	76.30
1950	A Philip	Vincent HRD	4	78.58
1953	G P Douglas	Vincent HRD	4	81.54

WINNER, FORMULA 500

1959	R McIntyre	Norton	3	97.77

WINNER, FORMULA 350

1959	A King	AJS	3	94.66

WINNERS, ZERO TT

2010	M Miller	MotoCzysz E1PC	1	96.82
2011	M Rutter	MotoCzysz E1PC	1	99.604
2012	M Rutter	MotoCzysz E1PC	1	104.056
2013	M Rutter	MotoCzysz E1PC	1	109.675
2014	J McGuinness	Shinden	1	117.366
2015	J McGuinness	Mugen	1	119.279
2016	B Anstey	Mugen	1	118.279
2017	B Anstey	Mugen	1	117.71
2018	M Rutter	Mugen	1	121.824
2019	M Rutter	Hickman Mugen	1	121.909

WINNER, TTXGP PRO

2010	R Barber	AGNI XOI	1	87.43

WINNER, TTXGP OPEN

2010	C Heath	Electric Motorsport		166.02

WINNERS, LIGHTWEIGHT (650CC)

2012	R Farquhar	Kawasaki	4	114.155
2013	J Hillier	Kawasaki	4	117.694
2014	D Harrison	Kawasaki	4	117.460
2015	I Lintin	Kawasaki	4	118.936
2016	I Lintin	Kawasaki	4	118.454
2017	M Rutter	Paton / Paton SC-Project Reparto Corse	4	118.645
2018	M Dunlop	Paton	4	120.601
2019	M Dunlop	Paton	4	121.646

ENCYCLOPAEDIA

ISLE OF MAN TT
FASTEST LAPS

www.dukevideo.com

ST JOHN'S COURSE

1907	C R Collier	Matchless single cyl	41.81
1907	H R Fowler	Norton Twin cyl	42.91
1908	J Marshall	Triumph single cyl	42.48
1908	W J Bashall	BAT twin	42.25
1909	H A Collier	Matchless	52.27
1910	H H Bowen	BAT	53.15

THE MOUNTAIN AND CLYPSE COURSES
*Races marked with an asterisk were run on the Clypse Course.

ULTRA-LIGHTWEIGHT (125CC)

1924	J A Porter	New Gerrard	52.61
1925	W L Handley	Rex-Acme	54.12
1951	W C McCandless	Mondial	74.85
1952	C C Sandford	MV	76.07
1953	R L Graham	MV	78.21
1954*	R Hollaus	NSU	71.53
1955*	C Ubbiali	MV	71.65
1956*	C Ubbiali	MV	70.65
1957*	T Provini	Mondial	74.44
1958*	C Ubbiali	MV	74.13
1959*	L Taveri	MV	74.99
1960	C Ubbiali	MV	86.10
1961	L Taveri	Honda	88.45
1962	L Taveri	Honda	90.13
1963	H R Anderson	Suzuki	91.32
1964	L Taveri	Honda	93.53
1965	H R Anderson	Suzuki	96.02
1966	W D Ivy	Yamaha	98.55
1967	P W Read	Yamaha	98.36
1968	W D Ivy	Yamaha	100.32
1969	D A Simmonds	Kawasaki	92.46
1970	D A Simmonds	Kawasaki	90.90
1971	C Mortimer	Yamaha	87.05
1972	C Mortimer	Yamaha	90.58
1973	T H Robb	Yamaha	89.24
1974	A Hockley	Yamaha	88.78
1974	C Horton	Yamaha	88.78
1989	R Dunlop	Honda	103.02
1990	R Dunlop	Honda	104.09
1991	R Dunlop	Honda	106.71
1992	J Dunlop	Honda	108.69
1993	J Dunlop	Honda	108.55
1994	J Dunlop	Honda	107.40
1995	M Baldwin	Honda	109.01
1996	J Dunlop	Honda	107.62
1997	I Lougher	Honda	109.25
1998	I Lougher	Honda	107.53
1999	I Lougher	Honda	107.43
2000	J Dunlop	Honda	108.56
2002	I Lougher	Honda	110.21
2003	C Palmer	Honda	110.41
2004	C Palmer	Honda	110.52
2008	C Palmer	Honda (Billown)	94.772
2009	I Lougher	Honda (Billown)	94.911

LIGHTWEIGHT (250CC)

1922	W L Handley	OK Supreme	51.00
1923	W L Handley	OK Supreme	53.95
1924	E Twemlow	New Imperial	58.28
1925	W L Handley	Rex-Acme	60.22
1926	P Ghersi	Moto Guzzi	63.12
1927	A Bennett	OK Supreme	64.45
1928	F A Longman	OK Supreme	64.65
1929	P Ghersi	Moto Guzzi	66.63
1930	W L Handley	Rex-Acme	66.86
1931	G E Nott	Rudge	71.73
1932	W L Handley	Rudge	74.08
1933	S Gleave	Excelsior	72.62
1934	J H Simpson	Rudge	73.64
1935	S Woods	Moto Guzzi	74.19
1936	S Woods	DKW	76.20
1937	O Tenni	Moto Guzzi	77.72
1938	E Kluge	DKW	80.35
1939	S Woods	Moto Guzzi	78.16
1947	M Cann	Moto Guzzi	74.78
1948	M Cann	Moto Guzzi	76.72
1949	R H Dale	Moto Guzzi	80.44
1949	T L Wood	Moto Guzzi	80.44
1950	D Ambrosini	Benelli	80.91
1951	F Anderson	Moto Guzzi	83.70
1952	B Ruffo	Moto Guzzi	84.82
1953	F Anderson	Moto Guzzi	85.52
1954	W Haas	NSU	91.22
1955*	WA Lomas	MV	73.13
1956*	H Baltisberger	NSU	69.17
1957*	T Provini	Mondial	78.00
1958*	T Provini	MV	79.90
1959*	T Provini	MV	80.22
1960	C Ubbiali	MV	95.47
1961	R McIntyre	Honda	99.58
1962	R McIntyre	Honda	99.00
1963	J Redman	Honda	97.23
1964	P Read	Yamaha	99.42
1965	J Redman	Honda	100.09
1966	M Hailwood	Honda	104.29
1967	M Hailwood	Honda	104.50
1968	WD Ivy	Yamaha	105.51
1969	K Carruthers	Benelli	99.01
1970	K Carruthers	Yamaha	98.04
1971	P Read	Yamaha	100.08
1972	P Read	Yamaha	100.61
1973	C Williams	Yamaha	102.24
1974	M Grant	Yamaha	97.85
1975	D Chatterton	Yamaha	103.54
1976	T Herron	Yamaha	103.55
1995	J Dunlop	Honda	117.57
1996	P McCallen	Honda	116.94
1997	J McGuinness	Aprilia	116.83
1998	J Dunlop	Honda	100.50
1999	J McGuinness	Honda	116.79
2000	J Dunlop	Honda	116.55
2002	B Anstey	Yamaha	118.03
2008	I Lougher	Honda (Billown)	102.321

JUNIOR (250CC)

1977	I Richards	Yamaha	101.45
1978	C Mortimer	Yamaha	102.06
1979	C Williams	Yamaha	106.83
1980	D Robinson	Yamaha	104.53
1981	G McGregor	Kawasaki	109.22
1982	C Williams	Yamaha	108.00
1983	C Law	EMC	110.03
1984	G McGregor	EMC	111.06
1985	B Reid	EMC	112.08
1986	P Mellor	EMC	111.42

JUNIOR (350CC)

1911	P J Evans	Humber	42.00
1912	E Rickman	Douglas	41.76
1913	H Mason	NUT	45.42
1914	E Williams	AJS	47.57
1920	C Williams	AJS	51.36
1921	E Williams	AJS	55.15
1922	H le Vack	New Imperial	56.46
1923	J H Simpson	AJS	59.59
1924	J H Simpson	AJS	64.65
1925	W L Handley	Rex-Acme	65.89
1926	A Bennett	Velocette	68.75
1927	W L Handley	Rex-Acme	69.18
1928	A Bennett	Velocette	70.28
1929	F G Hicks	Velocette	70.95
1930	G E Nott	Rudge	72.02
1931	P Hunt	Norton	75.27
1932	S Woods	Norton	78.62
1933	S Woods	Norton	79.22
1934	J Guthrie	Norton	80.11
1935	W F Rusk	Norton	79.96
1936	F L Frith	Norton	81.94

ENCYCLOPAEDIA

Year	Rider	Machine	Speed
1937	F L Frith	Norton	85.18
1937	J Guthrie	Norton	85.18
1938	S Woods	Velocette	85.30
1939	H L Daniell	Norton	85.05
1947	M D Whitworth	Velocette	81.61
1948	F L Frith	Velocette	82.45
1949	F L Frith	Velocette	84.23
1950	A J Bell	Norton	86.49
1951	G E Duke	Norton	91.38
1952	G E Duke	Norton	91.00
1953	W R Amm	Norton	91.82
1954	W R Amm	Norton	94.61
1955	W A Lomas	Moto Guzzi	94.13
1956	T K Kavanagh	Moto Guzzi	93.15
1957	R McIntyre	Gilera	97.42
1958	J Surtees	MV	95.42
1959	J Surtees	MV	97.08
1960	J Surtees	MV	99.20
1961	G Hocking	MV	99.80
1962	M Hailwood	MV	101.58
1963	J Redman	Honda	101.30
1964	J Redman	Honda	100.76
1965	J Redman	Honda	102.85
1966	G Agostini	MV	103.09
1967	M Hailwood	Honda	107.73
1968	G Agostini	MV	106.77
1969	G Agostini	MV	104.00
1970	G Agostini	MV	104.56
1971	P Read	Yamaha	100.37
1972	G Agostini	MV	103.34
1973	A T Rutter	Yamaha	104.22
1974	A T Rutter	Yamaha	106.39
1975	A George	Yamaha	106.29
1976	A T Rutter	Yamaha	108.69
1982	G McGregor	Yamaha	112.03
1983	C Law	Yamaha	109.71
1986	D Leach	Yamaha	112.05
1987	S Hislop	Yamaha	111.51
1988	S Hislop	Yamaha	113.41
1989	E Laycock	Yamaha	114.04
1990	I Lougher	Yamaha	117.80
1991	P McCallen	Honda	116.75
1992	S Hislop	Yamaha	117.51
1993	R Dunlop	Yamaha	116.75
1994	B Reid	Yamaha	115.97

JUNIOR/SUPERSPORT (600CC)

Year	Rider	Machine	Speed
1995	I Duffus	Honda	117.87
1996	P McCallen	Honda	118.94
1997	I Simpson	Honda	119.86
1998	J Moodie	Honda	118.49
1999	J Moodie	Honda	118.11
2000	A Archibald	Honda	121.15
2002	J Moodie	Yamaha	120.63
2003	R Farquhar	Kawasaki	122.30
2004	J McGuinness	Yamaha	122.87
2005	R Farquhar	Kawasaki	122.639
2005	J Griffiths	Yamaha	122.540
2006	J McGuinness	Honda	123.975
2007	G Martin	Honda	125.161
2008	S Plater	Yamaha	124.127
2008	B Anstey	Suzuki	125.359
2009	B Anstey	Suzuki	126.549
2009	S Plater	Yamaha	125.384
2010	K Amor	Honda	126.909
2010	M Dunlop	Honda	127.836
2011	B Anstey	Honda	126.595
2011	G Johnson	Honda	125.892
2012	M Dunlop	Yamaha	126.948
2013	M Dunlop	Honda	128.666
2015	I Hutchinson	Yamaha	127.571
2015	I Hutchinson	Yamaha	127.751
2018	M Dunlop	Honda	129.197

SENIOR (500CC)

Year	Rider	Machine	Speed
1911	F Phillips	Scott	50.11
1912	F A Applebee	Scott	49.44
1913	H O Wood	Scott	52.12
1914	H O Wood	Scott	53.50
1920	G Dance	Sunbeam	55.62
1921	F G Edmond	Triumph	56.40
1922	A Bennett	Sunbeam	59.99
1923	J Whalley	Douglas	59.74
1924	F W Dixon	Douglas	63.75
1925	J H Simpson	AJS	68.97
1926	J H Simpson	AJS	70.43
1927	S Woods	Norton	70.90
1928	J H Simpson	AJS	67.93
1929	C J P Dodson	Sunbeam	73.55
1930	W L Handley	Rudge	76.28
1931	J H Simpson	Norton	80.82
1932	J H Simpson	Norton	81.50
1933	S Woods	Norton	82.7
1934	S Woods	Husqvarna	80.49
1935	S Woods	Moto Guzzi	86.53
1936	S Woods	Velocette	86.98
1937	F L Frith	Norton	90.27
1938	H L Daniell	Norton	91.00
1939	G Meier	BMW	90.75
1947	A J Bell	Norton	84.07
1947	P Goodman	Velocette	84.07
1948	O Tenni	Moto Guzzi	88.06
1949	A R Foster	Moto Guzzi	89.75
1950	G E Duke	Norton	93.33
1951	G E Duke	Norton	95.22
1952	G E Duke	Norton	94.88
1953	W R Amm	Norton	97.41
1954	W R Amm	Norton	89.82
1955	G E Duke	Gilera	99.97
1956	J Surtees	MV	97.79
1957	R McIntyre	Gilera	101.12
1958	J Surtees	MV	100.58
1959	J Surtees	MV	101.18
1960	J Surtees	MV	104.08
1961	G Hocking	MV	102.62
1962	G Hocking	MV	105.75
1963	M Hailwood	MV	106.41
1964	M Hailwood	MV	102.51
1965	M Hailwood	MV	95.11
1966	M Hailwood	Honda	107.07
1967	M Hailwood	Honda	108.77
1968	G Agostini	MV	104.91
1969	G Agostini	MV	106.25
1970	G Agostini	MV	105.29
1971	G Agostini	MV	104.86
1972	G Agostini	MV	105.39
1973	M Grant	Yamaha	104.41
1974	C Williams	Yamaha	101.92
1975	M Grant	Kawasaki	102.93
1976	J Williams	Suzuki	112.27
1977	P Read	Suzuki	110.01
1978	P Hennen	Suzuki	113.83
1979	M Hailwood	Suzuki	114.02
1980	S Woods	Suzuki	111.37
1981	M Grant	Suzuki	112.68
1982	C Williams	Yamaha	115.08
1983	N Brown	Suzuki	116.19
1984	J Dunlop	Honda	118.47

SENIOR 1000CC

Year	Rider	Machine	Speed
1985	R Marshall	500 Honda	116.07
1986	T Nation	Suzuki	116.55
1987	J Dunlop	Honda	105.08
1988	S Cull	Honda	119.08
1989	S Hislop	Honda	120.69
1990	D Leach	Yamaha	116.47
1991	S Hislop	Honda	123.27
1992	C Fogarty	Yamaha	123.61
1993	P McCallen	Honda	120.65
1994	S Hislop	Honda	122.50
1995	S Ward	Honda	121.73
1996	P McCallen	Honda	122.14
1997	P McCallen	Honda	122.22
1998	M Rutter	Honda	123.04
1999	J Moodie	Honda	124.45
2000	D Jefferies	Yamaha	125.69
2002	D Jefferies	Suzuki	127.29
2003	A Archibald	Suzuki	126.82
2004	J McGuinness	Yamaha	127.19
2005	J McGuinness	Yamaha	127.326
2006	J McGuinness	Honda	129.451
2007	J McGuinness	Honda	130.354
2011	J McGuinness	Honda	131.248
2015	J McGuinness	Honda	132.701
2016	M Dunlop	BMW	133.962
2019	D Harrison	Kawasaki	130.842

ENCYCLOPAEDIA

PREMIER CLASSIC
1984	R McElnea	Suzuki	117.13

SIDECAR (500CC)
1923	H Langman	Scott	54.69
1924	F W Dixon	Douglas	53.23
1925	F W Dixon	Douglas	57.18
1954*	E S Oliver/L Nutt	Norton	70.85
1955*	W Noll/F Cron	BMW	71.93
1956*	W Noll/F Cron	BMW	71.72
1957*	F Hillebrand/M Grunwald	BMW	72.55
1958*	W Schneider/H Strauss	BMW	74.07
1959*	W Schneider/H Strauss	BMW	73.32
1960	H Fath/A Wohlgemuth	BMW	85.79
1961	M Deubel/E Horner	BMW	87.97
1962	M Deubel/E Horner	BMW	90.70
1963	F Camathias/A Herzig	BMW	89.42
1964	M Deubel/E Horner	BMW	89.63
1965	M Deubel/E Horner	BMW	91.80
1966	F Scheidegger/E Horner	BMW	91.63
1967	G Auerbacher/E Dein	BMW	91.70
1968	K Enders/R Englehardt	BMW	94.32
1969	K Enders/R Englehardt	BMW	92.54
1970	K Enders/W Kalauch	BMW	93.79
1971	G Auerbachar/H Hahn	BMW	87.27
1972	H Luthringshausar/J Cusnik	BMW	92.53
1973	K Enders/R Englhardt	BMW	95.22
1974	J Gawley/K Birch	Konig	93.36
1975	M Hobson/G Russell	Yamaha	96.71
1976	S Schauzu/W Kalauch	Aro	97.50

SIDECAR (750CC)
1968	C Vincent/K Scott	BSA	89.11
1969	S Schauzu/H Schneider	BMW	92.06
1970	K Enders/R Englehardt	BMW	92.37
1971	S Schauzu/W Kalauch	BMW	93.44
1972	S Schauzu/W Kalauch	BMW	91.33
1973	K Enders/R Englehardt	BMW	96.86
1974	R Steinhausen/K Scheurer	Konig	98.18

SIDECAR (1000CC)
1975	S Schauzu/W Kalauch	BMW	99.31
1976	M Hobson/M Burns	Yamaha	99.96
1977	G O'Dell/K Arthur	Yamaha	102.80
1977	M Hobson/S Collins	Yamaha	101.74
1978 'A'	R Biland/K Williams	Yamaha	103.81
1978 'B'	R Steinhausen/W Kalauch	Yamaha	96.14
1979 'A'	M Boddice/C Birks	Yamaha	103.26
1979 'B'	R Steinhausen/K Arthur	MSAI	102.17
1980 'A'	J Taylor/B Johannson	Yamaha	100.61
1980 'B'	J Taylor/B Johannson	Yamaha	106.08
1981 'A'	J Taylor/B Johannson	Yamaha	108.12
1981 'B'	J Taylor/B Johannson	Yamaha	107.54
1982 'A'	M Boddice/C Birks	Yamaha	107.52
1982 'B'	J Taylor/B Johannson	Yamaha	108.29
1983 'A'	D Greasley/S Atkinson	Yamaha	105.01
1983 'B'	M Boddice/C Birks	Yamaha	106.19
1984 'A'	M Boddice/C Birks	Yamaha	107.45
1984 'B'	M Boddice/C Birks	Yamaha	106.90
1985 'A'	M Boddice/C Birks	Yamaha	107.10
1985 'B'	M Boddice/C Birks	Yamaha	107.37
1986 'A'	L Burton/P Cushnahan	Yamaha	105.90
1986 'B'	D Hallam/J Gibbard	Yamaha	105.47
1987 'A'	M Boddice/D Williams	Yamaha	105.73
1987 'B'	L Burton/P Cushnahan	Yamaha	105.93
1988 'A'	M Boddice/C Birks	Yamaha	107.15
1988 'B'	L Burton/P Cushnahan	Yamaha	107.66
1989 'A'	K Howles/S Pointer	Yamaha	105.65
1989 'B'	M Boddice/C Birks	Yamaha	108.31

SIDECAR F2
1984 'A'	B Hodgkins/J Parkins	Yamaha	92.24
1984 'B'	D Saville/D Hall	Sabre	92.55
1985 'A'	D Saville/D Hall	Derbyshire	94.08
1985 'B'	D Saville/D Hall	Derbyshire	93.37
1986 'A'	D Saville/D Hall	Windle	96.34
1986 'B'	D Saville/D Hall	Windle	96.85
1987 'A'	D Saville/D Hall	Sabre	96.82
1987 'B'	D Saville/D Hall	Sabre	96.37
1988 'A'	D Saville/D Hall	Sabre	96.70
1988 'B'	D Saville/D Hall	Sabre	96.82
1989 'A'	D Saville/R Crossley	Sabre	99.23
1989 'B'	D Saville/R Crossley	Sabre	99.11
1990 'A'	D Saville/N Roche	Yamaha	100.97
1990 'B'	D Saville/N Roche	Yamaha	100.55
1991 'A'	M Boddice/D Wells	Honda	99.85
1991 'B'	M Boddice/D Wells	Honda	100.15
1992 'A'	G Bell/K Cornbill	Yamaha	102.54
1992 'B'	G Bell/K Cornbill	Yamaha	101.66
1993 'A'	D Molyneux/K Ellison	Yamaha	104.27
1993 'B'	D Molyneux/K Ellison	Yamaha	103.29
1994 'A'	R Fisher/M Wynn	Yamaha	106.49
1994 'B'	R Fisher/M Wynn	Yamaha	105.45
1995 'A'	R Fisher/B Hutchinson	Yamaha	107.16
1995 'B'	R Fisher/B Hutchinson	Yamaha	107.67
1996 'A'	D Molyneux/P Hill	DMR	110.63
1996 'B'	D Molyneux/P Hill	DMR	111.02
1997 'A'	R Fisher/R Long	Yamaha	109.23
1997 'B'	R Fisher/R Long	Yamaha	110.45
1998 'A'	Race cancelled		
1998 'B'	D Molyneux/D Jewell	Honda	108.2
1999 'A'	D Molyneux/C Hallam	Honda	111.90
1999 'B'	R Fisher/R Long	Honda	108.76
2000 'A'	R Fisher/R Long	Yamaha	109.94
2002 'B'	R Fisher/R Long	Yamaha	111.58
2003 'A'	I Bell/N Carpenter	DMR Yamaha	110.81
2003 'B'	D Molyneux/C Hallam	DMR Honda	108.99
2004 'A'	D Molyneux/D Sayle	DMR Honda	112.61
2004 'B'	D Molyneux/D Sayle	DMR Honda	113.17
2005 'A'	D Molyneux/D Sayle	DMR Honda	111.99
2005 'B'	D Molyneux/D Sayle	DMR Honda	116.044
2006 'A'	N Crowe/D Hope	DMR Honda	113.571
2006 'B'	N Crowe/D Hope	DMR Honda	112.315
2007 'A'	D Molyneux/R Long	DMR Honda	112.736
2007 'B'	N Crowe/D Sayle	DMR Honda	116.667
2008 'A'	N Crowe/M Cox	LCR Honda	115.066
2008 'B'	N Crowe/M Cox	LCR Honda	114.544
2009 'A'	D Molyneux/D Sayle	DMR Suzuki	115.132
2010 'A'	D Molyneux/P Farrance	DMR/DMR	115.284
2010 'B'	K Klaffenbock/D Sayle	LCR Honda	114.157
2011 'A'	J Holden/A Winkle	LCR Suzuki	114.861
2011 'B'	J Holden/A Winkle	LCR Suzuki	114.627
2012 'A'	D Molyneux/P Farrance	DMR/DMR	113.590
2012 'B'	D Molyneux/P Farrance	DMR/DMR	114.486
2013 'A'	T Reeves/D Sayle	LCR Honda	113.728
2013 'B'	B Birchall/T Birchall	LCR Hanni	114.387
2014 'A'	D Molyneux/P Farrance	Kawasaki	115.538
2014 'B'	D Molyneux/P Farrance	Kawasaki	113.756
2015 'A'	D Molyneux/B Binns	LCR	116.060
2015 'B'	D Molyneux/B Binns	LCR	116.785
2016 'A'	B Birchall/T Birchall	LCR	116.798
2018 'B'	B Birchall/T Birchall	LCR	119.197.250

50CC
1962	E Degner	Suzuki	75.52
1963	E Degner	Suzuki	79.10
1964	H H Anderson	Suzuki	81.13
1965	L Taveri	Honda	80.83
1966	R Bryans	Honda	86.49
1967	S Graham	Suzuki	85.19
1968	B Smith	Derbi	73.44

PRODUCTION MACHINES
1967	W A Smith	250 Bultaco	89.41
1967	N Kelly	500 Velocette	91.01
1967	J Hartle	750 Triumph	97.87
1968	T E Burgess	250 Ossa	87.89
1968	R L Knight	500 Triumph	91.03
1968	R Pickrell	750 Dunstall	99.39
1969	C S Mortimer	250 Ducati	85.13
1969	T Dunnell	500 Kawasaki	90.84
1969	M Uphill	750 Triumph	100.37
1970	C S Mortimer	250 Ducati	86.37
1970	F Whiteway	500 Suzuki	90.75
1970	P J Williams	750 Norton	99.99
1971	C Williams	250 Yamaha	84.64
1971	J Williams	500 Honda	91.45
1971	P Williams	750 Norton	101.06
1972	J Williams	250 Honda	85.73
1972	S Woods	500 Suzuki	93.61
1972	R Pickrell	750 Triumph	101.61
1973	E Roberts	250 Yamaha	84.06
1973	S Woods	500 Suzuki	94.44
1973	P Williams	750 Norton	100.52
1974	E Roberts	250 Yamaha	88.48
1974	K Martin	492 Kawasaki	95.21
1974	M Grant	741 Triumph	100.74
1975	A George	748 Triumph	102.82
1976	R Nicholls	900 Ducati	103.13
1984	P Mellor	250 Yamaha	94.01
1984	T Nation	750 Honda	102.97
1984	G Johnson	900 Kawasaki	106.13

ENCYCLOPAEDIA

1985	M Oxley	250 Honda	96.40
1985	G Williams	750 Suzuki	105.93
1985	B Simpson	900 Kawasaki	105.83
1986	M Oxley	250 Yamaha	100.82
1986	P Mellor	750 Suzuki	110.70
1986	T Nation	1100 Suzuki	113.26
1986	G Padgett	400 Suzuki	104.43
1987	B Woodland	400 Yamaha	103.36
1987	T Nation	750	103.79
1988	S Hislop	600 Honda	109.83
1988	G Johnson	750 Yamaha	112.98
1988	G Johnson	1000 Yamaha	116.55
1989	D Leach	750 Yamaha	116.91
1989	N Jefferies	1000 Yamaha	117.27
1996	P McCallen	Honda	118.93
1997	P McCallen	Honda	117.53
1998	J Moodie	Honda	120.70
1999	D Jefferies	Yamaha	119.50
2000	D Jefferies	Yamaha	99.34
2002	D Jefferies	1000 Suzuki	124.31
2002	I Lougher	600 Suzuki	120.25
2003	S Harris	1000 Suzuki	123.55
2003	S Harris	600 Suzuki	119.75
2004	B Anstey	1000 Suzuki	125.10
2004	R Farquhar	600 Kawasaki	118.94

SUPERSTOCK

2005	A Archibald	1000 Suzuki	126.641
2006	B Anstey	Suzuki	126.204
2007	B Anstey	Suzuki	128.400
2008	C Donald	Suzuki	127.544
2009	I Hutchinson	Honda	127.612
2010	I Hutchinson	Honda	130.741
2011	M Dunlop	Kawasaki	129.709
2012	M Dunlop	Kawasaki	129.253
2013	M Dunlop	Honda	128.218
2014	M Dunlop	BMW	129.778
2015	M Dunlop	Honda	128.666
2016	I Hutchinson	BMW	133.098
2018	P Hickman		134.403

FORMULA 750

1971	A Jefferies	Triumph	103.21
1972	R Pickrell	Triumph	105.68
1973	P Williams	Norton	107.27
1974	C Williams	Yamaha	106.61

CLASSIC 1000CC

1975	M Grant	Kawasaki	109.82
1976	J Williams	Suzuki	110.21
1977	M Grant	Kawasaki	112.77
1978	M Grant	Kawasaki	114.33
1979	A George	Honda	114.18
1980	J Dunlop	Yamaha	115.22
1981	J Dunlop	Honda	115.40
1982	C Williams	Yamaha	113.47

TTF1

1977	P Read	Honda	101.74
1978	M Hailwood	Ducati	110.62
1979	A George	Honda	112.94
1980	S McClements	Honda	106.88
1981	G Crosby	Suzuki	113.70
1982	M Grant	Suzuki	114.93
1983	J Dunlop	Honda	115.73
1984	J Dunlop	Honda	115.89
1985	J Dunlop	Honda	116.42
1986	J Dunlop	Honda	113.98
1987	J Dunlop	Honda	117.55
1988	J Dunlop	Honda	118.54
1989	S Hislop	Honda	121.34
1990	S Hislop	Honda	122.63
1991	S Hislop	Honda	123.48
1992	S Hislop	Norton	123.30
1993	M Farmer	Ducati	120.58
1994	P McCallen	Honda	122.08
1995	P McCallen	Honda	120.85
1996	P McCallen	Honda	120.84
1997	P McCallen	Honda	122.98
1998	I Simpson	Honda	122.28
1999	D Jefferies	Yamaha	121.35
2000	D Jefferies	Yamaha	123.18
2002	D Jefferies	Suzuki	126.68
2003	A Archibald	Suzuki	125.43
2004	J McGuinness	Yamaha	127.68

TTF2

1977	A Jackson	Honda	101.15
1978	A Jackson	Honda	103.21
1979	A Jackson	Honda	103.40
1980	C Williams	Yamaha	98.17
1981	A Rutter	Ducati	103.51
1982	A Rutter	Ducati	109.27
1983	A Rutter	Ducati	109.44
1984	G McGregor	Yamaha	110.01
1985	B Reid	Yamaha	110.46
1986	B Reid	Yamaha	111.75
1987	E Laycock	Yamaha	112.36

TTF3

1977	J Kidson	Honda	94.81
1978	WA Smith	Honda	96.13
1979	B Smith	Yamaha	99.37
1980	B Smith	Yamaha	95.82
1981	B Smith	Yamaha	101.31
1982	G Padgett	Yamaha	97.36

SUPERBIKE

2005	J McGuinness	Yamaha	126.879
2006	J McGuinness	Honda	127.933
2007	J McGuinness	Honda	128.279
2008	J McGuinness	Honda	129.517
2009	J McGuinness	Honda	127.996
2010	C Cummins	Kawasaki	131.511
2011	B Anstey	Honda	131.379
2012	J McGuinness	Honda	130.483
2013	J McGuinness	Honda	131.671
2014	B Anstey	Honda	132.298
2015	B Anstey	Honda	131.797
2016	M Dunlop	BMW	133.393
2018	D Harrison	Kawasaki	134.432

JUBILEE RACE

1977	J Dunlop	Yamaha	110.93

SUPERSPORT (400CC)

1989	E Laycock	Suzuki	106.90
1990	D Leach	Yamaha	109.39
1991	D Leach	Yamaha	109.39
1992	B Reid	Yamaha	112.27
1993	J Moodie	Yamaha	112.40
1994	J Moodie	Yamaha	110.77
1995	D Leach	Yamaha	109.13
1996	N Piercy	Yamaha	107.03
1997	N Piercy	Yamaha	107.39
1998	P Williams	Yamaha	90.11
1999	P Williams	Honda	110.79
2000	D Madsen-Mygdal	Honda	105.94
2002	R Quayle	Honda	110.57
2003	J McGuinness	Honda	111.36
2004	J McGuinness	Honda	112.04

SUPERSPORT (600CC)

1989	D Leach	Yamaha	113.60
1990	D Leach	Yamaha	114.21
1991	S Hislop	Honda	115.69
1992	S Hislop	Honda	117.01
1993	J Moodie	Honda	116.77
1994	J Moodie	Yamaha	116.71

SINGLES TT

1994	J Moodie	Yamaha	112.66

1995	R Holden	Ducati	111.66
1996	D Morris	BMW	109.08
1997	D Morris	BMW	112.07
1998	D Morris	BMW	109.68
1999	D Morris	BMW	110.56
2000	J McGuinness	Chrysalis AMDM	111.43

HISTORIC TT

1984	J Millar	350 Aermacchi	95.28
1984	D Roper	500 Matchless	97.21

LIGHTWEIGHT CLUBMANS

1947	W McVeigh	Triumph	65.95
1948	MV Lockwood	Excelsior	66.40
1949	CV Taft	Excelsior	68.71
1950	F Fletcher	Excelsior	67.48

JUNIOR CLUBMANS

1947	D Parkinson	Norton	72.92
1948	R Pratt	Norton	73.76
1949	H Clarke	BSA	75.81
1950	B A Jackson	BSA	76.12
1951	KRV James	Norton	76.55
1952	R McIntyre	BSA	80.09
1953	D T Powell	BSA	80.96
1954	D A Wright	BSA	83.05
1955*	D Joubert	BSA	69.78
1956	B D Codd	BSA	82.33

SENIOR CLUBMANS

1947	E E Briggs	Norton	80.02
1948	G Brown	Vincent HRD	82.65
1949	G E Duke	Norton	83.70
1950	I B Wicksteed	Triumph	79.48
1951	I B Wicksteed	Triumph	81.06
1952	B J Hargreaves	Triumph	83.05
1953	R D Keeler	Norton	84.50
1954	A King	BSA	87.02
1955*	J Drysdale	BSA	72.53
1956	B D Codd	BSA	86.52

1000CC CLUBMANS

1949	C Horn	Vincent HRD	85.57
1950	A Phillip	Vincent HRD	81.01
1953	GP Douglas	Vincent HRD	82.80

FORMULA 500

1959	R McIntyre	Norton	98.35

FORMULA 350

1959	A King	AJS	95.27

ZERO TT

2015	J McGuinness	Mugen	119.279
2017	Bruce Anstey	Mugen	117.710
2018	M Rutter	Mugen	121.824

LIGHTWEIGHT (650CC)

2015	J Hillier	Kawasaki	120.848
2018	M Dunlop	Paton	122.750

ENCYCLOPAEDIA

ISLE OF MAN TT LAP/RACE RECORDS

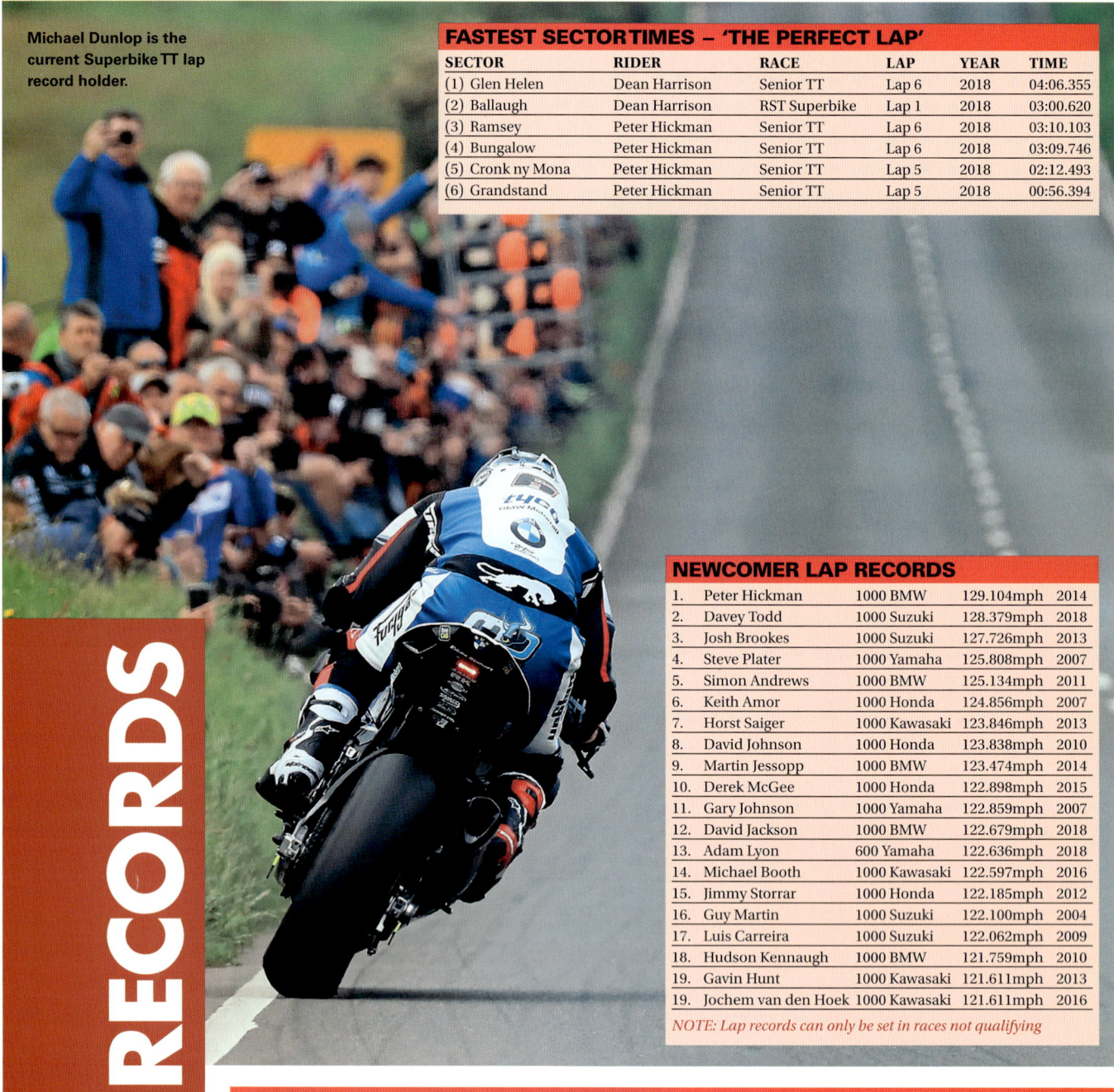

Michael Dunlop is the current Superbike TT lap record holder.

FASTEST SECTOR TIMES – 'THE PERFECT LAP'

SECTOR	RIDER	RACE	LAP	YEAR	TIME
(1) Glen Helen	Dean Harrison	Senior TT	Lap 6	2018	04:06.355
(2) Ballaugh	Dean Harrison	RST Superbike	Lap 1	2018	03:00.620
(3) Ramsey	Peter Hickman	Senior TT	Lap 6	2018	03:10.103
(4) Bungalow	Peter Hickman	Senior TT	Lap 6	2018	03:09.746
(5) Cronk ny Mona	Peter Hickman	Senior TT	Lap 5	2018	02:12.493
(6) Grandstand	Peter Hickman	Senior TT	Lap 5	2018	00:56.394

NEWCOMER LAP RECORDS

1.	Peter Hickman	1000 BMW	129.104mph	2014
2.	Davey Todd	1000 Suzuki	128.379mph	2018
3.	Josh Brookes	1000 Suzuki	127.726mph	2013
4.	Steve Plater	1000 Yamaha	125.808mph	2007
5.	Simon Andrews	1000 BMW	125.134mph	2011
6.	Keith Amor	1000 Honda	124.856mph	2007
7.	Horst Saiger	1000 Kawasaki	123.846mph	2013
8.	David Johnson	1000 Honda	123.838mph	2010
9.	Martin Jessopp	1000 BMW	123.474mph	2014
10.	Derek McGee	1000 Honda	122.898mph	2015
11.	Gary Johnson	1000 Yamaha	122.859mph	2007
12.	David Jackson	1000 BMW	122.679mph	2018
13.	Adam Lyon	600 Yamaha	122.636mph	2018
14.	Michael Booth	1000 Kawasaki	122.597mph	2016
15.	Jimmy Storrar	1000 Honda	122.185mph	2012
16.	Guy Martin	1000 Suzuki	122.100mph	2004
17.	Luis Carreira	1000 Suzuki	122.062mph	2009
18.	Hudson Kennaugh	1000 BMW	121.759mph	2010
19.	Gavin Hunt	1000 Kawasaki	121.611mph	2013
19.	Jochem van den Hoek	1000 Kawasaki	121.611mph	2016

NOTE: Lap records can only be set in races not qualifying

CURRENT ISLE OF MAN TT LAP RECORDS

CATEGORY	RIDER	MACHINE	YEAR	TIME	AVERAGE SPEED
Outright	Peter Hickman	BMW S 1000 RR	2018	16:42.778	135.452mph / 217.989km/h
TT Superbike	Dean Harrison	Kawasaki ZX 10R	2018	16:50.384	134.432mph / 216.347km/h
Supersport	Michael Dunlop	Honda CBR 600 RR	2018	17:31.328	129.197mph / 207.922km/h
Lightweight TT	Michael Dunlop	Paton 650	2018	18:26.543	122.750mph / 197.546km/h
TT Zero	Michael Rutter	Team Mugen	2018	18:34.956	121.824mph / 196.056km/h
Superstock TT	Peter Hickman	BMW S 1000 RR	2018	16:50.501	134.403mph / 216.300km/h
Sidecar TT	Ben & Tom Birchall	Honda CBR	2018	18:59.018	119.250mph / 191.914km/h
Fastest Newcomer	Peter Hickman	BMW S 1000 RR	2014	17:32.078	129.104mph / 207.772km/h
Female	Jenny Tinmouth	Honda CBR 1000 RR	2010	18:52.42	119.945mph / 193.032km/h

NOTE: Lap records can only be set in races not qualifying

CURRENT ISLE OF MAN TT RACE RECORDS

CATEGORY	RIDER	MACHINE	YEAR	TIME	AVERAGE SPEED
Senior TT (6 laps)	Peter Hickman	BMW S 1000 RR	2018	1:43:08.065	131.700mph / 211.951km/h
Superbike TT (6 laps)	Michael Dunlop	BMW S 1000 RR	2018	1:44:13.398	130.324mph / 209.736km/h
Supersport TT (4 laps)	Dean Harrison	Kawasaki ZX-6R	2018	1:11:28.059	126.703mph / 203.908km/h
Senior TT (4 laps)	John McGuinness	Honda CBR 1000 RR	2015	1:09:23.903	130.481mph / 209.988km/h
Superstock TT (4 laps)	Peter Hickman	BMW S 1000 RR	2018	1:08.49.976	131.553mph / 211.553km/h
Lightweight TT (4 Laps)	Michael Dunlop	Paton 650	2018	1:15:05.032	120.601mph / 194.088km/h
Sidecar TT	Ben & Tom Birchall	Honda CBR	2018	57:25.040	118.281mph / 190.355km/h
TT Zero	Michael Rutter	Mugen	2018	18:34.956	121.824mph / 196.056km/h

Subscribe to Classic Racer

SPECIAL OFFER! Expires 31/12/22

£20 for 6 issues

Get your FREE digital copy!

Classic Racer gives a passionate insight into the golden days of motorcycle racing.

Legendary riders are interviewed about their highs and lows in the saddle, their teams are profiled and the high-powered machines they rode are examined in exacting detail. Features from the world of classic racing are beautifully illustrated with dozens of rare period photographs and carefully reproduced original documents from the vast Mortons Archive. There's all the latest news about the growing racing revival movement right across the globe too and details of the festivals dedicated to the glory of classic two-wheeled motorsport.

SUBSCRIBE TODAY

Visit: www.classicmagazines.co.uk/CRIR22

Call: 01507 529529 and quote **CRIR22**

Download your FREE digital copy of Classic Racer! Visit: www.classicracer.com/islandracer

WHAT'S ON WHEN

ISLE OF MAN TT QUALIFYING SCHEDULE

QUALIFYING 1 – SUNDAY MAY 29, 2022
- 13:00 Roads Close
- 13:30 Newcomer's Speed Control Laps
- 13:50 Superbike / Superstock / Supersport Qualifying
- 15:30 Supersport / Supertwin Qualifying
- 16:30 Sidecar Qualifying

QUALIFYING 2 – MONDAY MAY 30, 2022
- 18:00 Roads Close
- 18:20 Superbike / Superstock / Supersport Qualifying
- 20:05 Sidecar Qualifying

QUALIFYING 3 – TUESDAY MAY 31, 2022
- 18:00 Roads Close
- 18:20 Superbike / Superstock / Supersport Qualifying
- 19:25 Supersport / Lightweight Qualifying
- 20:05 Sidecar Qualifying

QUALIFYING 4 – WEDNESDAY JUNE 1, 2022
- 18:00 Roads Close
- 18:20 Superbike / Superstock / Supersport Qualifying
- 20:05 Sidecar Qualifying

QUALIFYING 5 – THURSDAY JUNE 2, 2022
- 18:00 Roads Close
- 18:20 Superbike / Superstock / Supersport Qualifying
- 19:25 Supersport / Supertwin Qualifying
- 20:05 Sidecar Qualifying

QUALIFYING 6 – FRIDAY JUNE 3, 2022
- 12:30 Roads Close
- 13:00 Superbike / Superstock / Supersport Qualifying
- 14:10 Supersport / Supertwin Qualifying
- 15:05 Sidecar Qualifying

TT RACE SCHEDULE

TT RACE DAY 1 – SATURDAY JUNE 4, 2022
- 10:00 Roads Close
- 10:30 Solo Morning Warm Up [1 Lap]
- 12:00 RST Superbike TT Race [6 laps]
- 15:00 3wheeling.media Sidecar TT Race 1 [3 laps]

TT RACE DAY 2 – MONDAY JUNE 6, 2022
- 10:00 Roads Close
- 10:30 Solo Morning Warm Up [1 lap]
- 11:45 Monster Energy Supersport TT Race 1 [4 laps]
- 14:45 RL360 Superstock TT Race [4 laps]

TT RACE DAY 3 – WEDNESDAY JUNE 8, 2022
- 10:00 Roads Close
- 10:30 Solo Morning Warm Up [1 lap]
- 10:50 Sidecar Shakedown [1 lap]
- 11:45 Bennetts Supertwin TT Race [4 laps]
- 14:45 Monster Energy Supersport TT Race 2 [4 laps]

TT RACE DAY 4 – FRIDAY JUNE 10, 2022
- 09:30 Roads Close
- 10:30 3wheeling.media Sidecar TT Race 2 [3 laps]
- 12:45 Milwaukee Senior TT Race [6 laps]

For updates, go to: www.iomtt.com where you can also find out about the new digital channel, 'TT+' which – for a £14.99 'live pass' fee – gives more than 40 hours of TT action.